East Meets West in
Teacher Preparation

East Meets West in Teacher Preparation

Crossing Chinese
and American Borders

Edited by
Wen Ma

Foreword by
Allan Luke

Teachers College
Columbia University
New York and London

Published by Teachers College Press, 1234 Amsterdam Avenue, New York, NY 10027

Library of Congress Cataloging-in-Publication Data

East Meets West in Teacher Preparation : Crossing Chinese and American Borders / Edited by Wen Ma ; Foreword by Allan Luke.
         pages cm
    Includes bibliographical references and index.
    ISBN 978-0-8077-5521-1 (pbk. : alk. paper)
    ISBN 978-0-8077-5522-8 (hardcover : alk. paper)
    ISBN 978-0-8077-7278-2 (ebook)
    1. College teachers–China–Training of. 2. College teachers–United States–
Training of. 3. Chinese American college teachers–Training of. 4. Education–Aims
and objectives–China. 5. Education–Aims and objectives–United States. I. Ma, Wen.
    LB1738.E25 2014
    370.71'1–dc23   2013048613

ISBN 978-0-8077-5521-1 (paperback)
ISBN 978-0-8077-5522-8 (hardcover)
eISBN 978-0-8077-7278-2 (eBook)

Printed on acid-free paper
Manufactured in the United States of America

21 20 19 18 17 16 15 14   8 7 6 5 4 3 2 1

Contents

Foreword

In the context of contentious geopolitical and economic relations between China and the United States, how do we understand differences between Chinese and American education without lapsing into ideologically and culturally loaded stereotypes? There is a century of volumes by Western "experts" commenting on Chinese education—from the missionary period through what was called the "Cold War." And there is an established corpus of work on Asian American educational issues and perspectives. But this volume documents an emergent and new standpoint: the views of Chinese-born and trained educators working in American universities.

When Wen Ma approached me to read, review and comment on *East Meets West in Teacher Preparation: Crossing Chinese and American Borders,* it took me some time to grasp the complexities and subtleties of this project. This volume features the diverse analytic perspectives, critical commentaries, and standpoints on education of Chinese-educated scholars. It is in the tradition of Liping Ma's (2010) groundbreaking *Knowing and Teaching Elementary Mathematics.* The challenging and innovative essays here do not represent a single academic or disciplinary paradigm, nor do they represent an imaginary cultural homogeneity that might represent a "Chinese" view of American education. It is at once a simpler and a more complex matter than this. What brings these perspectives together is a shared biographical/historical moment: where Chinese-born and Chinese-educated teacher educators and educational researchers become academic and intellectual partners in the training of American teachers and the study of American education, while reflecting on the historical formation of their own schooling, university education, and teacher training.

Of course, the struggle to increase the cultural and linguistic-minority presence in North American teacher education and educational research continues—dominated by debates over African American, Latino, Asian American, Indigenous, and Native American standpoint and education. At the same time, the presence of Chinese-born and Chinese-educated teacher educators and educational researchers has grown over the past 2 decades, persisting through the unwinding of post-Tiananmen and post-9/11 visa restrictions. Given the current bilateral policy push to increase the flow of university students between China and the United States, this is quite likely the beginning of the largest scale cultural, intellectual, and technological exchange to date between the two countries.

Each one of these pieces begins from the lived intercultural experience of a Chinese-trained educator crossing the academic, institutional, and systemic divides between Chinese and American education. They are based on what they report is a shared autobiographical moment that Ma refers to as "pedagogy shock"—a moment where, analytic training aside, Chinese-trained academics face the challenge of intercultural explanation of the differences they perceive and experience in American schooling, university teaching, and pedagogical cultures.

The volume begins with Hu's synoptic overview of Chinese and American educational reforms—an extremely difficult task given the complex and diverse policy contexts of American and Chinese education in the face of economic and cultural globalization. The core of the volume is a series of comparative analyses that attempt to illustrate and reframe the differences in mathematics education (Chiu, Zhang, & Padilla), science teacher education (Liu), language teaching (Pu), and university research training (Wang & Wang). While some draw foundational perspectives from Anglo-European educational models and paradigms—ranging from constructivism to phenomenology and critical theory—others are bids to use Chinese analytic frameworks and definitions for explanation. These studies sit in the context of narrative accounts of transitions from China to the United States by He, Ma, Sung, Zhang, and Zheng. As Zheng's chapter insists, culture counts in the formation of traditions of pedagogy and curriculum. The Chinese teachers' focus on moral development and effort contrasts strongly with the current American focus on measurable standards-based performance.

But while cultural difference is a real and substantive phenomenon, it would be risky to conveniently fit these pieces into a binary China/America symmetry. As Angel Lin (2012) has consistently argued, these kinds of binary analyses have inevitably been produced by successive waves of colonialism and postcolonial backlash. But they are often predicated upon a flattening out of heterogeneity, diversity, difference, and conflict within the geographically separate "cultures" in question. The cultural and linguistic diversity of China is often overlooked, with 56 officially recognized ethnic minorities, at least ten groups with more than 7 million members, multiple dialects, and minority languages and religions. And, most readers would recognize, to treat American education as a singular and coherent cultural and institutional entity would be, at best, naïve and misleading.

Kuan-Hsing Chen's (2010) important volume *Asia as Method: Towards De-imperialization* calls for a new moment in transnational cultural studies and social sciences, where the binary analysis of the "West is best" is no longer the default mode of analysis. At the same time, his call for a "de-cold war" model would also preclude the kind of reverse-Orientalism that is increasingly popular in educational policy debates. Many policy think tanks, journalists, public intellectuals, and politicians have developed an acute case of "Asia-envy": calling for American, Canadian, and Australian schools to emulate the educational success of Shanghai and Singapore. Again, this requires a studied disregard of the complexities of cultures, histories, and political economies of education (Luke, 2011).

What is needed is a new wave of analysis that does not presuppose the existence or value of a singular, homogeneous cultural perspective or a unified set of pedagogical practices. We find models of this kind of analysis emerging in the literature that contests some of the longstanding Western psychological descriptions of Chinese learners and learning. A recent volume of the *Journal of Curriculum Studies* features a robust debate over neo-Confucianism and pedagogy in China (Wu, 2011). In that volume, Deng's (2011) analysis of Chinese educational traditions reminds us that the tensions and exchanges with the West began over a century ago and have moved through successive generational and ideological waves of reconciliation, reaction, and combination. In his critique of neo-Confucianism, Yongbing Liu (2011) reminds us that there is no pristine Chinese pedagogical tradition but that all pedagogies are the products of the merging of Indigenous and imported models, of politically reconstructed and selective versions of the educational past.

Situated alongside of these current debates, *East Meets West in Teacher Preparation: Crossing Chinese and American Borders* is part of new dialogic process of exchange and reconstruction in action: a kind of thinking aloud about the differences that have struck these writers in relation to their own changed speaking and writing positions as academics and teacher educators. The authors fastidiously avoid simple lessons for American and/or Chinese education. Rather than being a finished, summative statement, this volume is part of an intergenerational and intercultural exchange by historical players who are, quite literally, living and experiencing, teaching and learning a new, historically unprecedented moment of change and shifting power relations.

Allan Luke,
Brisbane, Australia

REFERENCES

Chen, K-H. (2010). *Asia as method: Towards de-imperialization*. Durham, NC: Duke University Press.

Deng, Z. (2011). Confucianism, modernization and Chinese pedagogy: An introduction. *Journal of Curriculum Studies, 43*(5), 561–568.

Lin, A.M.Y. (2012). Towards transformation of knowledge and subjectivity in curriculum inquiry: Insights from Chen Kuan-Hsing's "Asia as method." *Curriculum Inquiry, 42*(1), 153–178.

Liu, Y. (2011). Pedagogic discourse and transformation: A selective tradition. *Journal of Curriculum Studies, 43*(5), 599–606.

Luke, A. (2011). Generalizing across borders: Policy and the limits of educational science. *Educational Researcher, 40*(8), 367–377.

Ma, L. (2010). *Knowing and teaching elementary mathematics: Teachers' understanding of fundamental mathematics in China and the United States* [Anniversary ed.]. New York, NY: Routledge.

Wu, Z. (2011). Interpretation, autonomy, and transformation: Chinese pedagogic discourse in across-cultural perspective. *Journal of Curriculum Studies, 43*(5), 569–590.

Acknowledgments

Many individuals have contributed to the fruition of this book. First among them are the editors at Teachers College Press, Jean Ward, Aureliano Vazquez, and Meg Hartmann. Jean, thank you for your priceless trust and for your tireless guidance over the entire project. Aureliano and Meg, thank you for all of your efficient facilitation of the review and publication process and thoughtful feedback that helps to improve this book in so many ways.

I am grateful to the two anonymous reviewers, whose insights and critical comments and suggestions made the book stronger and better. I like to thank Allan Luke for sharing his works and writing the Foreword. Allan, thank you for your mentoring and support! I want to give my special thanks to Chuang Wang (who also wrote one of the chapters) for his helpful suggestions throughout the process. Patricia Schmidt read the whole manuscript and made detailed comments and suggestions. Patty, my sincere thanks for your help and mentoring! Needless to say, any errors that remain are entirely my own.

Above all, my deepest gratitude goes to all the chapter authors. It is their lived experience and scholarly inquiry that constituted the basis of the narratives detailed in the pages. Without their courageous pursuits and innovative reflections, this book would not have been possible. I truly enjoyed all of the teamwork behind this book!

Mapping Out Similarities and Differences in Teaching in China and the United States

Part I presents research and history that helps to understand differing American and Chinese perspectives and the benefits of learning from the strengths of both to reach for some "middle ground." These ideas also provide a broad context for understanding the rest of the chapters in the book. Specifically, Chapter 1 introduces the purpose and central themes of the book. It argues that the experiences and perspectives of Chinese university educators may help the American and Chinese educational community better learn about and from each other. In light of the rapidly increasing educational exchanges and economic ties between the two countries, such research is not only critically important, but also urgently needed. Chapter 2 gives an expansive review of research on learning and teaching in Chinese and U.S. educational institutions over the past 30 years. It offers conceptual lenses that help us better understand a host of issues related to social, cultural, and ideological differences and similarities in China and the United States.

Caring About the Chinese Educators' Experiences and Perspectives

Negotiating Toward the "Middle Ground"

Wen Ma

This book addresses the following questions: What experiences do disciplinarily diverse educators from Chinese backgrounds have in American classrooms? What fresh perspectives do they bring to the new educational context? Having lived in both worlds, how do they view the educational similarities and differences between China and the United States? In what ways may educational communities in both countries come to the "middle ground" through learning about and from each other?

Then, why should other teachers and teacher educators care about these questions? Because of their cross-cultural backgrounds and dual professional experiences, these Chinese educators are truly at a vantage point and may offer significant ideas and practices for both the United States and China. Therefore, their critical probing may reflect unique alternative viewpoints and fresh insights, meaningful to educational communities in both countries. Since their challenges, adaptations, and reflections directly impact what and how their students learn, these issues may be especially relevant to educators here in the United States.

WHY IS THIS BOOK NEEDED NOW?

This text is needed now for several reasons. First of all, thousands of Chinese students are studying, and hundreds of faculty members from Chinese backgrounds are teaching, at numerous American universities. Based on *Open Doors Report on International Educational Exchange* published by the Institute of International Education (2013), during 2011–2012, students from China made up 25.38% of the total international student population in the United States. During that same period, research scholars from China made up 27.5% of all the international scholars in the United States. Data from the National Center for Education Statistics (2010) show that American universities are not only having more scholars from diverse backgrounds entering natural sciences and engineering disciplines, but also various social sciences and humanities areas.

Despite the changing landscape in higher education, however, there are few systematic studies about how nonnative professors from Chinese and other backgrounds are doing as faculty members. Such a gap in research is unusual since they, as a significant cohort among the total faculty force, are recognized for having made irreplaceable contributions in terms of their research, teaching, and service across academic disciplines (Institute of International Education, 2009). Therefore, more research is needed to better understand what these newcomers' professional experiences and perspectives are, and how the U.S. educational community may benefit and also help them fit in and become more productive members in our shared profession.

Furthermore, China is increasingly being pushed to the forefront of conversations taking place globally. In addition to the complicated ideological, political, social, cultural, economic, and trade fronts, the educational field is no exception to such a "China complex." In the United States, this is evidenced by President Obama's (2009) unprecedented announcement to send 100,000 American students to study in China, the debates over the so-called Confucian-heritage learning culture and the paradox of the Chinese learner (Watkins & Biggs, 1996), the *Battle Hymn of the Tiger Mother* (Chua, 2011) controversy and Chinese-style parenting, the discussions around the national curriculum standards and the educational accountability movement, to the differing Program for International Student Assessment (PISA) results and the widening achievement gap between American and Chinese students (Duncan, 2010), and on and on.

This trend is reflected by fast growth both in the number of students taking Chinese as a foreign language and the number of K–12 schools and universities offering Chinese programs in the first decade of the 21st century. For example, the number of university students learning Chinese increased over 50% from 2002 to 2006, and the number of Chinese programs at K–12 levels increased 200% from 2005 to 2008 (Asia Society, 2008). Based on the Asia Society's 2010 special report, more and more U.S. states and cities have also come to "view the study of Chinese language and culture as an investment in economic competitiveness" (p. 11), and this trend is predicted to go on in the future.

Unfortunately, among the information out there about education, as well as in many other spheres related to China, much is unsubstantiated, partial, or lacking meaningful context. We hear hardly enough from insider perspectives to bring some analytical depths and cross-cultural insights into the heart of the issues under question. Moreover, the U.S. educational field is at a critical juncture right now, searching for new thinking to overcome the mounting challenges. Few would have keener understanding of the advantages and disadvantages of both Chinese and American educational theories and practices than professional educators who not only have firsthand educational experience and knowledge from China, but also have studied as learners and taught as professors in the United States. Equipped with their professional training and lived experiences in both settings, these bilingual educators are in a unique position to critically examine the pros and cons of Chinese education, reflected through the American education system, and vice versa.

There is relatively little research on how educators from China adjust, adapt, and transition to full-time faculty roles in the United States, and there have been even fewer systematic investigations or publications in this regard (Ma, 2010). This book fills in this research gap. By looking at the issues they face and the strategies they employ in their border-crossing, the two divergent systems may use each other as a mirror to reflect upon their own perspectives and practices. While both educational communities necessarily need to subscribe to their own traditions and sociocultural circumstances, they may find some good practices, even conceptual lenses, to draw from each other. Such research will be valuable in helping the entire educational community gain fresh ideas and move toward some "middle ground."

HOW IS THIS BOOK ORGANIZED?

In addition to the Foreword and Conclusion, there are 12 chapters written by a disciplinarily diverse team of educators from Chinese backgrounds who are currently teaching at various teachers colleges or education programs. These chapters are divided into four parts. Part I discusses why the educational community should care about such a book and what prior comparative research literature informs us about teaching and learning in China and the United States that moves us to the "middle ground." Part II showcases a cohort of Chinese educators' perspectives on the Chinese ways of teaching in the context of the conceptual framework promoted in the United States. This section demonstrates the challenges and benefits for teaching on reaching some "middle ground." Part III examines Chinese educators' professional practices across the educational spectrum. These perspectives will allow us to see ways to collaborate and establish some "middle ground." Part IV focuses on science and mathematics education in the United States and China and how we might select best practices from both countries to move toward the "middle ground." Finally, the Conclusion is an overview of how Chinese and American educational perspectives and pedagogical practices are shaped up by their own traditions, which serves as a meaningful context to look at many of the issues under discussion. By considering what the Chinese ways of thinking and practices are across a variety of disciplinary areas, alongside those in the United States, educators may find some "middle ground" that integrates the strengths from both to benefit all students. To this end, some final thoughts about possible implications are intended to further stimulate thinking about how the two systems may both be enriched by learning about and from each other

The chapters across the sections are thematically diverse, but they flesh out some discipline-specific Chinese ways of thinking and practices, alongside those in the United States. Taken together, these chapters present a picture of not only who the diverse educators from Chinese backgrounds are, but also what they are doing professionally to contribute to our educational enterprise. The individual narratives from these chapters add to the collective discourse about the challenges, as well as possibilities, for educators to bridge and transform seemingly opposing perspectives to aim for some "middle ground." This could help the educational community think about how to construct a more inclusive pedagogical framework across the Pacific shores.

REFERENCES

Asia Society. (2008). Chinese: An expanding field. Retrieved from http://asiasociety.org/education/chinese-language-initiatives/chinese-expanding-field#comment-24621

Asia Society. (2010). Meeting the challenge: Preparing Chinese language teachers for American schools. Retrieved from http://asiasociety.org/files/chinese-teacherprep.pdf

Chua, A. (2011). *Battle hymn of the tiger mother*. New Yo2rk: The Penguin Press.

Duncan, A. (2010). Secretary Arne Duncan's Remarks at OECD's Release of the Program for International Student Assessment (PISA) 2009 Results. Retrieved from http://www.ed.gov/news/speeches/secretary-arne-duncans-remarks-oecds-release-program-international-student-assessment

Institute of International Education. (2009). *Higher education on the move: New developments in global mobility*. New York: Author.

Institute of International Education. (2013). *Open doors report on international educational exchange*. Retrieved from http://www.iie.org/en/Research-and-Publications/Open-Doors/Data/Fact-Sheets-by-Country

Ma, W. (2010). From lecturing to impart information to presenting to facilitate class discussions: Pedagogical journey of a Chinese professor. *New England Reading Association Journal*, 46(1), 65–70.

National Center for Education Statistics. (2010). Digest of education statistics, 2008. Retrieved from http://nces.ed.gov/fastfacts/display.asp?id = 61

Obama, B. (2009, November 16). Remarks by President Barack Obama at town hall meeting with future Chinese leaders. Retrieved from http://www.whitehouse.gov/the-press-office/remarks-president-barack-obama-town-hall-meeting-with-future-chinese-leaders

Watkins, D. A., & Biggs, J. B. (Eds.). (1996). *The Chinese learner: Cultural, psychological, and contextual influences*. Hong Kong: The University of Hong Kong Press.

Learning About the Challenges of Teaching in Two Worlds

Ideologies and Beliefs in China and the United States

Ran Hu

Thirty years have passed since the establishment of Sino-U.S. diplomatic relations in 1979. In these 30 years, changes occurred both in China and the United States, noticeably in the field of education exchange. In 1979, the U.S. Embassy in China issued 4,700 nonimmigrant visas to Chinese citizens, 770 of which were for students. In 2009, the number of nonimmigrant visas issued increased to almost 500,000, of which 77,000 were for students. This is 100 times more than 30 years ago (Chen, 2011). In addition, data from the Institute of International Education's Open Doors 2010 report also revealed that of all the foreign students who enrolled in American universities in the 2009–2010 academic year, nearly 128,000 (18%) were Chinese. China exported more students to the United States than any other country in the 2010–2011 academic year, a 30% increase over the previous year (Spak, 2011).

It is also true the other way around. There were only 1,200 foreigners living in Beijing 30 years ago, but nowadays there are more than 1,200 Americans working just in the U.S. Embassy in Beijing, and more Americans are living in China than in the state of Montana. From 2008 to 2009, a total of 13,674 American students traveled to China to study (Chen, 2011). Under the status quo, it is imperative to understand education in these two countries.

This chapter is a review of the research literature on learning and teaching in China and the United States. The literature was selected based on three criteria: (1) articles and books that explained the mainstream ideologies that dominated the Chinese and U.S. societies, (2) articles that explained the differences in terms of learning and teaching in China and the United States, and (3) research studies, published in the past 30 years from 1980 to present, that investigated the learning and teaching challenges from two groups: Chinese students learning in Western countries and Western teachers teaching in China. It is worthy of mentioning that in selecting research studies investigating learning and teaching challenges, I extended the country of destination where Chinese students go to study to include other Western English-speaking countries, as the initial search based on China and the United States revealed limited number of studies. In addition, I did this as many Western English-speaking countries share similar social ideologies and hold similar beliefs about learning and teaching as the United States. Therefore, the Chinese students in those Western countries and the teachers from those countries teaching in China face similar challenges. This chapter begins with an introduction of prevalent ideologies that have historically caused the social, cultural, and value differences between the United States and China. Next, it summarizes the learning and teaching pathways and beliefs, and then explains the cross-cultural challenges of learning and teaching. It concludes with a discussion of the problems and issues and offers suggestions in terms of how to support cross-cultural students and teachers.

PREVALENT IDEOLOGY IN THE UNITED STATES AND CHINA

Social ideologies shape the beliefs and values of the individuals within a society in all aspects, and education is directly influenced by a society's social ideology. It has been well recognized that individualism is central to the American character (Chen & Uttal, 1988; Spence, 1985) and self-reliance and self-confidence are highly valued (Elkins, 1994). Contrary to the American freedom of social ideologies, Confucianism traditionally has dominated Chinese minds and determined the collectivist nature of the Chinese society. The following sections briefly examine American Individualism, Confucianism, and Chinese Collectivism.

American Individualism

Individualism is found in many Western cultures, particularly the North American societies. As Spence (1985) defined it, individualism is "the belief that each of us is an entity separate from every other and from the group and as such is endowed with natural rights" (p. 1288). According to Triandis (1994), individuals are the basic units of perception in individualist cultures, and personal achievement, freedom, competition, and autonomy are highly valued. Behavior is more likely to be guided by attitudes and personality traits. Hence, members in an individualist society are more likely to pursue personal goals over group goals, and the construct of self is centered on self-reliance and self-confidence (Elkins, 1994).

Confucianism and Chinese Collectivism

Confucianism is a complex system of moral, social, and political thought that has influenced China for centuries. Confucian thoughts centered on achieving harmony and emphasized the proper ritual of the society (Ames & Rosemont, 1998). According to Confucius, it is important to educate the young to make following rituals a tradition of their own and not to challenge the authority, which usually refers to the elders, teachers, and the rulers. Confucius put the greatest emphasis on education and emphasized unification and the idea of the whole; hence, individuality was not appreciated (Yang, 2008).

The Confucian thoughts explain the collectivist nature of the Chinese society. Collectivism refers to "a perception of self that is embedded within social roles and social relationships; separate selves are de-emphasized with an orientation toward others and the welfare of the group or community" (Le & Stockdale, 2005, p. 682). When collectivism is highly appreciated in a society, individuals take on a particular location within the society. Individual equality, rights, and freedom become subordinate to moral conduct, public benefit, and social duty and responsibility (Zhang, 1988). Effort and diligence are highly valued in a collectivist society and human beings achieve the goal of self-perfection through self-criticism and self-cultivation (Chen & Uttal, 1988).

TEACHING AND LEARNING IN THE UNITED STATES AND CHINA

Not surprisingly, teaching and learning activities in the United States and China reflect the aforementioned differences in values and expectations. According to the literature, the differences in teaching and learning result in complexities in four aspects: the relevance of the curriculum and pedagogy, students' preferred learning styles, the social positions of teachers and students, and the expected patterns of teacher-student interaction (Chan, 1999; Ellsworth, 1997; Holmes, 2005; Li, 2003; Pratt, 1992; Redding, 1980; Zhou, 1988).

Differences in the Relevance of the Curriculum and Pedagogy

Hofstede (1986) explained that the education curriculum in one country might have little benefit to students coming from a different culture. In the early 1950s, China's higher education institutions followed the Soviet model in order to strengthen specialized education, but it resulted in a series of unfavorable outcomes (Jiang, 2005). More recently, students' achievement has become the emphasis of curriculum development. Zhao (2009) explains that American policymakers who praised Chinese students' academic achievement are drawing wrong lessons to excessively emphasize high-stakes testing in the American education system.

Ellsworth (1997) further argued that pedagogy is also context-dependent. The best practice of teaching in one country may not produce the expected results with students from a different country. For example, the traditional Chinese rote learning method has been regarded as surface-level learning in the West (Samuelowicz, 1987), but it has been proved that this method produced favorable results on Chinese learners (Cortazzi & Jin, 1996; Pratt, Kelly, & Wong, 1999; Winser, 1996).

Differences in Students' Preferred Learning Styles

Research suggested that students in the United States and China have different preferred learning styles and that this preference toward one method over the other is largely influenced by their different understandings of learning (Li, 2001, 2003). Li (2003) compared the understanding of learning between American and Chinese students and found that students from the two cultures emphasized different aspects of learning. While students in the United States valued critical thinking, learning through inquiry, practical and real-life experience in education (Boyles, 2006), Chinese students regarded learning as a lifelong pursuit that requires that they hold a modest attitude, endure hardship, and go through with diligence, perseverance, and dedication (Li, 2001). In addition, Chinese students believed that the purposes of learning were to improve the social status of self, bring honor to family, and contribute to society. In this last regard, Chinese and U.S. values coincide, though they are felt to a lesser degree in the United States.

The different understandings toward learning resulted in the different preferred learning styles. Most students in the United States believe in innate ability, prefer an open-ended and unstructured learning environment, value discussion, and do not expect their instructors to necessarily know all the right answers. In contrast, many Chinese believe that ability is an accumulation of skills and knowledge. Innate ability only decides the rate at which students acquire new knowledge; effort is the key to the ultimate level of achievement (Chen & Uttal, 1988; Dweck, 1999; Stevenson et al., 1990; Tweed & Lehman, 2002). Many Chinese students prefer to follow strict rules, to have a structured and defined learning environment, and expect their instructors to be the expert on the subject—to have the right answers to their questions and be the authority in classroom (Tapanes, Smith, & White, 2009).

Differences in the Social Positions of Teachers and Students

The social positions of teachers and students differ in the United States and China. Teachers are classified as professionals in the United States. Similar to a physician who treats patients and a lawyer who serves clients, a teacher serves students (Robb, 2006). Although teachers are respected as a profession, it is acceptable for teachers to acknowledge uncertainty and the lack of knowledge to students' questions.

Situations differ in China. Teachers in China have enjoyed a long-honored social status in history. Traditionally, they were one of the five categories of being who were more adored by society: the God of Heaven, the God of the Earth, the emperor, parents, and teachers (Zhou, 1988). They were expected to be the authority, the expert, the role model—the one that both students and parents looked up to (Pratt, 1992). Contemporarily, the Chinese curriculum has called for a change in terms of the roles teachers should play in classrooms. According to the Ministry of Education in China (2001), teachers were encouraged to be facilitators, guides, and task participants under the new English curriculum. However, this government-initiated call did not change how students perceive their teachers. Teachers are still respected as the knowledgeable ones (Björkell, 2011). The Confucian values of modesty and following rituals keep putting teachers at center stage in classrooms as the authority and the expert (Xie, 2009).

Differences in the Expected Patterns of Teacher-Student Interaction

The differences in mutual role expectations between teachers and students affect the learning process. According to Hofstede (1986), the roles teachers and students play under different cultures are guided by the values rooted in these cultures, and "lead to feelings of good and evil, right and wrong, rational and irrational, proper and improper" (p. 305). In individualist societies, teachers are expected to suppress emotion to be strictly impartial. They respect the independence of students, interpret intellectual disagreement as a stimulating exercise, openly praise students, and expect students to initiate communication and find their own ways of learning. Students, on the other hand, believe that knowledge and truth can be obtained from any competent person (it does not necessarily have to be the teacher). Students speak up spontaneously in large groups and are sometimes allowed to contradict or criticize teachers. They regard failure in school as a minor accident, and the effectiveness of learning is related to the amount of two-way communication in class.

In collectivist societies, teachers usually form a more personal relationship with students and are expected to give preferential treatment to some students. They avoid openly praising students and accept their role as the expert of their subject area. They demand respect from students both inside and outside class and interpret intellectual disagreement as personal disloyalty. Students, alternatively, value the wisdom from teachers and do not contradict or criticize teachers in public. They believe that a formal harmony in learning situations should be maintained at all times. Students also behave modestly, expect teachers to initiate communication, and speak up only when teachers invite them to do so. The students interpret silence in the classroom as being respectful and willingness to listen (Holmes, 2005). They prefer the structured question-answer format, think highly about unity, and expect teachers to outline the rules for them to follow. They consider failure in school a severe blow to their self-esteem.

In conclusion, ideology and cultural differences have a significant impact on learning and teaching. With the different beliefs and values appreciated by the two different cultures, and the different conceptions and styles of learning and teaching, cross-cultural students and teachers face many challenges.

CROSS-CULTURAL CHALLENGES
OF LEARNING AND TEACHING

As globalization has become a key idea for education in the 21st century, there are more students and teachers coming to different countries to study and work. The aforementioned data from the Institute of International Education's Open Doors 2012 report have made evident the increase of Chinese students in universities in the United States. China has become one of the largest countries to import Western teachers and has provided job opportunities for hundreds of thousands of Americans (Sina News Center, 2011). With these increased numbers of cross-cultural students and teachers, it is imperative to understand their needs and challenges, so they can be better supported academically, socially, and culturally. The following sections are devoted to reporting those challenges.

Challenges of Chinese University Students Learning in Western Countries

Studying in a different country can be an exciting but challenging experience for international students. In particular, the struggle of transitioning into a new learning environment is dependent upon how significant a change the new environment is to their home academic and pedagogical tradition (Mehdizadeh & Scott, 2005). The review of literature on Chinese students' learning experiences in Western countries suggested that although students overall were satisfied with their learning experiences in terms of educational quality, teaching styles, and support, they faced many challenges and went through an arduous process of adjustment. These challenges can be grouped into three categories: language incompetency, academic unfamiliarity, and cultural intricacies.

Language Incompetency. Among all the challenges and difficulties reported by international students academically, socially, and culturally, language incompetency was not surprisingly the most prevalent (Campbell & Li, 2008; Dillon & Swann, 1997; Feng, 1991; Gu & Maley, 2008; Heikinheimo & Schute, 1986; Holmes, 2005; Wan, 2001; Wan, Chapman, & Biggs, 1992). Ward and Masgoret (2004) studied international students' academic difficulties in New Zealand, which is like the United States in terms of its primary language being English, and found the top five challenges for students were related to language: making oral presentations, taking tests or exams, expressing themselves in English, expressing opinions to the teacher, and writing assignments.

Students reported their weaknesses in terms of English listening and speaking skills (Wan, 2001), and others mentioned the feeling of insecurity and academic pressure in a foreign country due to the lack of confidence in English communication (Dillon & Swann, 1997; Wan, Chapman, & Biggs, 1992). Campbell and Li (2008) summarized Asian students' language difficulties and stated that language barriers prevented students from effectively communicating with teachers and peers, following instruction, understanding lectures, evaluation criteria and procedures, completing assignments and examinations, and socializing with native residents. The lack of confidence in language skills has been shown to be one of the most daunting barriers for a positive adjustment experience. As explained by Takahashi (1989), long periods of hard studying, strong linguistic ability, and an extensive knowledge of the adopted culture are all necessary for adult learners to acquire foreign language proficiency, especially academic English proficiency.

Academic Unfamiliarity. Many Chinese students pass language tests with good scores; however, good scores on the tests by no means guarantee that a student is academically competent (Pederson, 1991). Campbell and Li (2008) used the term *academic illiteracy* to refer to the lack of knowledge on academic norms and conventions, and reported that many Chinese students in Western countries were academically illiterate (Campbell & Li, 2008). As learning is context-dependent and value-laden, some Chinese students may have limited understanding about the norms and conventions that are embedded in cultural values and beliefs.

Many researchers found that it was hard for some Chinese students to understand why plagiarism was a serious issue in academia in the West (Getty, 2011; Özturgut, 2007; Sapp, 2002; Simpson, 2008). Getty (2011) stated that the Chinese mind interprets learning as gathering all the relevant information on a subject rather than presenting one's own ideas in the context of others. Simpson (2008) also offered an explanation from the perspective of Chinese learning tradition. He argued that the Chinese education focused on students' ability of quoting, interpreting, and recognizing the Classics; hence, it is unnecessary to reference those acknowledged thinkers. And in fact, citing the reference may even be considered a sign of insufficient study.

Academic writing is another challenge to many international higher education students. In Campbell and Li's study (2008), students found academic writing most difficult, reporting lack of preparation in writing literature reviews, essays, research proposals, and making references.

Sociocultural Intricacies. Studying and living in a different country can be challenging. As a matter of fact, students encountered more sociocultural difficulties than language difficulties, such as unfamiliarity with the learning and living environment, and lack of understanding about the host country's cultural values and beliefs (Holmes, 2005). The difficulties in this category include sociocultural differences between students' home country and the host country, such as learning styles and motivations, understanding about assignments and teacher supports, and making friends with local students.

In addition to challenges discussed earlier related to Chinese learning styles, learning motivation and expectation have also caused Chinese students learning discomfort (Boyer & Sedlacek, 1986; Campbell & Li, 2008; Gu & Maley, 2008; Gu & Schweisfurth, 2006; Heikinheimo & Shute, 1986). Generally speaking, Chinese students possess higher achievement motivation as they believe in learning through effort rather than fixed ability (Dweck, 1999; Stevenson et al., 1990; Tweed & Lehman, 2002). To be the best brought pride not only for themselves but also for the entire family, including extended family members, such as uncles and aunts (Chang, 1999). Hence, competition and ranking are the greatest motivators. The students preferred to be pressured, controlled by teachers, and be compared with other students. However, this was incompatible with the values embedded in Western education. Therefore, Chinese students have felt dissatisfied with the unstructured and loose study atmosphere and felt disoriented by the light study load (Campbell & Li, 2008; Chen & Uttal, 1988).

Discussion and group assignments are another challenge for Chinese students (Campbell & Li, 2008; Holmes, 2005; Maley, 1983; Tan & Goh, 2006). Many Chinese students indicated that they did not know how to get involved in group discussion and were afraid that their input was not appreciated (Holmes, 2005). Furthermore, because discussion with teachers and peers in the classroom was not considered part of the learning process in traditional Chinese classrooms (Holmes, 2005), some Chinese students regarded discussion as a waste of time (Gu & Maley, 2008). As Maley (1983) explained, the imperial examination system in China has led teaching to be "didactic and text-bound, with very little or no time allowed for discussion" (p. 101).

In terms of group assignments, Chinese students found it frustrating to work with Western students in groups, as the Chinese conceived the group as an interdependent network in which members worked together and made decisions considering everyone's input. Group members in the Western classrooms, however, divided the task into pieces and each member was only responsible for her/his part. The information gathered independently was then gathered together to make a whole (Holmes, 2005). In addition, many Chinese hardworking students also considered group assignments unfair, unreasonable, and fruitless because group members, regardless of members' attitude and contribution, all received the same score (Campbell & Li, 2008).

Many Chinese students report lack of support from teachers outside classrooms as a difficulty in their learning. In China, most of the time in class was devoted to teachers' lecture, but students continued learning interactions with teachers after class in a social context beyond classrooms, and teachers were expected to provide support to students whenever needed (Biggs, 1996). In Western culture, however, teachers were rarely available after class except during the limited office-hour time, which caused the feeling of "being abandoned" or "hav[ing] to rely on the self" among Chinese students (Campbell & Li, 2008; Holmes, 2005).

Because of the language barriers, different ways of thinking and behaving, and the lack of common background and interest, Chinese students in Western countries also face social problems, such as homesickness and difficulty forming friendships with local students (Campbell & Li, 2008; Gu & Maley, 2008; Heikinheimo & Shute, 1986; Holmes, 2005). Many students reported the homesickness of being alone in a different country. Some students shared that they did not have much to talk to the local students about, some chose to stay in the homogeneous culture friendship because they considered themselves harder working than the locals, and some others regarded close friendship with local students as being disloyal to their Chinese peers. Additionally, one student described his socialization with local students as artificial, compared to his personal understanding of friendship (Holmes, 2005). In explaining the Chinese conception of friendship, Tan and Goh (2006) stated that Chinese students built highly personal relationships with each other once friendship was developed. They anticipated the receiving and returning of favors between friends and regarded it as an important obligation to foster and sustain the relationship. Western conception of friendship, on the other hand, valued individuality: Students asserted their individuality when communicating with friends and family members. While there was the need to affiliate with others, it was more of a result of common interests. Emphasis was on the individual and his or her unique inner qualities. The different style of interaction explained why many Chinese students preferred to stay within their own Chinese circle.

Challenges of Western Teachers Teaching in China

Just like cross-cultural Chinese students, Western teachers in China were facing many of the same challenges. Different understandings about knowledge and the ways to pursue it led to the discrepancy between students' learning style and teachers' teaching style (Zhou & Fan, 2007), which brought student-teacher relationship problems as well. Moreover, the Chinese also seemed to have different interpretations about the role that Western teachers needed to perform. In addition to these academic related issues, many Western teachers also reported their unfamiliarity with the politics in the school administration.

Styles Mismatch. Research suggested that Chinese learners were more analytic, imaginal (visual), concrete, and reflective in terms of their preferred learning style whereas Western teachers preferred the global, verbal, abstract, and TEF (trial, error, and feedback) teaching style (Zhou & Fan, 2007). Western teachers favored being facilitators in classrooms, encouraging questions and discussions. Teachers provided general direction, got students involved in activities, and pushed students to think and defend what they know. Chinese students, on the other hand, expected to follow teachers' lead or step-by-step guidance to find the definite correct answer to their question, and they were used to copying, drilling, and memorizing (Degen & Absalom, 1998; Pratt, Kelly, & Wong, 1999; Rao, 2010).

The style mismatch has caused misunderstandings. Many Western teachers portrayed Chinese students as unmotivated, passive learners, who demanded specific correct answers from the teacher and were unwilling to think deeply (Chu & Morrison, 2011; Simpson, 2008). Conversely, students were also frustrated with their Western teachers, thinking that they were disorganized, ignorant of proper teaching methods, lacked the subject knowledge, and talked aimlessly in class (Simpson, 2008).

Teacher-Student Relationship Problems. Effective teachers in the Chinese culture are characterized as having a close, protective relationship with students, just like a parent. A good teacher cares about students in and outside school and the care is not limited to the academic aspect of students' lives. Western teachers, however, tended to frame their relationship with students in terms of the institutional roles and responsibilities and avoid being too close (Pratt, Kelly & Wong, 1999). In addition, many Western teachers were also uncomfortable with the Chinese style of expressing feelings (Chu & Morrison, 2011; Simpson, 2008). Because harmony is central to the Chinese culture, many Chinese students tended not to express their real feelings when there were conflicts or disagreement. Sometimes a student's laugh and smile could be an expression of embarrassment (Gu & Maley, 2008). Furthermore, because "face" (self-image or respect from others) is very important in Asian culture, many students did not want to endanger the teacher's face personally or in public when problems arose. In this case, students usually reported the problem to a third person, who was usually the teacher's supervisor. All these normal cultural behaviors of the Chinese students have caused Western teachers dissatisfaction and discomfort.

Westerners' Roles. Having a misunderstanding about the role that foreign teachers should play was another difficulty for many Western teachers. When

China opened its door to modernization, Westerners were invited as foreign experts to teach English to Chinese (Cortazzi & Jin, 1996). This invitation was misinterpreted by many Western teachers as an invitation to bring their pedagogical expertise in language teaching (Lam, 2002). Many Western language teachers intended to be the "change agents," helping Chinese teachers develop innovative and competent language pedagogies (Chu & Morrison, 2011, p. 491). As Bodycott and Walker (2000) explained, "Many see themselves as savior, that is, bringing the best of the West to a developing country" (p. 81). This misinterpretation about the roles they should play in the classroom led to Western teachers' dissatisfaction when they found Chinese schools hesitant and unsupportive toward the changes they initiated. As a matter of fact, Chinese welcomed Western teachers' language authenticity and cultural familiarity and hoped for opportunities to enrich their English and learn about the Western culture (Rao, 2010).

Unfamiliarity with the Politics of the Administration. Just like many teachers who are the authority in classrooms, administrators are also the authority in their schools in China. For the Western teachers who did not have a full understanding of the school culture, working with the Chinese administrators could be a challenging process. Getty (2011) stated that many administrators in Chinese schools were accustomed to changing their minds constantly without being challenged. For examples, the class schedule was determined at the last minute, but then rescheduled just a few days before the start of the class; the semester holiday schedule was made available a month after the semester began; class time was changed without notice ahead of the time. Furthermore, Western teachers complained about the lack of democracy in the Chinese workplace and felt that the principals were like dictators of the school (Chu & Morrison, 2011).

To conclude, the challenges and difficulties reported by cross-cultural students and teachers resulted from the different values, beliefs, and cultures that are rooted in the Eastern and Western worlds. Knowing these challenges, apparently, helps schools and institutions provide support to facilitate their cross-cultural adaptation.

CROSS-CULTURAL TEACHING AND LEARNING: IMPLICATIONS AND SUGGESTIONS

Cross-cultural adaptation is a challenging process for everyone. For students, studying in a different culture requires courage, determination, and persistence (Wan, 2001). Living and studying in a different country meant that students did not only have to adjust and change, but sometimes had to give up their identity to assume a new one in order to be accepted in a different culture.

Research suggested that good preparation in the home country is positively related to the satisfaction level with the study abroad experience (Wang, 2011).

Those better-prepared students who were more familiar with the new learning environment tended to be more satisfied with their abroad learning experiences. Öztugut and Murphy (2009) provided several recommendations about how the universities can support international students, such as providing intercultural and multicultural communication programs, courses devoted to learning about different cultures, and English as a Second Language (ESL) support throughout the entire program of study.

For Western teachers, on top of adapting to a different culture, they also have the responsibility of providing effective instruction to Chinese students—those who share different values and beliefs about teaching and learning. Wong (2000) explained that Western teachers usually go through three stages of acculturation. The first stage is related to prior experience and expectations. At this stage, Western teachers bring their expectations to China and then get frustrated knowing the reality is different from what they expect. The Chinese, at the same time, get frustrated as well, noticing the unacceptability of Western practice. The second stage is the awakening stage in which Western teachers start to understand the reality and context of China and become accepting. Finally, in the last stage, Western teachers compromise and negotiate decisions with local teachers to be professionally productive.

In order to support international teachers transitioning into a new workplace, a two-level model based on capacity building was developed (Brown, Dashwood, Lawrence, & Burton, 2010). At the first level, international teachers should have access to key professional systems, knowledge, and the pedagogical expectations of an institution. It is the responsibility of the institution to be aware of the difficulties international teachers may encounter and help them overcome these barriers. The institution should make explicit the expected roles, duties, type of communication, and engagement level to international teachers. In addition, the sharing of successful practices from other teachers would also help provide a clear picture of the pedagogical expectation and practices of the institution. The second level involves strategies to help build staff and institutional capacity. International teachers should have opportunities to learn about the different pedagogy and cultural context, and be scaffolded in their adaptation process. The institution, on the other hand, should not only develop new pedagogical expectations and practices, but also value the strengths and tools that international teachers bring with them for the greater good of the organization.

MOVING TOWARD THE "MIDDLE GROUND"

As the world becomes increasingly culturally diverse, the internationalization of education has become a major goal in many countries. Learning from the literature in the past 30 years, this chapter provides conceptual views that help us better understand the issues related to social, cultural, and ideological differences in China and the United States.

Although challenges exist, cross-cultural students and teachers bring international perspectives, cultural diversity, and innovative learning and teaching methods. They are valuable assets to the globalization of education. An increased awareness, flexibility, and open-mindedness are keys to ensure a successful cross-cultural experience for both students and teachers.

SUMMARY OF IMPLICATIONS

- Individualism is the main social ideology in the United States and it values personal achievement, competition, self-reliance, and self-confidence.
- Confucianism explains the collectivist nature of the Chinese society. Under the culture of collectivism, effort and diligence are valued. Individual rights and freedom become subordinate to social duty and responsibility.
- Education in China and the United States is under the influence of the two main social ideologies in four aspects: differences in the relevance of the curriculum and pedagogy, students' preferred learning styles, the social positions of teachers and students, and the expected patterns of teacher-student interaction.
- The challenges for Chinese university students to study in Western countries include language incompetency, academic unfamiliarity, and sociocultural intricacies.
- The challenges of Western teachers teaching in China include styles mismatch, teacher-student relationship problems, misunderstanding about Westerners' role, and unfamiliarity with the politics of the administration.

REFERENCES

Ames, R. T., & Rosemont, H. Jr. (1998). *The Analects of Confucius: A philosophical translation.* New York: The Random House Publishing Group.

Bigg, J. (1996). Western misperceptions of the Confucian heritage learning culture. In D. Watkins & J. Biggs (Eds.), *The Chinese learner: Cultural, psychological, and contextual influences* (pp. 45–67). Hong Kong/Melbourne, Australia: Comparative Education Research Center/The Australian Council for Education Research Ltd.

Björkell, S. (2011). *Perspectives on teaching.* Retrieved from http://radio86.com/lifestyle/education/perspectives-teaching

Bodycott, P., & Walker, A. (2000). Teaching abroad: Lessons learned about inter-cultural understanding for teachers in higher education. *Teaching in Higher Education, 5*(1), 79–94.

Boyer, S. P., & Sedlacek, W. E. (1986). *Attitudes and perceptions of incoming international students.* (Research Report #4-86). College Park: Maryland University Counseling Center. (ERIC Document Reproduction Service No. 278935)

Boyles, D. (2006). Dewey's epistemology: An argument for warranted assertions, knowing, and meaningful classroom practice. *Educational Theory, 56,* 57–68.

Brown, A., Dashwood, A., Lawrence, J., & Burton, L. (2010). "Crossing over": Strategies for supporting the training and development of international teachers. *International Journal of Learning, 17*(4), 321–333.

Campbell, J., & Li, M. S. (2008). Asian students' voices: An empirical study of Asian students' learning experiences at a New Zealand University. *Journal of Studies in International Education, 12*(4), 375–396.

Chan, S. (1999). The Chinese learner—a question of style. *Education + Training, 41*(6/7), 294–304.

Chang, J. (1999). *Transforming Chinese American literature: A study of history, sexuality, and ethnicity.* New York: Peter Lang Publishing.

Chen, C. S., & Uttal, D. H. (1988). Cultural values, parents' belief, and children's achievement in the United States and China. *Human Development, 31,* 351–358.

Chen, Q. (2011). 中美历史教育交流的新篇章—记美国《社会教育》中国特刊. [A new chapter in the history of Sino-U.S. educational exchange.] Retrieved from http://www.pep.com.cn/gzls/js/xsjl/xsdt/201108/t20110817_1064388.htm

Chu, C. K., & Morrison, K. (2011). Cross-cultural adjustment of native-speaking English Teachers (NETs) in Hong Kong: A factor in attrition and retention. *Educational Studies, 37*(4), 481–501.

Cortazzi, M., & Jin, L. (1996). English teaching and learning in China. *Language Teaching, 29,* 61–80.

Degen, T., & Absalom, D. (1998). Teaching across cultures: Considerations for Western EFL teachers in China. *Hong Kong Journal of Applied Linguistics, 3*(2), 117–132.

Dillon, R. K., & Swann, J. (1997, November). *International students' adjustment studying in America: Assessing how uncertainty reduction and communication satisfaction influence international students' adjustment.* Paper presented at the National Communication Association Convention, Chicago, IL.

Dweck, C. S. (1999). *Self-theories.* Philadelphia: Psychology Press.

Elkins, M. (1994). *Chinese students avoid interpersonal communication: An analysis of the problem and suggestions for retentions.* (ERIC Document Reproduction Service No. ED374474)

Ellsworth, E. (1997). *Teaching positions; Difference, pedagogy, and the power of address.* New York: Teachers College Press.

Feng, J. H. (1991). *The adaptation of students from the People's Republic of China to an American academic culture.* (ERIC Document Reproduction Service No. Ed 329833)

Getty, L. J. (2011). Points of departure. False assumptions: The challenges and politics of teaching in China. *Teaching in Higher Education, 16*(3), 347–352.

Gu, Q., & Maley, A. (2008). Changing places: A study of Chinese students in the UK. *Language and Intercultural Communication, 8(4),* 224–245.

Gu, Q., & Schweisfurth, M. (2006). Who adapts? Beyond cultural models of "the" Chinese learner. *Language, Culture and Curriculum, 19*(1), 74–89.

Heikinheimo, P. S., & Schute, J.C.M. (1986). The adaptation of foreign students; Student view and institutional implications. *Journal of College Student Personnel, 27,* 399–406.

Hofstede, G. (1986). Cultural differences in teaching and learning. *International Journal of Intercultural Relations, 10,* 301–320.

Holmes, P. (2005). Ethnic Chinese students' communication with cultural others in a New Zealand University. *Communication Education, 54*(4), 289–311.

Institute of International Education. (2012). *Open doors 2012: Report on international exchange.* Retrieved from http://www.iie.org/en/Research-and-Publications/Open-Doors

Jiang, K. (2005). The centre-periphery model and cross-national educational transfer: The influence of the US on teaching reform in China's universities. *Asia Pacific Journal of Education, 25*(2), 227–239.

Lam, A. (2002). English in education in China: Policy changes and learners' experiences. *World Englishes, 21,* 245–256.

Le, T. N., & Stockdale, G. D. (2005). Individualism, collectivism, and delinquency in Asian American adolescents. *Journal of Clinical Child and Adolescent Psychology, 34*(4), 681–691.

Li, J. (2001). Chinese conceptualization of learning. *Ethos, 29*(2), 111–137.

Li, J. (2003). U. S. and Chinese cultural beliefs about learning. *Journal of Educational Psychology, 95*(2), 258–267.

Maley, A. (1983). Xanadu—"A miracle of rare device": The teaching of English in China. *Language Learning and Communication, 2*(1), 97–104.

Mehdizadeh, N., & Scott, G. (2005). Adjustment problems of Iranian international students in Scotland. *International Education Journal, 6,* 484–493.

Ministry of Education. (2001). 全日制义务教育普通高级中学英语课程标准(试验稿). [National English Curriculum Standard—Experimental version.] Beijing: Beijing Normal University Press.

Özturgut, O. (2007). Teaching West in the East: An American university in China. *International Journal of Teaching and Learning in Higher Education, 19*(3), 228–237.

Özturgut, O., & Murphy, C. (2009). Literature vs. practice: Challenges for international students in the U.S. *International Journal of Teaching and Learning in Higher Education, 22*(3), 374–385.

Pederson, P. B. (1991). Counseling international students. *Counseling Psychologist, 19,* 10–58.

Pratt, D. D. (1992). Chinese conceptions of learning and teaching: A westerner's attempt at understanding. *International Journal of Lifelong Education, 11*(4), 301–319.

Pratt, D, D., Kelly, M., & Wong, W.S.S. (1999). Chinese conceptions of "effective teaching" in Hong Kong: Toward culturally sensitive evaluation of teaching. *International Journal of Lifelong Education, 18*(4), 241–258.

Rao, Z. H. (2010). Chinese students' perceptions of native English-speaking teachers in EFL teaching. *Journal of Multilingual and Multicultural Development, 31*(1), 55–68.

Redding, S. G. (1980). Management education for Orientals. In B. Garratt & J. Stopford (Eds.), *Breaking down barriers: Practice and priorities for international management education* (pp. 193–214). Farnborough Hants, UK: Westmead.

Robb, K. C. (2006). An uncertain position: Examining the status of teaching as a profession. *Essays in Education, 18.* Retrieved from http://www.usca.edu/essays/vol182006/robb%20revised.pdf

Samuelowicz, K. (1987). Learning problems of overseas students: Two sides of a story. *Higher Education Research and Development, 6,* 121–134.

Sapp, D. A. (2002). Towards an international and intercultural understanding of plagiarism and academic dishonesty in composition: Reflections from the People's Republic of China. *Issues in Writing, 13*(1), 58–79.

Simpson, S. T. (2008). Western EFL teachers and East-West classroom-culture conflict. *Regional Language Centre Journal, 39*(3), 381–394.

Sina News Center. (2011). 老外新职业 来华当外教. [New career for foreigners, come to China to teach.] Retrieved from http://news.sina.com.cn/w/2011-10-25/053623356389.shtml

Spak, K. (2011). Chinese students enrolling in U.S. colleges in record numbers. Retrieved from http://www.suntimes.com/news/education/4266771-418/chinas-new-crop-of-exports-students.html

Spence, J. T. (1985). Achievement American style: The rewards and costs of individualism. *American Psychologist, 40*(12), 1285–1295.

Steven, H. W., Lee. S. Y., Chen, C., Stigler, J. W., Hsu, C. C., Kitamura, S., & Hatano, G. (1990). Contexts of achievement: A study of American, Chinese, and Japanese Children. *Monographs of the Society for Research in Child Development, 55*(1–2), 1–116.

Takahashi, Y. (1989). Suicidal Asian patients: Recommendations for treatment. *Suicide and Life-Threatening Behavior, 19,* 305–313.

Tan, J.K.L., & Goh, J.W.P. (2006). Why do they not talk? Towards an understanding of students' cross-cultural encounters from an individualism/collectivism perspective. *International Education Journal, 7*(5), 651–667.

Tapanes, M. A., Smith, G. G., & White, J. A. (2009). Cultural diversity in online learning: A study of the perceived effects of dissonance in levels of individualism/collectivism and Tozer tolerance of ambiguity. *Internet and Higher Education, 12,* 26–34.

Triandis, H. C. (1994). *Culture and social behavior.* New York: McGraw-Hill.

Tweed, R. G., & Lehman, D. R. (2002). Learning considered within a cultural context: Confucian and Socratic approaches. *American Psychologist, 57,* 89–99.

Wan, G. (2001). The learning experience of Chinese students in American Universities: A cross-cultural perspective. *College Student Journal, 35*(1).

Wan, T., Chapman, D. W., & Biggs, D. A. (1992). Academic stress of international students attending U.S. university. *Research in Higher Education, 33*(5), 607–622.

Wang, W. G. (2011). Chinese students' satisfaction of the study abroad experience. *International Journal of Educational Management, 25*(3), 265–277.

Ward, C., & Masgoret, A. (2004). *The experiences of international students in New Zealand: Report on the results of the national survey.* Thorndon, Wellington: New Zealand Ministry of Education.

Wenzhong, H., & Cornelius, L. G. (1999). *Encountering the Chinese: A guide for American.* New York: Intercultural Press.

Winser, W. N. (1996). Literacy development and teaching East and West: Culture and Context—Text relations. *Hong Kong Journal of Applied Linguistics, 1,* 19–37.

Wong, M. S. (2000). *The influence of gender and culture on the pedagogy of five western teachers in China.* (Unpublished doctoral dissertation). University of Southern California, Los Angeles.

Xie, X. Y. (2009). Why are students quiet? Looking at the Chinese context and beyond. *ELT Journal, 64*(1), 10–20.

Yang, S. H. (2008). Narrative of a cross-cultural language teaching experience: Conflicts between theory and practice. *Teaching and Teacher Education, 24,* 1564–1572.

Zhang, D. (1988). Chinese culture and Chinese philosophy. *Chinese Studies in Philosophy, XIX*(3), 69–95.

Zhao, H. (2009). *Catching up or leading the way: American education in the age of globalization.* Alexandria, VA: Association for Supervision & Curriculum Development.

Zhou, L., & Fan, Z. Z. (2007). Discrepancy between native English speaker teachers' teaching styles and Chinese English learners' learning styles. *US-China Education Review, 4*(9), 15–20.

Zhou, N. Z. (1988). Historical contexts of educational reforms in present-day China. *Interchange, 19*(3/4), 8–18.

PART II

Drawing on Chinese Educators' Perspectives to Reflect on the "Middle Ground"

This section presents a group of Chinese professors' perspectives on Chinese educational thinking and practices, and explores how these ideas may be adapted for learning and instruction in a U.S. context. Chapter 3 centers on seven sets of educational relationships, each addressing one specific area of Chinese ways of teaching and learning. This chapter also gives tips to help other Chinese educators adopt and adapt them in teaching diverse learners in America's multicultural and multiethnic classrooms, thus helping them reconcile differences between the two perspectives on some common ground.

Chapter 4 illustrates the complexities extant in negotiating educational expectations and opportunities for Chinese teachers, parents, and children in the Southeast of the United States, and also makes suggestions for supporting recent Chinese immigrants' bicultural and bilingual development. The chapter gives recommendations for administrators, teacher educators, and teachers to better serve first- and second-generation Chinese immigrants to address cross-cultural conflicts in the United States. These ideas highlight the importance of cross-cultural education on the "middle ground."

Chapter 5 addresses the identities, values, and beliefs held by a Chinese language teacher. The teacher was found to carry many notions and teaching practices situated in Chinese culture, including teaching students in accordance with their aptitude, willingness to work hard, and respect for teachers. Interestingly, her classroom practices sometimes depart from Chinese cultural values and beliefs in keeping with the new American sociocultural realities. This demonstrates how one's professional beliefs may change over time and move toward a more balanced "middle ground."

Chapter 6 examines the experiences and perspectives of four educators from Chinese backgrounds. Their stories can not only help the educational community better understand these Chinese educators' lived experiences, but also encourage other nonnative faculty to similarly reflect on and sort out their own pedagogical journeys. Their hybrid experiences and perspectives showcase the benefits of cross-cultural integration and transformation.

3

Being Culturally Relevant in Teaching

Binyao Zheng

U.S. demographics are projected to change dramatically during the next 50 years, and more and more learners from diverse backgrounds will enter our schools (Martin & Nakayama, 2010). Accordingly, teachers need to practice culturally relevant pedagogy to better connect with diverse students, build on what they bring to school, and encourage them to become self-directed thinkers within a caring and democratic society (Pang, 2005). Research has shown that culturally responsive teachers understand and value the role of diversity in schools. They can infuse cultural knowledge and adapt their curricula and pedagogy to more adequately fulfill the needs of the diverse population of students. As a result, teacher educators are increasingly called upon to prepare school teachers with these competencies (Prater & Devereaux, 2009; Siwatu, 2011).

It has been more than 20 years since I came to the United States as a graduate student. Prior to that, I taught English at the secondary and university levels in China. In addition, I worked as a translator and coordinated international exchange programs at Central China Normal University. I believe I have benefited from Chinese cultural traditions and educational perspectives, which in turn have guided and supported my work as a teacher educator in the United States.

In 1997, I joined the teacher education faculty at Kennesaw State University, one of the largest teacher producers of Georgia. Since then, I have been teaching in the areas of educational psychology, research methods, and multicultural education. In this chapter, I use an analytical and reflective approach to explore how cultural elements can be integrated to facilitate learning, and how I as a teacher educator used my background, experience, and expertise to model culturally relevant teaching. I also draw on Confucianism and Daoism as traditional Chinese thoughts, while exploring some of the contemporary educational practices in China.

This chapter includes seven sections, each addressing an area in education:

1. Cultural differences in attribution and expectations;
2. A modest learning attitude;
3. A harmonious learning environment;
4. Diverse styles in teaching and learning;
5. Learning theories and language arts;
6. Conceptions of student behavior management; and
7. Roles of a parent and an educator.

In the following, each of these areas will be discussed, with concrete details or personal examples, starting with an exploration of cultural differences in attribution and expectations between Chinese and American teachers. The chapter concludes with a call for other educators and teachers to similarly adopt culturally relevant teaching.

CULTURAL DIFFERENCES IN ATTRIBUTION AND EXPECTATIONS

Attribution to Success and Failure

Attribution theory is a systematic analysis of the possible ways that people perceive the courses of their success or failure in terms of achievement. Accordingly, how to perceive the success or failure as a consequence of past experience becomes critical in the individual's decision making for current and future practices.

As psychology defines, there are three key elements that contribute to success or failure: ability, effort, and luck. *Ability* is relatively constant and does not change rapidly overnight; therefore, it is beyond the individual's control. *Luck* is the opportunity unknown to the individual, and it is also out of the individual's control. The only element that the individual can manage is *effort*. For example, if I receive some math homework, such as solving equation problems, I can spend 2 hours or possibly more reviewing all of the equation patterns before deciding on the correct ones to solve the problems. Or, if I just want to fulfill the task, I can simply apply the equations that I assume would work and spend 10 or 15 minutes finishing the assignment. Obviously, my effort of spending 2 hours devoted to mastery and comprehension of all the equation patterns will lead me to greater success in math performance.

Researchers (e.g., Eccles & Wigfield, 2002) found that children from different cultures may hold varying perspectives toward academic achievement since they are influenced by unique motivational beliefs, values, and goals. For example, Indo-Chinese students, as opposed to American and Caucasian students, have stronger beliefs that failure is due to lack of effort. Latino students have similarly strong beliefs. On the contrary, African American and Caucasian students often attribute failure to inability to understand and perform.

Graduate students who are inservice teachers frequently report difficulties working with children who believe that they simply could not do the work. Typical statements are: "I am not a math person. I just cannot do it." "I am not a musician. I cannot join the performance." A more interesting argument would be, "I am a visual person, and this paperwork is not for me!" and so on. Actually, these learners are overemphasizing the power of ability in completing a task. The idea is, "I am unable to do it, so why should I try?" In dealing with these perspectives, I introduced the Chinese perspective, which emphasizes *effort*.

I asked an M.Ed. Educational Psychology class: "If one of your students fails a math test, and you ask the student's mother what she thought the major reason was, what reason might you get?" Many said, "She would say that was hard and it was not for my child." I shared with my students that while the American mother's response highlights ability, most Chinese mothers would say, "My child just did not study it. If he had spent some more time on it he should be able to do it!"

Expectations for Learning Achievement

Expectations align with perspectives in attribution. If someone greatly values *effort*, then that person would believe that more effort will lead to success. Remember, among the three elements in attribution, *effort* is the only aspect that the individual can really control. Chinese parents, as well as educators, have high expectations for their children and students, believing that if they work hard they will succeed. In the United States, we often hear students saying that they "just cannot do it." Parents and teachers are more likely to underestimate the ability of the children with the dominating perspective of respecting the nature and needs that the children have. In addressing the topic of expectations, I shared a story about a Chinese mother's demand and the misunderstanding of an American teacher.

A 6th-grade Chinese girl was achieving straight As. At the teacher-parent conference, the mother asked the teacher: "Could you please raise the standards for my child?" "Sure," the teacher replied readily. In China, when a parent asks a teacher to "raise the standards," what the parent hopes is that the teacher will have higher standards with the child and help the child learn more, such as with more challenging tasks. Unfortunately, this middle school teacher did not understand that. She did not do anything to provide the child with higher-level learning; what she did instead was simply to give the child Bs rather than As.

When I told this true story to an M.Ed. Educational Psychology class and asked them: "What do you think the Chinese mother was asking the teacher to do?" A female middle school science teacher said, "Maybe the parent thought that the school's standards were low?" A male math teacher said honestly, "I really don't understand what she meant." When they finally got the message that the mother was asking for higher expectations for her daughter, they were excited, and commented, "That's nice!"

In American education, high standards and expectations are also advocated. AP classes, Honors programs, and Governor's Schools, for example, encourage students to advance their studies for a higher level of achievement. Scholarships, like the Hope Scholarship in Georgia, support hardworking high school students to get into a university. It is important that teachers hold high expectations and value students' *effort*. To foster a learning perspective, I also advocated *modesty* from the thoughts of the Chinese educator Confucius.

A MODEST LEARNING ATTITUDE

There is a consensus among many scholars: Chinese culture values *modesty* while American culture encourages *self-confidence*. The Chinese perspective is rooted in the Confucian attitude of learning, which encourages being humble as Confucius once taught his students: "Three people traveling together, there must be someone who could be my teacher." It is important to learn from others, and students can learn from each other.

In America, *modesty* is not highlighted in education, particularly in the early stages of development. Growing up, children are taught to be brave and confident in their own abilities. Consequently, if a child feels overly confident about his/her own abilities, then that child may not want to learn from others.

Learning from others makes people more capable, while feeling positive about the self may also be necessary especially when facing difficulties and challenges. Then, which is more beneficial? The answer of most educators would be "both." In most cases, a balanced combination of the American *self-confidence* coupled with the Chinese *modesty* might be most beneficial.

Our Master of Arts in Teaching (MAT) program includes a sequence of two courses that focus on research methods and reflection. Students produce autoethnographies as capstone projects. It is easy for students to mistake the purpose of the courses and think that they are solely for completing their projects for graduation. To facilitate the students' learning from each other, I adopt the Confucian learning attitude.

"How many of you know anything about the Chinese educator Confucius?" I asked an MAT Capstone Seminar class. Many raised their hands. I then asked: "Do you know any of his thoughts?" There was a silence. "Well," I introduced, "one of his famous quotes is, 'Three people traveling together, there must be someone who could be my teacher.'" I continued, "Then, look around, how many do we have as a class?" They looked around and laughed. "We have many more than three, and we do not just travel together for a while, we study together for an entire semester, actually a year!" They looked excited. I believed they were quick in getting the message—we can learn from each other!

With great enthusiasm they shared their field experiences in groups, and each group recommended a representative to share with the class. Questions were raised, comments were shared, and new approaches were explored. A student later wrote in the course evaluation: "I enjoyed the cultural relevance that the professor used in his teaching. It broadened my view toward learning and teaching."

In Confucius's time, the teacher was respected as the authority of knowledge, and it was the student who needed to learn from the teacher. To make sense with the contemporary *student-centered* educational philosophy, I applied the concept of *modesty* to myself. With students' questions, comments, and presentations I identified their wisdom and creativity. I used their ideas as sample research topics and told them I had learned a great amount from them, including many things that I had never thought about. Students have taken my attitude positively, as one of them wrote: "The professor treated us as teachers and colleagues. He is such a great role model for my teaching profession."

In American education, learning from others is also emphasized and put into practice, particularly at the advanced levels. In teacher education, for example, we apply a variety of learning theories to engage learners to study together. These theories and approaches include Albert Bandura's (1977) social cognitive theory and the cooperative learning approach. While the social cognitive theory facilitates learning through observation and models, the cooperative learning approach provides opportunities for the learners to share authority and build on the knowledge that is distributed among other people. These contemporary theories and approaches have American roots in the work of psychologists, such as John Dewey (1913), and they echo the traditional Chinese thoughts that value a modest learning attitude.

Modesty contributes to learning achievement, but alone it may not be effective. A harmonious learning environment is also needed to ensure that all students learn and succeed.

A HARMONIOUS LEARNING ENVIRONMENT

Education that is multicultural provides an environment that values diversity and portrays it positively (Gollnick & Chinn, 2004), and the general purpose of multicultural education is to foster mutual understanding of and respect for each other

(Pang, 2005). Such beliefs and expectations are explained by the Chinese philosophy of Daoism, which emphasizes harmony and unity.

To explain the idea of harmony, I introduced the Chinese character 道 [dao]. I wrote the character on the board in calligraphy style and asked the class what image they could associate it with. That was a hard task. Then, I illustrated the component of 首 [shou], literally a person's head, and the other component of 走 [zou], which shows the walking motion of the person. I walked across the room for students to perceive the meaning of the character. Putting their perceptions and imaginations together, they eventually understood the Chinese word 道 [dao] as they said: "You walk." "You move forward." "When you walk, you walk on the road." "You need the road, and Dao means the road, right?"

"Exactly," I agreed. "Accordingly, there is the Dao, the nature of everything, of doing things, and that's what Daoism means!" I explained that the soul principle of Daoism is the notion of *harmony*, which ensures the existence and development of all species within a welcoming environment for all.

Then, the class examined ten general purposes of multicultural education, with the last one being, "Students, teachers, and parents will work together to eliminate racism, sexism, classism, homophobia, and other types of social oppression in schools and society" (Pang, 2005, p. 285). When one group presented the reasons why they had chosen this purpose as one of the most important ones, someone said, "This purpose emphasizes *Harmony* in school and society, and it echoes the Chinese Daoism." They applied ancient Chinese thoughts in understanding and addressing current educational issues.

DIVERSE STYLES IN
TEACHING AND LEARNING

In the educational methods courses, major topics include instructional strategies and learning styles. When looking at the nature of various types of content knowledge and the preferred ways of performance by individual teachers and students, there is a wide array of diverse approaches in teaching and learning. What is amazing beyond these specific choices is that the diversity may be rooted in cultural traditions. Some cultures value spiritual knowledge, while others prefer scientific knowledge. Some emphasize theoretical knowledge, while others are more practically oriented (Zion & Kozleski, 2005). For example, mainstream American students tend to favor a learning mode that is based on logical analysis of written work. On the other hand, African American, Native American, and rural White students prefer an oral mode. To demonstrate how teaching and learning styles differ across cultures, I used the example of automation used in China in math problem solving.

Automation in Math Problem Solving

There are a number of issues in the study of cognition, including the issue of understanding, memorization, association, brain-based learning, and so forth, and teachers confront various challenges in pedagogical and cultural aspects (Schunk, 2012). Researchers have reported that Chinese schools, as well as schools in other Asian countries (such as Korea and Japan), encourage quick studies and the use of automation, with which the learner gets the answer immediately without going through the step-by-step procedures.

The following is a scenario with an undergraduate Educational Psychology class with the topics of cognition and problem solving.

I gave the class a math problem and asked them how an American math teacher would solve it. They demonstrated the "typical" American way in solving this subtraction:

$$\begin{array}{r} 6^5\ 7^{17} \\ -\ 2\ \ 8\ \ \\ \hline 3\ \ 9 \end{array}$$

Knowing that 7 is not enough to be subtracted by 8, borrow 1 from 6. The problem-solver would go through the steps:

A. Cross 6 to borrow from it, write 5 as the remainder by 6 and write 17 by 7.
B. Get the answer: $17 - 8 = 9$; $5 - 2 = 3$; the answer is 39.

"Perfect!" I commented on the procedures. Then I asked, "This is the typical American way of doing it. Do you want to know how a Chinese math teacher would do it?" "Yes!" They looked at me curiously. I demonstrated the way a Chinese math teacher would do the problem using the skill of automation. The basic approach is very similar, but Step A is greatly simplified. Rather than crossing out 6 and writing a 5 and a 17, a simple dot above 6 would be just enough to remind the problem-solver that there has been a "borrowing" action there, and then he can use the invisible image of 17 to get 9 and the invisible image of 5 to get 3. I asked the class: "How can you get the invisible images?" They said, "Use the brain, cognition!" "Exactly," I approved. "It is actually a highly brain-based approach that trusts the effect of short-term memory and ability in quick study. It also helps develop the learner's ability of intuition in math acquisition." "This is amazing!" one of the students commented.

Gradual progression is also practiced in China, particularly at the beginning of learning to solve new kinds of problems. The difference is that the Chinese math teacher would then put more emphasis on developing students' automated problem-solving skills. This is identified as a major feature and strength in Chinese math teaching. I claimed to the class that in America we often underestimate the ability of the learner. Using too much procedure, such as crossing a number and writing the remainder number is logical, but the procedure does not facilitate cognition and high-level thinking. Researchers have reported that Asian students perform better in mathematics and have a more positive attitude toward learning math. One of the reasons is that from the beginning of math learning they have trusted their ability in solving the problems. Thus, math is not really difficult to them and solving a problem can be fun.

Deductive vs. Inductive Inquiry

Another notable difference in instructional strategies and learning styles is the way of inquiry—*deductive* inquiry versus *inductive* inquiry. As Bennett (1990) reported, Native American students prefer the deductive learning model as opposed to the inductive procedure. They perform better if lessons begin with an overview and then proceed to a detailed examination of the specifics. In contrast, Chinese and Asian students in general are more accustomed to the inductive approach. When the teacher begins a topic by telling a story, the students know that the teacher is making a point. They try to understand the story and figure out what is behind it. At the end of the story, the students get the message or the teacher highlights what he/she really wants to say.

I advised a class by explaining why American students may not be very receptive to the inductive approach: "Well, you may not want to use the inductive way easily since the American students won't be that patient. They might ask: 'What are you talking about?'" They all laughed, but they became aware that knowing the cultural differences is interesting and helpful. This knowledge led them to feel more comfortable while choosing instructional techniques and organizing learning activities with students from different cultures.

Intercultural learning is not always easy or comfortable. Sometimes intercultural encounters make people aware of their own ethnocentrism—a tendency to think that one's own culture is superior to other cultures (Martin & Nakayama, 2010). To guard against my potential bias or ethnocentrism, I tried to explore the pros and cons of both sides. Actually, *deductive* inquiry and *inductive* inquiry are both meaningful and useful, and I encouraged students to use both to vary their instructional styles. The popular *advance organizer* is a typical *deductive* strategy in instruction, which presents an overview of a lesson plan at the beginning of a class, and I use it a lot. I commented that I was being *deductive* with the *advance organizer*, and there was laughter when I claimed, "You see, I am becoming more Americanized!"

To American teachers and many other people in the Western world, the Chinese culture is unique and mysterious. For example, its linguistic system appears to be so different in perceiving and presenting the world, and it can be used in culturally relevant teaching.

LEARNING THEORIES AND LANGUAGE ARTS

In learning theories, sensory register is the first component of the dual-store model of memory, which holds incoming information long enough for it to undergo preliminary cognitive processing. Forms of storage make the difference in whether the learner will encode the information for long-term memory. The important implication for teachers is that information that is meaningfully presented during sensory register is likely to be encoded and retained by the learner. This concept of learning is discussed in the educational psychology courses at all levels: undergraduate, M.Ed./MAT graduate, and doctorate.

According to Prater and Devereaux (2009), teacher educators need to obtain knowledge about diversity and how it affects the schools for which they are preparing future teachers, while at the same time acquiring culturally responsive dispositions. To illustrate the effect of a meaningful presence of information with sensory register, I used the Chinese translation for Coca-Cola as a form of language arts. Here is a scenario with an M.Ed. Learning Theories class. The topic under study was information processing view of human learning.

"How many of you like Coca-Cola?" I asked. Many raised their hands.

"Why do you like Coca-Cola?"

"Because it tastes good."

"Now imagine, if you don't know anything about Coca-Cola, and *Coca-Cola* is a new word you see for the first time, are you going to memorize this word?"

"No." "Definitely not."

"Well, you don't know how popular Coca-Cola is in China now, not just because it tastes good, but also because the way the Chinese language puts it is so attractive."

I wrote 可口可乐 on the board with the phonetics *Ke Kou Ke Le* and asked students to try to say it. They tried curiously. I explained: "*Ke* means okay or good for, *Kou* means mouth, *Kekou* then means delicious. *Le* means happiness. What impresses you when you first see or hear the name? It is going to be good for your mouth—to enjoy, and good for your happiness!"

"That's cool!" "Interesting!" said the students.

I concluded: "Since it is such a good drink, you definitely want to try it and will memorize the name *KeKouKeLe*, or for short, *KeLe*—Be happy!"

Every time I used this example I was touched by students' enthusiasm in learning a new language and their support for my cultural relevance. In addition, the illustration demonstrated that a daily item such as Coca-Cola can be so impressively portrayed with another language. Language arts are embedded in all content teaching, and I believe the linguistic integration can be performed by all teachers, no matter what subjects they teach and what backgrounds they have.

Despite the many differences between Chinese and American cultures, such as those presented by the Chinese and English languages, I found that Chinese and American educators share many common tasks and challenges. Student behavior management is one of these common challenges.

CONCEPTIONS OF STUDENT
BEHAVIOR MANAGEMENT

Classroom management is critical for effective teaching. Whether students are learning and how much they are learning largely depends on the classroom management by the teacher. Chinese and American teachers take student behavior management as their common responsibilities and challenges. However, their approaches in practice are different.

In working with children and students, there are four different styles—authoritarian, authoritative, neglectful, and indulgent (Santrock, 2008). Research has found that American classrooms are generally more democratic, with plenty of freedom for student needs, but still with rules and regulations. This aligns with the *authoritative* style and contrasts with the more authoritarian Chinese classrooms, in which the students are more disciplined, with an emphasis of student *self-regulation*. Once, I asked a class what type of teachers and parents they wanted to be. Almost all students raised their hands for the second type—*authoritative*, since the *authoritative* style is especially important for helping children construct their individual identities and begin to function more autonomously as they develop into and through adolescence.

It is good that most American teachers, as well as parents, prefer to be *authoritative*, but some may go overboard by giving children too much freedom that can result in behavior problems. In American schools, teachers often ask for smaller-sized classes. Thirty may be too many, and 25 may be still too many to manage. I told a class that I had 45 or more students in my classes while teaching in China, and they asked: "How can you manage that many?" I then introduced the Chinese traditions and practices that include discipline, parental expectations, and intrinsic motivation that lead to self-regulated behavior. I shared with them a conversation between an American teacher and a Chinese high school principal.

In May 2001, I was visiting a high school in Nanjing with the U.S. Education Delegation to China (organized by the National Board for Professional Teaching Standards and the People to People Ambassador Program). At a meeting, a

National Board–certified teacher asked the Chinese principal: "In our country we have behavior problems with students, particularly with those from disadvantaged families. Do you have similar problems in your school?" The principal smiled and said, "We don't have many problems with these students. Students from poor families actually study harder and behave better than other students. These students know it is not easy for their parents to send them to high school and they want to be successful to return their parents' support." When I told this story the class was quiet, and some were in tears. I asked them: "What does this mean? High expectations and value of academic work can bring out good behavior!" This supportive and expecting perspective does not fit within any of the four parenting styles, but represents the traditional Chinese value of hard work and achievement.

In comparing the educational and parenting styles in China and in the United States, I told my classes that in China many educators and parents like the American *authoritative* style. They are becoming more *authoritative* by providing children with more freedom and choices with guidance and control. At the same time, many other Chinese parents are very *indulgent*, considering that many families have only one child. These parents try to meet all the needs and demands from their children, not knowing that their "love" in such a manner is not really beneficial. It is apparent that both systems have their strengths and weaknesses, and many times what we are doing here in the United States is highly commented on by people elsewhere, like the *authoritative* style being embraced by many Chinese educators and parents.

ROLES OF A PARENT AND AN EDUCATOR

As many educators have done, I also draw from my cultural background and experiences to enrich my teaching. I have used many examples from the growth and experiences of my daughter Sharon as well.

Sharon was 6 years old when she came to this new land with her mother. One month after her arrival she was put in an elementary school in Memphis, Tennessee, instead of in Wuhan, China, as she had expected. My wife and I worried a lot about her first school days since she spoke very little English. To our surprise she returned home very happy the first day of school. That semester was hard, but she was happy all the time. In the second semester, she was talking to peers freely, even being "a little too talkative" in class, as we were told by her teacher. Again, to our surprise, the next year she volunteered to join the school's reading competition and won third place based on the number of books she read outside of school that semester.

I shared with my classes that Sharon has enjoyed schooling from the beginning. Her story has been a happy one, not necessarily because she is a smart girl or because her parents have supported her, but largely because she had a wonderful

1st-grade teacher, Ms. Turner, who understood what she needed and did everything possible to help her. The most beneficial things Ms. Turner did included getting a student assistant to tutor Sharon's English and arranging for another girl in the class, Amanda, to sit by Sharon and help her. Sharon learned vocabulary and basic grammar from picture books during the tutoring sessions and enjoyed talking with Amanda. Without the English tutoring and help from Amanda, Sharon could not have easily adapted herself to the new environment.

Researchers have found that students who do not speak English or have limited English ability cannot fully participate in classroom activities or instruction. Educators have argued that without some special help in learning English, non-English-speaking or limited-English-speaking children are actually deprived of an equal educational opportunity (Bodur, 2012). I told my students that I was grateful for the school system and teachers like Ms. Turner for the wonderful educational opportunities that they created for Sharon.

Another story that I shared with my classes was about Sharon's cultural identity. It was a nice autumn afternoon, and at that time she was a 3rd-grader. My wife and I were waiting for her by the road, along with many other parents, and we were talking in Chinese. When Sharon came and heard our conversation, she covered her mouth and whispered: "Shuuuuu . . . no Chinese!" Apparently, she felt some peer pressure since all of the other parents were talking in English!

That year, at the time of the Chinese New Year, Sharon reported that her homeroom teacher asked her to talk about the Chinese New Year to the class. A little later her teacher invited me to come to the class, and I performed *Erhu* (Chinese violin). The following semester the school had an international art gallery. With her art teacher's help Sharon learned how to take pictures and came up with a presentation of our family. I then noticed that Sharon became more confident in being a Chinese girl, and she no longer stopped us when we talked in Chinese in a public place. Research (e.g., Bodur, 2012) has proven that culturally responsive programs are most effective with institutional support. Sharon's cultural identity developed positively because her school valued diversity.

When I told these stories, I was being *inductive*, and the message was loud and clear: My daughter was happy and successful in school because she was fortunate to be in a caring environment. Her teachers had wonderful multicultural perspectives and competencies, and I hoped that my students would perform like those teachers.

FINAL THOUGHTS

Being culturally relevant in teaching has been both interesting and rewarding for me. It has greatly benefited me in establishing my teaching effectiveness with my background, experience, and expertise. More important, it has informed me that this can be an effective way to help preservice and inservice teachers develop their multicultural competencies, which may further enable them to adapt curricula and pedagogy more effectively in addressing the learning needs of their diverse students.

In summary, this chapter has raised both theoretical and pedagogical questions for other teachers and teacher educators to (re)consider their practices for teaching diverse learners in America's multicultural and multiethnic classrooms. The ideas and practices from this chapter may serve as useful responsive teaching models for other educators in their exploration of culturally responsive teaching. It is clear that culturally relevant teaching can be implemented by every teacher regardless of his/her background. Such teaching can be applied in all subject areas, useful in broadening all learners' pluralistic and positive perspective of the world, while making the instruction informative, interesting, and effective.

SUMMARY OF IMPLICATIONS

For U.S.-Born Educators

- While working with nonnative colleagues/professors, try to understand the cultural elements they bring in, and see how you may benefit from them.
- Identify different perspectives and approaches that people elsewhere use in dealing with common topics. Keep your curiosity, since a "foreign" idea may be insightful.
- Understand how a U.S. practice is highly commented on by people in another culture. Such practice may have been ignored or taken for granted in the United States.
- You are a cultural person; you can be culturally relevant in teaching with your background and knowledge about other cultures.

For Foreign-Born Educators

- Be confident as being a nonnative educator. You are an asset for U.S. schools and society with your background, experience, and expertise.
- Be interesting when you are cultural relevant. Make sure your students understand the point that you are making and how it relates to the topics under study.
- Remind yourself that the purpose of being culturally relevant is to make teaching effective rather than commenting on a culture. Be positive while referring to a culture.
- Everybody may hold cultural bias, and so do you and I. Guard against your possible bias, develop a balanced perspective, and try to achieve the "middle ground" for educational excellence.

REFERENCES

Bandura, A. (1977). *Social learning theory*. Englewood Cliffs, NJ: Prentice-Hall.

Bennett, C. I. (1990). *Comprehensive multicultural education: Theory and practice* (2nd ed.). Boston: Allyn & Bacon.

Bodur, Y. (2012). Impact of course and fieldwork on multicultural beliefs and attitudes. *The Educational Forum, 76*(1), 41–56.

Dewey, J. (1913). *Interest and effort in education*. Cambridge, MA: Houghton-Mifflin.

Eccles, J. S., & Wigfield, A. (2002). Motivational beliefs, values, and goals. *Annual Review of Psychology, 53*, 109–132.

Gollnick, D. M., & Chinn, P. (2004). *Multicultural education in a pluralistic society* (6th ed.). Columbus, OH: Pearson Merrill Prentice Hall.

Martin, J. N., & Nakayama, T. K. (2010). *Intercultural communication in contexts* (5th ed.). Boston: McGraw-Hill.

Pang, V. O. (2005). *Multicultural education: A caring-centered, reflective approach* (2nd ed.). Boston: McGraw-Hill.

Prater, M. A., & Devereaux, T. H. (2009). Culturally responsive training of teacher educators. *Action in Teacher Education, 31*(3), 19–27.

Santrock, J. W. (2008). *Adolescence* (12th ed.). Boston: McGraw-Hill.

Schunk, D. H. (2012). *Learning theories* (6th ed.). Boston: Pearson.

Siwatu, K. O. (2011). Preservice teachers' culturally responsive teaching self-efficacy-forming experiences: A mixed methods study. *Journal of Educational Research 104*, 360–369.

Zion, S., & Kozleski, E. (2005). *Understanding culture*. Tempe, AZ: National Institute for Urban School Improvement.

4

Becoming a Chinese Teacher Educator in the Southeastern United States

Ye He

As noted elsewhere, as a result of globalization in various industrial fields and in educational markets, Chinese students have increasing opportunities to enter the U.S. K–16 educational system. The pattern of Chinese immigrant settlement has also shifted from the traditional gateway metropolitan areas such as New York, Los Angeles, Houston, Miami, and Chicago to less populated regions, including Southeastern states (Massey, 2010). Even though the relative number of Chinese immigrants is much smaller in the Southeastern United States compared to the west coast, the growth rate is significant. This immigration pattern has presented distinctive challenges for teacher educators if teachers in the Southeast are to be prepared for the diverse needs of the recent Chinese immigrant population that are significantly different from those of the Latino immigrant populations with whom they are more familiar.

With teaching and learning experiences both in China and the United States, and as a recent Chinese immigrant myself, I have learned from colleagues, students, and parents from both countries while becoming a teacher, teacher educator, and researcher. Learning and teaching in the Southeastern United States, I have developed greater understanding of the complexities in negotiating educational expectations and opportunities for recent Chinese immigrants, and have developed a sense of responsibility in sharing my learning with other teachers and teacher educators working with Chinese students and their parents. In this chapter, I describe what I have learned from teachers, and from Chinese parents. I looked backward at my experiences in order to move forward (Kitchen, 2005).

Having teaching and learning experiences in both China and the United States, I compare similarities and differences from both learners' and teachers' perspectives, and offer recommendations to leverage Chinese teacher educators' backgrounds in better preparing teacher candidates for the globalized teaching context.

BECOMING A TRANSNATIONAL TEACHER EDUCATOR

Our expectations and practices of teaching and learning are shaped by our experiences, or what Lortie (1975) described as the "apprenticeship of observations." Even though in teacher education programs there are specific courses designed to introduce teacher candidates to pedagogical knowledge and content-pedagogical knowledge for teaching, coursework is definitely not the only source of teacher knowledge that guides decision making and actions in the classrooms (Clandinin & Connelly, 2000; He & Levin, 2008; Levin & He, 2008). Clandinin and Connelly (2000) define teacher knowledge holistically to include the ways teachers understand themselves and teaching as impacted by a temporal continuum, a personal-social continuum, and place. In other words, our past learning and teaching experiences, current teaching practices, future goals as teachers, our social interactions with others within and beyond teaching settings, and our teaching contexts all contribute to our teacher knowledge. This three-dimensional knowledge reflects the ongoing reflective nature of the process of becoming a teacher (Xu & Connelly, 2009).

Becoming a teacher educator entails a similar evolving process, where one's experiences, social interactions, and teaching contexts are critical components in forming the knowledge base for the practice of teaching about teaching. Teacher educators with teaching and learning experiences from China, therefore, face unique challenges in reconciling conflicts in values, beliefs, and practices to embrace differences across the teaching contexts as they become teacher educators in the United States. On the other hand, such experiences across national boundaries also provide these teacher educators with unique transnational perspectives. Transnational teacher educators could bring "two societies into a single social field" (Glick Schiller, Basch, & Blanc-Szanton, 1992, p. 1) and introduce discussions based on broader global contexts into teacher education courses.

BECOMING AN ENGLISH TEACHER IN CHINA

Growing up in the late 1970s in Shanghai, I witnessed the opening up of the People's Republic of China (PRC) and the increasing emphasis on English language education as part of the national modernization process (Adamson & Morris, 1997). As a result of the earlier decade-long Cultural Revolution when most English programs had been eliminated and few English language teachers were prepared, in the 1980s there was a significant shortage of qualified teachers who could take on the task of reviving English language education in China (Higher Education Research Center, 1993). In response to this teacher shortage, there was an effort to recruit students from middle schools affiliated to normal universities to become future English language teachers. Always yearning to become a teacher, I signed up for the cohort and was selected to attend a special class in the middle school where everyone was prepared to enroll in the Foreign Languages College in a normal university to become a middle or high school English teacher.

Although most classes were teacher-centered and grammar-focused and we had to memorize and recite innumerable passages and were tested on dictation daily, several of my teachers taught us English songs and used role-plays, games, and communicative activities in class. Each unit in the textbook was taught over several days, typically starting with the definition of vocabularies and grammatical points, and followed by explanations of the text, and completion of the vocabulary and grammar exercises after each unit. Although we had a standardized curriculum and used the textbook that was the same for all schools in Shanghai, in 6th and 7th grade, our English teacher also introduced us to passages from one of the popular English learning textbooks used in China called *New Concept English*, published by Longman. Similar to our English textbook, it also contained a number of drills, repetitions, and grammar exercises. The images and texts, on the other hand, were quite different. There was one lesson in the book about buying shoes. I still remember how I got confused with the notion of "size five" and the salesman's comment that "women always wear uncomfortable shoes." That is when I started to realize that English is more than just vocabulary and grammar. I could understand every single word in a sentence, yet still have no idea what people were referring to.

Because English was one of the core subjects in schools, we had a lot of English exams and tests. English proficiency was measured mainly through written exams that contained a section on listening comprehension. Multiple-choice items and closed-text were commonly used formats. We were also tested on essay writing in high school and university. Even though I started to pay more attention to some of the cultural differences noted in our readings, our tests were generally more focused on the conventional use of terms and phrases rather than cultural implications and inferences. I remember thinking that the better I was at English, the better an English teacher I could become.

The enhanced demand for English language skills as a result of China's rapid economic development and educational reforms that recognized English as one of the core elementary and secondary subjects led to the development of local training institutes that offered English language classes to both K–12 students and adults who wanted to improve their English proficiency. As an English teacher, I had many teaching opportunities beyond the public school setting. The experience of teaching the same level of English to a group of students ranging from 2nd-graders to middle-aged adults using the same textbook, such as *New Concept English*, really challenged me and greatly impacted my understanding of teaching. Although the expectation was still teacher-centered, grammar-focused English lessons, I learned to supplement textbooks with different materials, use visuals and realias, build background knowledge, and provide choices of different activities and assignments for students at different ages or with different interests. I started to realize that teaching is not just about the content, and language teaching is not just about the language. As my desire to become a better teacher increased, I started to be much more intentional in reflecting on my teaching and the impact of my instruction on students' learning.

BECOMING A CHINESE TEACHER EDUCATOR IN THE SOUTHEASTERN UNITED STATES

It was not until I started the doctoral program in the United States that I started to have the opportunity to officially work with preservice teachers through teacher education courses.

Preparing English as a Second Language (ESL) teachers in the Southeastern United States presents different challenges from teaching English as a Foreign Language (EFL) in China. Needless to say, the English language teaching contexts are very different in terms of purpose, audience, instruction format, assessment, and teacher preparation (Table 4.1).

In China, with EFL established as a core subject in all secondary schools and in the primary schools in developed regions (Liu & Gong, 2000), the goal is to prepare all students to be proficient in English to meet the demand of the globalized economy. Though some schools experimented with content-based English instruction (Brinton, Snow, & Wesche, 1989; Wesche & Skehan, 2002), English is mainly taught as a core subject and is assessed using national standardized tests. At the college level, non-English majors can obtain the College English Certificate (CET), and English majors can obtain the certificate for the Test for English Majors (TEM). CET-4 and TEM-4 are required certificates that students must obtain to graduate.

In the United States, on the other hand, English as a Second Language (ESL) is taught only to students whose first language is not English and who are determined to be non-proficient in English. Even though the benefits of bilingualism have been recognized by many researchers and educators, there has been a debate about whether bilingual programs are efficient in preparing students (Rossell, Snow, & Glenn, 2000). In the Southeastern United States, with the Chinese immigrant population being relatively new, comprising mainly first-generation immigrants, ESL instruction is typically conducted in an add-on fashion in a pull-out format by

Table 4.1. Comparison of English Education for Nonnative Speakers in China and the United States

	China—EFL	United States—ESL
Purpose	Become bilingual in Chinese and English Be able to use English in work environment to meet the needs of increasingly globalized economy	Become proficient in English language Be able to learn content in other academic areas using English
Audience	All students	Nonnative-English-speaking students
Format	As one of the core subject just like science or math	As an add-on in the format of pull-out instruction, inclusion or sheltered instruction
Assessment	Focus on listening, reading, and writing abilities in ongoing formal assessments	Focus on speaking, listening, reading, and writing abilities in placement and progress monitoring assessments
Teacher Preparation	Focus on English language proficiency	Focus on understanding of language development and language instruction methods

ESL teachers. The fact that students are pulled out of their regular classrooms for ESL instruction could result in ESL students' missing content-area instruction, which in turn impacts their overall academic development. There is a recent effort to encourage regular classroom teachers to deliver sheltered instruction so that content instruction can be comprehensible for ESL students in regular classrooms as well (Echevarria, Vogt, & Short, 2007). In terms of assessment, ESL students take a placement test during initial identification and take annual assessments to monitor their English language development until they exit the ESL program (No Child Left Behind [NCLB], 2002).

Because of the differences in the teaching contexts, teacher preparation programs also have different emphases. In China, preservice teachers are all fluent Chinese speakers, so the emphasis for EFL teacher education program is to enhance the English proficiency of teachers. In the United States, on the other hand, the majority of the ESL teachers are native English speakers. The wide range of linguistic and cultural backgrounds students bring into the classrooms also present challenges for teachers to assess students' background knowledge and build relationships with them.

Having studied English as a foreign language in China and experienced cross-cultural differences in the United States, my background provided me with unique strengths as I started to work in ESL teacher education. Through sharing of our English language learning experiences, for example, I learned that most native-English-speaking teachers I work with have not studied the International Phonetic Alphabet (IPA). As a result, they were not aware of the use of IPA in facilitating students' phonological awareness development and leveraging ESL students' understanding of IPA in language instruction. By introducing IPA in the ESL linguistics and methods course, I was also able to share EFL learning experiences that many teachers were not familiar with and to discuss how students' prior EFL learning could be leveraged and built upon in their U.S. classrooms. Personal examples of cross-cultural misunderstandings were also shared in my courses to engage teachers in reflections on our assumptions. For example, I was able to use personal examples to explain that some students may not be able to participate in group discussions because they have not learned the nonverbal signal for their turn to speak due to their cultural background, rather than because of limited knowledge, language, or motivation to participate.

Such sharing of personal experiences encouraged more teachers to share their backgrounds as well through the teacher education courses. Instead of only focusing on English language content or pedagogical issues, I learned to become a teacher educator who facilitates teachers' reflections on their personal experiences, strengths, and assets; goals and visions as teachers; and ways to monitor the impact of their teaching for future growth. Through this type of interaction between and among the participating teachers, experts' voices from the assigned readings, and myself as the instructor, we bring various perspectives of teaching and learning to help one another better understand education beyond our own viewpoint.

CHINESE PARENTS IN THE SOUTHEASTERN UNITED STATES

As a teacher educator from China, I have often been positioned to bridge the cultural differences for colleagues between Chinese families and American schools, teacher candidates, and the parents with whom I work. Speaking the Chinese language also afforded me opportunities to work with Mandarin-speaking Chinese students and families directly. Although there has been a long history of Chinese immigrants in the United States, over half of this population resides in metropolitan areas in California and New York (U.S. Census Bureau, 2008). Different from these metropolitan populations, Chinese immigrants in the Southeastern United States tend to be first-generation. The majority of the parents I have worked with came to the United States to pursue graduate education and then resettled in the Southeast United States. Some of them have children who were born and educated in the United States, while others have children who were initially educated in China and then continued middle or high school in the United States.

My interaction with these Chinese parents extended my understanding of education in the United States for recent Chinese immigrants. I would like to highlight what I have learned from four parents in particular in this chapter. They participated in focus group discussions on transnational educational experiences for a larger project inviting voices from parents with different linguistic and cultural backgrounds. All of them came from mainland China with children who were attending public schools. Both Lin and Daisy came to pursue graduate degrees in the late 1980s. Lin is the only male participant, and he has two daughters who were in 6th grade. Daisy married an American and her daughter was in 10th grade. Hai came to the United States for her post-doc and has an 8-year-old son. Different from Lin, Daisy, and Hai, Dong came to the United States in 2002 to work, and her daughter came later, in 2005, as a high school student. Through our discussions, I have learned more about the challenges Chinese parents face and their expectations for education.

Comparing their own learning experiences in China with their children's current learning experiences in the United States, all four parents recognized the different expectations for teaching and learning in the two countries. They reflected on the much greater emphasis on grades in China, especially when they themselves were in school. They recalled that they were told that 书中自有黄金屋 [The gold is hidden in the books] or 学会数理化, 走遍天下都不怕 [You can do everything anywhere around the world if you master math, physics, and chemistry]. Dong, however, also pointed out that "Now it's changing. We are talking about *our* education. Since then, a lot of things have changed."

Wanting their children to be more "well rounded," as Daisy called it, they appreciated the various student projects and activities in the U.S. school settings and "the freedom to be creative." Growing up being prepared only for academic success, parents wanted their children to have different experiences. Hai, for example, reflected:

> In our generation in China, teachers tell us [to] work hard, get good point, good grades. We worked really hard and get really good points, and went outside to get good degree. We don't know how to cook. We don't know how to raise a family. We don't know how to do garden work. We don't know that. Right now we know that. We don't want our kids to do the same.

Although the parents were pleased that their children were not merely measured by their academic achievement at schools, Lin pointed out that it is important for teachers to challenge the students in addition to providing praise. He commented that "In China, they always say you are not doing enough. In the

United States, it's always good job, good job." Emphasizing the balance between academics and other skills, Lin felt that in the United States teachers "need to establish an environment that you are good at science, you are cool. It's just too much emphasis in China and too little emphasis here."

With the expectation to provide the "best education they can afford" and support their children in their development, the four Chinese parents also shared their concerns for selecting Advanced Placement (AP) programs for their children. Daisy's daughter was enrolled in the Early College program. Daisy said, "she is doing all the As, but every night she goes to bed very late at night, which is my concern. I don't want her to exchange her sleeping hours with all the As." Similarly, Lin noted that

> AP students also study until 12, 1 o'clock. I don't know about American students, but for Chinese immigrant kids, they all do that. The Americans, I think they just think B is fine, so you don't have to study till 1 o'clock to try to get an A; B is fine. . . . For a lot of Chinese parents, B is not good.

Except for Dong, whose daughter is fluent in Chinese since she has already started high school in China, the other three parents are facing the challenges of preparing their children to be bicultural and bilingual. Hai, for example, deliberately spent time in China so that her son can learn the language:

> I try my best to use Chinese at home. Before 6 years old, my son couldn't speak Chinese. I know for kids, 7 years [of age] is the language window. So I switch my time to bring my child to China. After 1 week, miracle, he could speak some words and after 1 month, he can express himself. Then I came back here, I sent him to the Chinese School [a community-based Chinese language school organized by the local Chinese association]. I am so proud of him that he can speak Chinese and can write some now.

Daisy also spent time in China and sent her daughter to a Chinese school, but she shared her struggle that "she [her daughter] has different thinking about school than the Chinese kids or the American kids." Even though her daughter has been exposed to Chinese culture through 4 years of schooling in China and "wanted to study Chinese," her Chinese language skills are limited. Daisy "wish[es] my [her] daughter would speak Chinese" and " [tries] to have Chinese influence on her any chance I [she] get[s]." Daisy revealed that her daughter "has her way with Chinese culture"—"She put ketchup on her rice. She enjoys that and she created that herself." Also wanting his daughters to speak Chinese and learn Chinese culture, Lin urged schools to help emphasize the importance of heritage language:

The critical issue for speaking Chinese is that the kids do not see the value. Good cheerleader; good football player. That's something you can show off. But she speaks Chinese. What is that? The kids won't see that's the cool stuff, so there is no reason why they would do that.

Conversely, Dong's daughter's preference for Chinese is "the problem" and she worried about her daughter's English development.

Interestingly, when asked about what they would like the teachers to do to help support their children's development, parents commented that "I don't think they can do much." Hai said, "You just try your best at home."

IMPLICATIONS AND RECOMMENDATIONS

These experiences may not be representative of all recent Chinese immigrants in the Southeastern United States. However, they are by no means idiosyncratic, either. Summarizing my teaching and learning experiences, I would like to share the following recommendations with administrators, teachers, and teacher educators working with and advocating for recent Chinese immigrants in the United States.

First, teachers' and teacher educators' diverse linguistic and cultural backgrounds and teaching experiences are great assets that could be leveraged to enhance our understandings of education in the global setting and seek mutual learning opportunities through comparisons of different educational systems. Although the distinctions between the Chinese and American educational systems present challenges for teachers to adapt to the teaching context, these differences also afforded teachers from both countries opportunities to seek alternative perspectives in advancing teaching and learning efforts. Examining the recent educational reforms in China and the United States, Preus (2007) observed that "China and the US are moving in opposite directions" (p. 116) with the United States emphasizing a more centralized education, while China is moving toward a more decentralized model to encourage the development of curriculum and materials at the local level. She pointed out that "the American and Chinese education systems have been at opposite ends of the continuum in many respects, so these opposing trends might be considered a movement by each toward the center" (p. 116). As both systems are trying to take a more balanced approach toward education, teachers and teacher educators with experiences in both settings may have unique insights to contribute. Engaging teachers and teacher educators from both countries intentionally in discussions and collaborative research activities on educational issues of common interest may further extend the impact of such research pursuits.

Second, in the past, many immigrants may have wanted their children to focus on English language development at school, but today, most parents are more concerned about their children's bilingual and bicultural development (Liao & Larke, 2008). Daisy, Lin, and Hai's stories clearly illustrated the Chinese parents' efforts. Even though there are some Chinese-English bilingual or immersion programs at the elementary level, Chinese language education is very scattered. Most parents rely mainly on community-based Chinese language programs or teaching at home to encourage their children's Chinese language learning. Further development of Chinese language programs would not only benefit Chinese-speaking students, but English-speaking students as well. In addition to learning a foreign language, language learning enables students to expand their ways of thinking. Based on a comprehensive literature review, for example, Rao and Ngan Ng (2010) found that learning number words in the Chinese language affords benefits for mathematics learning. Given the existing community resources, intentional connections between university-based teacher education programs, K–12 schools, and community-based language programs could help further these efforts. Parents who are interested in teaching Chinese, for example, could be encouraged to get their certificate in teaching so that they could further enhance the quality of Chinese language curriculum and schools could have more qualified bilingual teachers to sustain and extend such programs as well.

Third, with more and more students coming from diverse linguistic and cultural backgrounds, teachers need to be better prepared to understand and appreciate students' backgrounds and be able to facilitate their individual development (Cooper, He, & Levin, 2011). Providing opportunities for teachers to extend their social interactions beyond traditional classroom settings in teacher education programs would enhance their teacher knowledge and cultural competence. With the increasing availability of technology tools, teachers' interactions with people from other countries are made possible. With connections in local communities and in China, Chinese teacher educators could identify mutually beneficial opportunities for teacher candidates from both countries to collaborate through field experiences and coursework. These types of cross-cultural interactions would also help prepare teachers for teaching opportunities abroad through which they could further obtain valuable experiences and share their teaching beliefs and practices. As education becomes increasingly globalized, teacher education also needs to include more transnational experiences in order to better prepare qualified teachers for the 21st century.

Finally, accompanying such community-based, transnational experiences, teachers need to be encouraged to be engaged in critical reflections. Using narrative inquiry as a method, as illustrated by the reflections and parent voices presented in this chapter, would help teachers and teacher educators document our journeys and deepen our dialogues for the development of the field (Clandinin & Connelly, 2000; Xu & Connelly, 2009). Projects that encourage teachers to reflect on their own beliefs, values, and teaching experiences; explore learning experiences from different cultural perspectives; and conduct comparisons of cross-cultural similarities and differences could be valuable experiences for all teachers and teacher educators (He & Cooper, 2009).

Learning to become a teacher educator is a reciprocal process that involves "knowing through relationship to self and others" (Hollingsworth, Dybdahl, & Minarik, 1993, p. 8). While many teacher educators draw from their own teaching and learning experiences that may be similar to those of the teacher candidates to develop understanding, respect, and empathy with teachers (Kitchen, 2005), Chinese teacher educators in the United States offer unique insights with their learning and teaching backgrounds through interactions with their American colleagues and teachers. Building upon their experiences and language skills, they are also often positioned to link U.S. teacher education programs, K–12 schools, and local Chinese communities.

SUMMARY OF IMPLICATIONS

For Teachers and Teacher Educators from Diverse Cultural Backgrounds

- The distinction between educational systems and learning backgrounds presents challenges for Chinese teachers and teacher educators to adapt to U.S. teaching contexts.
- These differences offer unique opportunities for teachers and teacher educators to seek alternative perspectives in advancing teaching and learning efforts.
- It is important to engage in discussions and collaborative efforts with teachers and teacher educators from various cultural backgrounds.

For Universities and Schools with Students from Diverse Cultural Backgrounds

- Teachers and teacher educators need to be sensitive to issues of students' bilingual and bicultural development in addition to their English language development.
- Heritage language or bilingual programs are essential in promoting immigrant students' academic success and preparing all students to become global citizens.
- Universities and schools need to take initiatives in leveraging existing community resources to prepare more qualified bilingual teachers and sustain heritage or bilingual programs at the schools or in the communities.

For Teachers Working with Diverse Student Populations

- Teachers can become better prepared to understand and appreciate students' diverse backgrounds if they have more opportunities to interact with education professionals and students from other countries.
- Narrative inquiry is one method that teachers and teacher educators can use to deepen the dialogues with one another and with the local and global communities.

REFERENCES

Adamson, B., & Morris, P. (1997). The English curriculum in the People's Republic of China. *Comparative Education Review, 41,* 3–26.

Brinton, D. M., Snow, M. A., & Wesche, M. B. (1989). *Content based second language instruction.* New York: Newbury House.

Clandinin, D. J., & Connelly, F. M. (2000). *Narrative inquiry: Experience and story in qualitative research.* San Francisco: Jossey-Bass.

Cooper, J. E., He, Y., & Levin, B. B. (2011). *Developing critical cultural competence: A guide for 21st century educators.* Thousand Oaks, CA: Corwin Press.

Echevarria, J., Vogt, M. E., & Short, D. (2007). *Making content comprehensible for English learners: The SIOP model* (3rd ed.). Boston: Pearson Allyn & Bacon.

Glick Schiller, N., Basch, L., & Blanc-Szanton, C. (1992). *Towards a transnational perspective on migration: Race, class, ethnicity and nationalism reconsidered.* New York: Academy of Science.

He, Y., & Cooper, J. E. (2009). ABCs for preservice teacher cultural competency development. *Teaching Education, 20*(3), 305–322.

He, Y., & Levin, B. B. (2008). Match or mismatch? How congruent are the beliefs of teacher candidates, teacher educators, and field mentors? *Teacher Education Quarterly, 35*(4), 37–55.

Higher Education Research Center. (1993). *Zhongguo waiyu jiaoyu yaoshilu.* [Chronicle of foreign language education in China.] Beijing: Foreign Language Teaching and Research Press.

Hollingsworth, S., Dybdahl, M., & Minarik, L. (1993). By chart and chance and passion: Learning to teach through relational knowing. *Curriculum Inquiry, 23*(1), 5–36.

Kitchen, J. (2005). Looking backward, moving forward: Understanding my narrative as a teacher educator. *Studying Teacher Education, 1*(1), 17–30.

Lakoff, G., & Johnson, M. (1980). *Metaphors we live by.* Chicago: University of Chicago Press.

Levin, B., & He, Y. (2008). Investigating the content and sources of preservice teachers' personal practical theories (PPTs). *Journal of Teacher Education, 59*(1), 55–68.

Liao, L. J., & Larke, P. J. (2008). The voices of thirteen Chinese and Taiwanese parents sharing views about their children attending Chinese heritage schools. *US-China Education Review, 5*(12), 1–8.

Liu, D., & Gong, Y. (2000). *Foreign language education in Chinese schools.* Paper presented at the International Symposium on 21st Century Foreign Language Education in Schools, Beijing, China.

Lortie, D. C. (1975). *School teacher: A sociological study.* Chicago: University of Chicago Press.

Massey, D. S. (2010). *New faces in new places: The changing geography of American immigration.* New York: Russell Sage Foundation.

No Child Left Behind (NCLB) Act of 2001, Pub. L. No. 107-110, § 115, Stat. 1425 (2002).

Preus, B. (2007). Educational trends in China and the United States: Proverbial pendulum or potential for balance? *Phi Delta Kappan, 89*(2), 115–118.

Rao, N., & Ngan Ng, S. S. (2010). Chinese number words, culture, and mathematics learning. *Review of Educational Research, 80*(2), 180–206.

Rossell, C. H., Snow, C. E., & Glenn, C. (2000). The federal bilingual education program. *Brookings Papers on Education Policy, 3*, 215–264.

U.S. Census Bureau. (2008). 2008 American community survey. Retrieved from http://www.census.gov/

Wesche, M. B., & Skehan, P. (2002). Communicative, task-based, and content-based language instruction. In R. B. Kaplan (Ed.), *The Oxford handbook of applied linguistics* (pp. 207–228). Oxford, UK: Oxford University Press.

Xu, S., & Connelly, F. M. (2009). Narrative inquiry for teacher education and development: Focus on English as a foreign language in China. *Teaching and Teacher Education, 25*, 219–227.

5

Identities, Values, and Beliefs

Listening to a Chinese Teacher's Narratives

Ko-Yin Sung

In order to promote cultural and educational exchanges between China and the international community, and to promote Chinese language teaching internationally, China's Confucius Institute Headquarters, also called *Hanban*, sends numerous Chinese language teachers and teaching consultants to K–12 schools and colleges across the world every year. By the end of 2008, Hanban had sent more than 5,000 volunteers to 48 countries in Asia, Europe, America, Africa, and Oceania. The applicants are required to be current college-graduate teachers teaching either Chinese, foreign languages, or education-related fields in China. They are also required to be citizens of China under the age of 55. The selected teachers stay in the assigned school and country for 2 years and are eligible to reapply for another teaching abroad task after returning to China from the prior assignment.

In the United States, the need for Chinese-speaking teachers from overseas is steadily rising with the demand for Chinese language programs. According to the Modern Language Association (2009), at the university level, Chinese enrollment grew by 18% since 2006, with about 61,000 students studying it. With the intention of cultivating U.S. students' language skills to fulfill needs in business, government, and education, the U.S. educational community has devoted much effort and funding to Chinese language learning. For example, the state of Utah has seen the fastest growth in K–12 Chinese bilingual programs. Utah passed the International Initiatives to implement 100 dual-language programs throughout the Utah public school system by 2014, in which Chinese is recognized as one of three target languages (Language Policy, 2012). As more and more Chinese language teachers come to the United States from China each year, more research is needed to better understand any cultural clashes and conformities confronting these teachers. This chapter examines the identities, values, and beliefs a Hanban teaching abroad Chinese teacher held while her teaching environment changed from one sociocultural context to another.

THE CONSTRUCTION OF ONE'S IDENTITY

From a social constructivist's view, one's identities are constructed through discourses available to him or her at a particular point in time and place. According to Pavlenko and Blackledge (2004), the relationship between language and identity are mutually constitutive in two ways. First, languages offer linguistic resources with which identities are constructed and negotiated. Second, individuals' language ideology and identity determine ways in which they use language to index their identities and to evaluate the language use of others. Scholars have contested the notion of a singular and fixed identity and have argued that identity needs to be seen as multiple and dynamic (Ha, 2007). For instance, Hall (1987) stated that identity is not "tied to fixed, permanent, unalterable oppositions. It is not wholly defined by exclusion" (p. 46). Moreover, Pavlenko and Blackledge (2004) point out that the nature of multiplicity of identity is constructed through one's age, race, class, ethnicity, gender, generation, geopolitical locale, institutional affiliation, and social status. In addition, each factor adjusts and readjusts all others. Hence, identity is always changing and is a process that never ends. Taking into consideration the plural nature of identity, identity is best understood when examined in its entirety rather than through a single aspect or position.

One's identity is defined and redefined in relation with others. The notion of "self" versus "other" suggests that identity indexes sameness and difference between self and other. By defining who one is, he or she automatically defines who he or she is not. In other words, the marking of sameness and difference is constructed through the inclusion or exclusion of different groups of people (Ha, 2007). An example of the "self" versus "other" identity is the English-only debate in the United States (Blackledge, 2004). Advocates of English-only think that all American citizens should be literate in spoken and written English and they seem to fear that being literate in other languages jeopardizes the dominance of English. The language ideology of the English-only advocates therefore reveals their position on national identity in which only people who know English are considered "American." By defining those who are legitimate Americans, the advocates also have defined the illegitimate ones—people who are not literate in English. The type of identity used in the aforementioned example is called cultural identity, which refers to the strong tie between individuals and their country. Cultural identity assumes the effect of culture on an individual's ways of doing things. For instance, Ha (2007) pointed out that Vietnamese scholars investigating Vietnamese identities have found the belief of a shared identity among Vietnamese people, in which every Vietnamese acts and thinks with reference to Vietnamese culture.

This chapter and its underlying study draw upon the identity theories described above to examine a Hanban teacher's identity construction and negotiation while her teaching location moved from one context to another and how her identity construction shapes her teaching and learning beliefs. As such, this study may make readers more aware of the differences between teaching and learning beliefs in China and those in the United States. The study also makes suggestions to teachers and education administrators on how to reach for the "middle ground" when the two cultures are involved.

WHO WAS THE TEACHER?

Lili has taught Chinese as a second language for 20 years. She began teaching abroad in 2000 at the University of Weishan, Korea. Her second teaching abroad assignment was in Romania from 2002 to 2003. Her third assignment was from 2006 to 2007 in the United States. Lili holds a bachelor's degree in Chinese literature and a master's degree in world literature and comparative studies from a teacher-training university in China. Lili was selected for this study because of her rich teaching experience in various teaching environments in different cultures.

Lili's 2-hour interview was conducted in her preferred language, Mandarin Chinese, and was recorded and translated into English.

WHAT WAS DISCOVERED?

Teach Students in Accordance with Their Aptitudes

There exists a Chinese idiom 因材施教 (yīn cái shī jiào), which means "teaching students in accordance with their aptitudes." It is derived from the book *Analects of Confucius*, in which Confucius's pupils indicated that he knew them very well. For example, Confucius was able to describe his pupils' personalities, characteristics, and levels of intelligence. According to his understanding of his pupils, Confucius utilized different means to educate them individually. In Excerpt 1, Lili used this idiom when she described a teaching challenge she faced in an American classroom.

Excerpt 1

Actually, this should be my biggest challenge. I mean, my workload is a lot. When I was in my home country, there were around 20 people in a class. I was able to be familiar with every single student and taught them in accordance with their aptitudes. [In America] I sincerely wanted to be a teacher who helped everyone but I really couldn't; there were too many students.

Lili expressed her sincere desire to be a teacher who helps everyone in her class in accordance with their aptitudes. Her teaching values and beliefs follow the Chinese cultural script; in particular, they follow the Confucian idea of education described in *Analects of Confucius*. In Excerpt 2, Lili extended the concept of 因材施教 (yīn cái shī jiào).

Excerpt 2

As a student, you must think of ways that suit [your learning abilities]. You must find your own ways of learning. The final goal is to master learning. No matter what means you use, you must have your own methods [of learning].

Lili believed that not only teachers but also students should recognize their characteristics and find suitable ways of learning.

Hardworking

In several statements, Lili used the term *hardworking* to define a good teacher and a good learner. According to Chan (1999), for many Chinese people, hard work is one of the main ways of moving up the social ladder. This is due to the imperial examination system set up in the 7th century, which provided commoners with opportunities to advance in society. Since then, the Chinese social norm is for citizens to act in the traditional role of being hardworking people (Yang, Zheng, & Li, 2006). In terms of the role of education, "Education is viewed as an instrumental entity to cultivate noble persons in order to fulfill its social responsibility" (Yang, Zheng, & Li, p. 348).

In addition to working hard, Han Yu, a precursor of Confucius during the Tang Dynasty, stated a now common idiom in his book, *On the Teacher*, to describe a teacher's role, "师者，所以传道授业解惑也" (shī zhě suǒ yǐ chuán dào shòu yè jiě huò yě). This means that "only through the teacher can the doctrine be propagated, professional knowledge imparted and doubts dispelled." One can see from this description of a teacher's role that teachers carry important responsibilities at the social level. Hard work and dedication are required to take on such responsibilities.

Excerpt 3

I feel I am especially hardworking. My personality has a very obvious characteristic, which is working hard for others. By nature, [I] like to help with other people's work. If other people need me, I will work very hard. It is just such a personality trait that is suitable for being a teacher.

The fact that Lili explicitly stated that one of her personality traits is "working hard for others" (in her case, working hard for her students) and not just "working hard" shows that she believed she not only had a good trait defined by Chinese society, but was also seen as a good teacher as defined by Chinese culture.

In Excerpt 4, the concept of working hard appears again in describing the learning of a new language.

Excerpt 4

If you don't want to make an effort, you sure can't learn [a language] well, no matter what language.

Effort is linked to success in learning a new language. The concept of working hard leading to academic success is related to the hardworking value derived from the Chinese imperial examination system mentioned earlier. Only people who studied hard would pass the exam and join the ruling class.

Hardworking/Self and Other

The notion of working hard emerged again when Lili discussed her teaching workload in America.

Excerpt 5

I have many students, and to me the biggest difficulty is that I spend too much time [preparing for class] after class. Like yesterday, I spent 4 to 5 hours continuously in the office reading students' homework. . . . An American teacher told me he wouldn't do it if he reads homework for more than an hour. He only gives students grades with A, B, C, and D's. How could I [do that]? If [the student] makes an error, I must correct his pinyin and tones, so for many students I rewrite what they wrote. My son said, "Mom, if you want to be a good teacher, you must bear hardship without complaint. You can't say you are tired." You want to help others, that is your willingness to do so, then you can't say that you are tired. These 2 days I said I was tired. I think I have said it a bit too much. I mean, I have been very, very tired.

To Lili, being a good teacher is more about showing responsibility to others in society than about self-fulfillment. For example, her own physical condition is less important than the mission of helping students. She even criticized herself because she had complained about her tiredness too much; this is more evidence of social responsibility outweighing personal conditions. In terms of the construction of "self" vs. "other," Lili separated herself from American teachers by contrasting her work ethic with an American teacher's lack thereof. For example, Lili spent 4 to 5 hours correcting students' assignments. Lili's "self" and "other" construction has defined a Chinese teacher as hardworking and an American teacher as not hardworking.

Respect and Harmony Toward Teachers

Yang, Zheng, and Li (2006) explain the importance of achieving harmony in Chinese society: "It places social harmony as one of the key priorities and emphasizes social hierarchy and stability in order to achieve such harmony" (p. 349). In order to achieve harmony, younger and less experienced people are expected to respect seniors or more experienced people by obeying them and acting in a socially appropriate way in front of them. Challenging or acting inappropriately in front of seniors or more experienced people is seen as disrespectful. With respect to the relationship between teachers and students, teachers are seen as knowledge providers and experts. Therefore, students are expected to respect teachers and to avoid challenging them (Chan, 1999). Students who challenge or do not act appropriately in front of their teachers in Chinese society are seen as destroying harmony with, and being disrespectful to, their teachers. The level of respect toward teachers is evident with the common Chinese idiom 一日为师，终身为父 (yī rì wéi shī, zhōngshēn wéi fù), which means "a teacher for a day is to be respected like a father for a lifetime." In Excerpt 6, while Lili followed the Chinese cultural script of respect and harmony, the student did not. This resulted in a cultural conflict between Lili and her student.

Excerpt 6

When I am teaching, A non-Chinese student may not face the teacher. He may appear to be doing something else while he is in fact listening. But being Chinese, you must look at the teacher to show that you are serious [about learning]. It shows you are listening to the lecture. Teachers are also learning and slowly understand students. This culture characteristic we didn't know before, so when I just started teaching for a few years, I was in class, actually I didn't make comments to a particular individual, I only said "listen to the lecture seriously, everyone." I noticed this American student, who was leaning on his desk, so I said, "listen to the lecture seriously, everyone," then he wasn't happy about it. He felt that [I] corrected him in front of everyone. To him, this was a personal offense. He was very unhappy and later, after class, he asked me to the side and asked why [I] did such and such things and explained that actually [he] was doing XYZ. I think it was a kind of cultural conflict. My explanation to him was that I said it to everyone in class. I didn't say that it was [he who didn't listen to the lecture]. But he thought that he had a little bit of uncomfortable feeling. At that time I felt that, because he was very upset, his face was angry. This foreigner was the only one [who confronted me as a teacher]. I was very young and just started teaching. I didn't know what to do at that moment. I was a person who easily cries, so I started crying at that moment.

In a traditional Chinese class, the teaching is teacher-centered. Students are expected to listen while teachers are expected to provide knowledge (Chan, 1999). Lili's narrative confirms her culturally embedded teaching values and beliefs. When a student broke the cultural expectation of student listening behaviors, Lili reminded her class to follow the cultural expectation by saying "listen to the lecture seriously, everyone." She did not expect a confrontation from the student after class. In Chinese society, students are expected to preserve harmony and to avoid questioning teachers. When the student confronted Lili about the statement she made earlier, Lili did not know how to react to the situation because it does not exist in her cultural teaching script.

Active Learning

Chan (1999) compared teaching and learning in the United States with China and identified key differences influenced by the cultures of the two nations. For example, in the United States, good learners are characterized as active learners who interact socially with others. Conversely, good Chinese learners quietly listen to teachers' lectures and are characterized as passive learners. When Lili was asked to identify a good language learner, she described several characteristics that matched the U.S. teaching and learning beliefs.

Excerpt 7

First, [an] outgoing personality and the desire to socialize with people. These are very important. This kind of person can learn languages well. It depends on whether or not one really wants to learn. A good learner depends on his or her desire and motivation [to learn]. Another [factor] is if you have friends around you who speak the language. It will help you a lot. Another [factor] is to look for materials yourself.

Phrases that Lili used to describe a good language learner, such as "outgoing personality and loving to socialize with people," "have the motivation to learn," "really want to learn," "have friends around you who speak the language," and "look for materials yourself" are all behaviors of an active learner promoted in the U.S. education system.

Lili continues with her description of a good learner.

Excerpt 8

[A student] needs to listen to the lecture seriously. For example, I have a Japanese student who came to see me at every office hour for 15 minutes. He brought his questions with him and left after [we solved] his problems. He would discover problems.

Lili repeated the behavior of listening to the lecture as a good learner behavior. However, later she gave an example of a good learner's behavior in which the student was actively involved in his learning by asking Lili questions at each set of office hours. Another good learner behavior defined by Lili is to "discover problems," another active learner trait. The majority of the characteristics and behaviors she identified involve being active in learning, which represent the traits of a good learner in the U.S. cultural script.

Sincerity/Creativity/Comprehensive Study of the Subject

Three main themes emerged while Lili described being a good teacher.

Excerpt 9

First, a teacher must treat students with sincerity. For example, have you prepared your lessons? Whether or not a teacher is serious, students know it, correct? First, you have to do it well, then you will use creative ways to teach and these ways are flexible. You have to learn continuously. In fact, I learn different teaching methods from different people. No matter which country I was at, I tried my best, except that I don't have time in America. I tried my best to listen to other foreign language teachers' classes. I didn't necessarily want to learn the languages, but I wanted to learn the methods the teachers used. I would try to understand the methods that different people and different foreign language teachers use. So I feel that my method is to combine all the methods together. In addition, I like to read. At first I couldn't read in English. I couldn't reach the [English] level to read, but during the 2 years in Romania, there was a library across the street from me. I borrowed a massive number of books that talked about all kinds of English teaching methods. I read the books and then I thoroughly integrated them into my own methods. [I] constantly advance myself.

Sincerity, which Lili mentioned as a key quality of a teacher, is identified as one of the five constant virtues in human relationships by Confucius (Chan, 1999). For Lili, being sincere to her students means being prepared for the class and being serious about teaching. The second quality of a good teacher is being creative and flexible. Lili's identification of being creative as a good teacher quality does not follow traditional Chinese teaching values and beliefs.

The third good teacher quality identified by Lili is 融会贯通 (róng huì guàn tōng), which means "achieving mastery through a comprehensive study of the subject." In Lili's case, this means improving her methods of teaching Chinese. This idiom originates from the book *Works of Zhu Xi*, written by Zhu Xi, a Confucian writer of the Song Dynasty. It suggests that one acquires extensive knowledge of the subject from different sources and makes inferences and generalizations of the knowledge gained in order to achieve mastery of the subject. Lili quoted this idiom and follows this Chinese teaching value and belief.

WHAT ARE THE IMPLICATIONS?

In terms of Lili's values and beliefs, her narratives have shown that she carries a lot of culturally embedded concepts of teaching, including teaching students in accordance with their aptitudes, working hard, harmony and respect, sincerity, and achieving mastery through a comprehensive study of the subject. In addition, most of these concepts are derived from Confucius, who is considered to be the master of learning in China. However, some concepts of teaching and learning that do not follow Chinese cultural values and beliefs also emerged. The sociocultural factors that reshaped Lili's definition of the identity of a good learner may include her frequent contacts with students from different cultural backgrounds and her years of teaching experience in different sociocultural contexts.

In terms of Lili's identity formation, it is apparent that she used the Chinese cultural identity to separate Chinese from non-Chinese students, and to separate herself, a Chinese teacher, from American teachers. In Lili's narratives, the difference between "self" and "other" in terms of teaching is the difference between the work ethics of Chinese and American teachers.

Many of Lili's narratives reflect the ideals of Chinese culture, which is dominated by Confucianism. Confucianism holds distinct beliefs concerning teaching and learning compared to the Western philosophy of education.

One implication of the findings is the need for teacher training to raise teachers' cultural awareness. For example, teachers who are teaching overseas need to be knowledgeable about the culture of the place in which they are situated. On the other hand, teachers who might not necessarily be teaching overseas, but have students with different cultural backgrounds, need to be aware of the cultures their students bring to the class. A lack of cultural training may result in cultural conflict between teachers and students.

Another implication is that educational administrators who host overseas teachers should take advantage of the unique cross-cultural backgrounds and dual professional experiences these teachers have. For example, administrators could hold workshops in which local and overseas teachers exchange teaching ideas. As mentioned in Chapter 1, in the multicultural society of the United States, teachers from different cultural backgrounds learn from each other and work together as a team. The unique viewpoints and insights of overseas teachers bring critical thinking and alternative ways of teaching that local educators may find useful.

SUMMARY OF IMPLICATIONS

- Teachers need to be knowledgeable about the culture of the place in which they are situated.
- Teachers who have students with different cultural backgrounds need to be aware of the cultures their students bring to the class.
- Educational administrators who host overseas teachers should take advantage of the unique cross-cultural backgrounds and dual professional experiences these teachers have.
- Hosting cross-cultural workshops and activities in which local and overseas teachers can meet and exchange ideas would help reach the "middle ground."
- Local and overseas teachers should work together as a team, and share their different viewpoints and alternative ways of teaching.

REFERENCES

Blackledge, A. (2004). Constructions of identity in political discourse in multilingual Britain. In A. Pavlenko & A. Blackledge (Eds.), *Negotiation of identities in multilingual contexts* (pp. 68–92). Clevedon, UK: Multilingual Matters LTD.

Chan, S. (1999). The Chinese learner—A question of style. *Education + Training, 41*(6/7), 294–304.

Ha, P. H. (2007). Australian-trained Vietnamese teachers of English: Culture and identity formation. *Language, Culture and Curriculum, 20*(1), 20–35.

Hall, S. (1987). *Minimal selves in identity: The real me* (ICA Documents 6). London,UK: Institute of Contemporary Arts.

Language Policy. (2012). *Utah dual language immersion.* Retrieved from http://www.lan guagepolicy.org/documents/Utah%20Dual%20Language%20Immersion.pdf

Modern Language Association. (2009). *Enrollments in languages other than English in United States institutions of higher education.* Retrieved from http://www.mla.org/pdf/2009_enrollment_survey.pdf

Pavlenko, A., & Blackledge, A. (2004). *Negotiation of identities in multilingual contexts.* Clevedon, United Kingdom: Multilingual Matters LTD.

Yang, B., Zheng, W., & Li, M. (2006). Confucian view of learning and implications for developing human resources. *Advances in Developing Human Resources, 8*(3), 346–354.

6

Integration and Transformation

The Teaching Experiences and Pedagogical Journeys of Four Chinese Professors

Wen Ma

The prevalent social constructivist perspective on teaching and learning in the United States depicts the classroom as a setting in which the teacher should engage students as active meaning-makers, where the learner's understanding may be explored, negotiated, and constructed through participatory learning activities. Such a decentralized, learner-oriented view contrasts sharply with the more teacher-directed, content-based educational practices in China and other Asian countries. Within a Chinese educational-cultural milieu, the teacher often takes the center stage to present all he or she is intellectually capable of offering, while the students are expected to put out their best efforts to listen attentively and wrestle with the content internally in order to comprehend the texts and other curricular materials elaborated by the more knowledgeable teacher.

Although there may be strengths (and weaknesses) in both models, students and educators shaped by one model may encounter some "pedagogy shock" if they are thrown into the other setting. In particular, such differences may pose unique challenges to faculty members from nonnative backgrounds. In spite of the changing landscape in higher education, there are relatively fewer studies about how nonnative professors from Chinese and other backgrounds adjust, adapt, and transition to becoming full-time faculty members (Lang, 2004). Consequently, more research is needed to better understand how nonnative professors juggle pedagogically in their classrooms, what challenges they face during their transition, what fresh perspectives they bring to the American educational scene, and how the educational community may help these newcomers fit in and contribute to our collective educational undertaking.

The research that underlies this chapter explored the teaching experiences, transitional challenges, and coping strategies of four teacher educators from Chinese backgrounds. Specifically, the study addressed three research questions: (1) What are the major challenges for these nonnative faculty? (2) What strategies do they use to help them survive and thrive in the competitive academe? (3) What lessons might their experiences suggest to the educational community and other diverse faculty?

THEORETICAL FRAMEWORKS

This study is informed by the social constructivist perspective on teaching and learning in the United States and by Chinese educational thinking and practice.

Social Constructivism and Participatory Dialogue

The social constructivist theory depicts knowledge as socially situated and collectively constructed (Windschitl, 2002). In a school setting, all teaching and learning activities must center on the learners, who acquire the curricular content not as any tangible form of information to be transmitted by the teacher. Instead, differentiated pedagogical practices, "social spaces," and hands-on opportunities should be used to engage the learners as active meaning-makers, resulting in their thinking and learning developing in the process of problem solving (Dewey, 1902). As Applebee (1996) put it, when the learner reflects upon what is said, heard, read, written, done, or viewed in any particular learning context and finds his or her particular niche to engage with the content, he or she is participating in "the larger curricular conversation that stretches over time and space" (p. 53).

While knowledge construction encompasses a variety of language-mediated, meaning-making endeavors and activities, dialogic interactions provide the needed social context for the students to cognitively attend to the specific curricular content or learning task (Applebee, Langer, Nystrand, & Gamoran, 2003). Consequently, discussion is tapped as a participatory learning tool in the language arts, literature, and various content areas and programs. For example, McMahon and Raphael (1997) proposed *book clubs*, which center on student discussion of literary texts as the cornerstone for English language arts programs at the elementary level. Daniels (2001) further specified the roles and steps of student discussions through *literature circles* for learning at the secondary level.

University professors regularly employ discussions in their discipline-specific instruction as well. For instance, Fishman and McCarthy (1998) followed Dewey's pedagogical principles to use free writing and class discussion to teach the philosophy curriculum to college students, and Addington (2001) illustrated the discipline-specific theoretical orientations and pedagogical practices in discussions at the graduate level. Not surprisingly, students in the United States often expect to learn through participatory discussions, whereas students from Chinese and other East Asian countries may not be accustomed to class discussions and oral presentations (Ma, 2008).

Chinese Educational Thinking and Practices

In contrast, China's educational tradition is rooted in a Confucian-heritage learning culture, and the practices often reflect marked hierarchical relations between the learned and the learner. As summarized in the widely studied essay "On Teachers" by Han Yu (768–824 A.D.), a teacher's roles are viewed to be threefold: to spread truth, to impart knowledge, and to untangle students' puzzlement and confusion. Reciprocally, the student's roles are also threefold: to be exposed to truth, to learn knowledge, and to solve their puzzlement and confusion (Ma, 2008). Therefore, the teacher, as an expert of the curricular content, is expected to organize the content systematically before class, lecture rigorously during class, and mentor students by answering their questions after lecturing. Meanwhile, the students are required to diligently review the texts before class, listen to the more knowledgeable teacher during class, and review the lessons after class. Whereas the students are required to be mentally engaged with the content, not many opportunities are offered for them to do hands-on projects; to discuss their understanding, confusion, or wonders; and to use other expressive forms to externalize their thoughts.

Paradoxically, while students from Confucian-heritage cultures (Stevenson & Stigler, 2006; Watkins & Biggs, 1996) are often taught in teacher-directed classrooms that deviate from the learner-oriented, social constructivist principles (e.g., extensive teacher lecturing, big class size, required memorization and repetition), they often turn out to be able to outperform their U.S. counterparts. The Program for International Student Assessment (PISA) 2009 data offered a more recent example (National Center for Education Statistics, 2010). Five thousand 15-year-old students from Shanghai and 2,000 from Zhejiang Province scored considerably higher than their U.S. counterparts in reading, mathematics, and science.

Some comparative studies attribute the differing test results to China's longstanding tradition of civil service examination (*Keju*). Because of the intense competition in the national examinations for college education in China, tests are frequently built into core subject areas and each grade level, and neither the teachers nor the students dare to deviate from the mandated curriculms prescribed by high-stakes tests (Ma, 2010; Zhao, 2009). Although not all Chinese teachers subscribe to this model of instruction, just as not all American schools embrace social constructivist views to the same degree (especially amid the test fever), the historically formed tradition and uneven educational realities provide useful conceptual lenses, not rigid frames, for understanding the educational thinking and practices in China.

Previous research has explored the unique learning experiences and socialization issues for students of Chinese descent in diverse American school settings (e.g., Igoa, 1995; MaKay & Wong, 1996). However, there is little research that has investigated how professors from Chinese cultural and linguistic backgrounds adjust, adapt, and transition to the role of full-time faculty members in the United States. The present study set off to address this gap by focusing on the experiences and perspectives of four teacher educators from China.

THE PARTICIPANTS AND THE RESEARCHER

This research followed an ethnographic case study design (Creswell, 2008). Four participants were purposefully selected. These participants' information is summarized below (all names are pseudonyms).

As shown in Table 6.1, the four participants come from different areas of education, and are teaching at the graduate school of education within geographically different university settings. Ming is the only male participant, and Jing is the youngest, who became a teacher educator just 2 years ago. All of them had at least 1 year of teaching experience at the university level before coming to the United States. Ming, Lian, and Haiping each have more than 20 peer-reviewed publications. In addition, they all speak English fluently, and are professionally active on the national scene, making presentations in refereed national or international conferences, reviewing for refereed journals or conferences, as well as serving as journal editors.

As the researcher, I grew up in China and taught there at the secondary and university levels for over 10 years, completed my doctoral study in the United States, and have been teaching as a teacher educator at an American liberal arts college. Thus, I was able to use my dual backgrounds as a strength, rather than a weakness, to build rapport with the participants throughout the research process.

DATA SOURCES

The primary sources of data included survey, interview, informal conversation, and email communication with each participant. These data cover a variety of topics, ranging from what prior educational and professional experiences the participants have both in China and in the United States; what theoretical perspectives they believe in; what pedagogical practices they follow; what unique strengths

Table 6.1. Participants' Profiles

Name	Age	Gender	PhD Major	Employer	Years of Teaching in the United States	Tenure Status	Rank
Jing	Early 30s	F	School Psychology	Private University in the Northeast	2	Tenure-Track	Assistant Professor
Ming	Mid 40s	M	Educational Research	State University in the Southeast	7	Tenured	Associate Professor
Lian	Mid 40s	F	Educational Leadership	State University in the Southeast	11	Tenured	Professor
Haiping	Mid 40s	F	Literacy	State University in the West	15	Tenured	Professor

they bring to the mainstream classrooms; what major challenges they face in their teaching, research, and service; what professional aspirations they have; to how their pedagogical practices have been transformed in the process (see the note at the end of the chapter for the specific data collection and analysis procedures). Three emergent themes were substantiated and triangulated by the data.

WHAT ARE THE MAJOR FINDINGS?

Nonnative Backgrounds: Inconvenient Luggage

The impact of the participants' nonnative backgrounds on them is reflected in three areas: nonnative English, lack of native cultural experience, and culture-specific perspectives.

Nonnative English. Despite the participant's native-like proficiency in English and their remarkable scholarly accomplishments, there is still the infrequent slip of the tongue in some participants' speech, and the even rarer ungrammatical use of words or sentences in their writing. There are traces of accent detectable in all four participants' spoken English as well. Although such slip-ups appeared insignificant and did not affect the meaning, this can be a challenge for some monolingual students who are not accustomed to having nonnative professors. In Haiping's experience, most students are willing to tolerate her accent, but occasionally a few students may exhibit an impatient attitude, for example, seeking clarifications with an exaggerated tone or subtle facial expressions. Ming admitted that one or two students even tried to use his accent as an excuse to avoid doing all the homework.

Related to "foreigner accent," there is another issue: an imperfect grasp of idioms and colloquialisms in English to be used freely (i.e., whenever and wherever appropriate). In the surveys and during the interviews, Haiping, Lian, and Ming all acknowledged "lacking a ton of humorous expressions," which all three felt would help build rapport with students or liven up the classroom atmosphere. In contrast, they noticed that their native-born colleagues are often more adept in using some quick and witty remarks to connect with the students at a personal level. Lian even felt that some of her students probably judged her to be reserved or indifferent.

Lack of Lived Experiences of Growing Up in America. The four participants all acknowledged a lack of insider perspective, both at the broad sociocultural level and at a personal level, whether it is about some celebrity's anecdotal story or a taken-for-granted reference in connection with a movie, song, book, event, or a joke, as none of them grew up in the United States to be socialized to the same system of reference. Yet the lack of lived K–12 school experience had the biggest impact on them as teacher educators. For example, both Jing and Ming admitted that there had been occasions when some students casually mention certain names, events, or experiences, and all the other students seem to get it, just leaving them clueless. These participants largely compensated for such inadequacy through reading about them over time, although to read to know something is obviously different from having lived experiences. As Jing put it, not having direct knowledge of the books discussed, the shows watched, or the events experienced, it is often difficult to tap such a reservoir of sociocultural information to make a point more vivid or entertaining during teaching or informal conversation.

Culturally Shaped Educational Beliefs and Practices. All the participants self-reported to have worked hard both as former international students and now as faculty members, and the courses they teach similarly demand the acquisition of foundational knowledge and skills by their students. They all have made conscious efforts in switching from a more teacher-directed, lecture-based instructional style to a more student-responsive, participatory style. While Jing and Haiping have moved to having more student discussions and hands-on group projects, Ming and Lian's classes still contain a significant lecture component on what they view as "core stuffs of the course," without which students cannot have a thorough grasp of the content. Lian felt that she is probably perceived by her students as a "harsh professor," because "I not only have heavy assignments and strict grading policies, but also have high expectation for the content." She routinely typed up a whole page of comments and suggestions for each major assignment, trying to help each student revise and improve his or her work, although some of her students could not take her well-meant criticisms easily.

In a similar vein, Haiping argued for a meaningful balance between content-based mini-lectures by the professor and hands-on learning activities by the students. When I asked her to elaborate on this, she maintained that "the educator must do her job actually presenting the content, whatever the subject matter it is, but the students should be given some opportunities to wrestle with the information in order to internalize it, too. It [Solid curricular content and innovative methods of delivery] should be balanced" (Haiping's Interview).

Strategies for Transition and for Teaching: Hard Work Pays Off

What strategies did they use to help them make the transition to the role of full-time faculty and to survive and thrive in a competitive nonnative environment?

Persistent and Hardworking. Based on self-reporting, each participant's department or program has some good mentors, especially in terms of explaining tenure requirements and committee service expectations. In addition, they regard it as important to have informal collegial study groups for discussing work-in-progress, to prepare drafts before submission to a journal, or to collaborate for a grant application. Interestingly, none of them mentioned having a colleague visiting their class, discussing course design, or analyzing student course evaluation.

Besides the Chinese work ethic, these participants also share a set of work habits, such as being well organized, having a weekly plan, setting an annual goal, and being hardworking. Without extended families or big social circles, as their native colleagues have, all of the participants lead a relatively simple lifestyle: Their lives seem to revolve mainly around home and work, centering on their teaching, research, and service responsibilities. In Ming's words, it is a "work-driven life." Many of them reflected on their professional achievements as a result of countless hours and unspeakable efforts devoted to teaching and research, not just because they are Chinese or particularly smart. Unfortunately, many of their own students are not as committed to hard work, even though they are widely expected to be the next generation of effective teachers.

Haiping believes that good time management is key to good professional planning, and it is more efficient to be proactive than to be reactive. This point is also echoed by Jing. After reflecting on her goal-oriented mentality, Jing lamented on some of her students' "unacceptable" lack of planning. Whether it is a major paper, a dissertation topic, or a conference proposal,

> You don't wait until the deadline approaches before taking any action. For you cannot expect to do the best job in so short time. Life is fair to everyone: If you don't put in the time and efforts to work on it today, simply because you don't feel like doing it now, then don't be sorry tomorrow when it may be too late to get it done. (Jing's Interview)

Jing maintained that a mature person should refrain from doing things "based on the feel of the moment rather than responsible planning." In her view, any future teacher needs to have the strong will to do whatever is needed to follow through on his or her goal. Like the other participants, Jing poured a lot of energy and confidence into her work. As the Chinese proverb goes, *Tian dao chou qin* (The dao of heaven is to reward diligence).

Drawing on Chinese Cultural Knowledge as Asset. All the participants agree that their Chinese linguistic and cultural knowledge is an asset. They also try, although sometimes rather inconveniently, to draw on their prior experiences and familiar referents from China to better inform their students' curricular work. For example, Jing reported that her U.S. students are curious about how it felt to be a girl growing up and going to college in China, and she would convey her experiences to them in light of how native language and culture help shape a student's cognitive and psychological development. Haiping drew on words from Mandarin Chinese to illustrate inter-language interference. Sometimes she told Chinese jokes, four-character proverbs, or popular adages in her literacy methods course. Haiping felt that her students enjoy the alternative ways to look at other people and things in the world. Such activities not only add "personal touches" to the literacy theories, but also help expand the cross-cultural dimension of her students' intellectual horizon.

Experimenting with Different Strategies. To cope with the demand of teaching as nonnative professors, these participants have experimented with a variety of methods. For example, all four participated in some campus-based ESL or Chinese courses, or organized study abroad programs to take their students on an educational tour to China. Working as resourceful teacher educators, all of them have used group projects, educational games, social media, and visuals, such as PowerPoint, YouTube, or videos in their respective course delivery. Lian also tried online teaching and coteaching with another colleague. In addition, all of them reported that they carefully read and responded to course assignments, made themselves available for student questions, and always gave quick and substantive feedback to help them.

Collective Musing:
Can We Meet in the Middle?

Although these participants managed to adapt to the American classroom norms, their prior experience in China is hardly exploited. How do they integrate the two approaches?

Balancing Student Participation and the Required Content. According to Ming and Lian, in a Chinese classroom, the knowledgeable educator puts all he or she knows on the table, usually in the form of a thoughtfully prepared lecture in connection with the particular textbook chapter or topic of learning. Just as there is more food put on the table than each individual's appetite has room for, there is more thoughtful and in-depth instruction in a lecture than each student's developing ability is capable of reaching, and an individual student's intellectual appetite is thus satisfied by having a rich body of information to wrestle with. This buffet-style learning often helps the Chinese students gain deeper foundational knowledge and skills on the given subject, although they may be relatively weaker in applying what is learned creatively to problem-solve.

In contrast, the participatory, hands-on approach offers a clear strength in Ming's view, in that with such a self-centered, inductive approach the curricular content is made more personally relevant and each learner is involved in some fashion, whereas its constraint is that the total amount of information to which the students are cognitively exposed in the same length of time could be significantly less substantive than that for their Chinese counterparts. This single-order style, on the other hand, often allows the U.S. students to be more eloquent in speech and creative in applying whatever they know, although their grasp of solid foundational knowledge and skills may be relatively weaker.

With personal learning and teaching experiences in both settings, these participants wrestled with this question: Can we strike a dialectical balance between these opposing models and get the most out of both? This question first emerged from the survey or interview like some kind of private hunch by each participant, but then converged to become a collective musing.

Appreciating the U.S. and Chinese Practices from the Other End. Regarding the differing conceptualization of the teacher-student relationship in the two countries, Ming summarized:

1. Teachers are not expected to teach everything in the United States. Instead, they serve more as facilitators, and students are expected to read the assigned materials, do the projects, participate in discussions, and get the information themselves. Consequently, teachers do not teach as much as their counterparts do in China.
2. U.S. students want more fun in the classroom. Some of them cannot concentrate on the lecture for longer than 30 minutes, and they think they are entitled to the teacher's attention because they paid the tuition. Chinese students know that they have to earn the teacher's attention by excelling in the coursework, and they are more respectful to the teacher and to knowledge itself, and are more accustomed to being lectured to by the knowledgeable teacher. (Ming's Survey)

In addition to these general categorizations, how did the other participants perceive and articulate their observations of things that may be learned by the U.S. and Chinese educational communities from each other? Haiping felt that academic freedom and critical thinking skills should be among the priorities to be learned from the United States. Jing and Lian similarly proposed that social learning theories and student-centered teaching practices would be worth learning by Chinese educators. Other agreements are that students in China should go beyond textbook(s)-based work and do more hands-on projects, as well as being more encouraged to question the professors and textbooks, in order to have more opportunities to problem-solve real-world issues to become critical and original thinkers. On the other hand, the participants concur that U.S. students may gain from being more diligent, less self-absorbed, and getting more foundational knowledge and skills. Their teachers should probably commit themselves to more direct teaching of substantive curricular content.

WHAT DO THE FINDINGS MEAN FOR OTHER EDUCATORS?

The data showed that there are both challenges and potentials for the nonnative professors, their students, and the educational community alike. The findings revealed that the nonnative accent and lack of cultural knowledge is a weakness for the participants, yet their native language and culture may give them pluralistic perspectives. After they overcome the nonnative linguistic and cultural hindrances, the added language proficiency and cultural insight from their Chinese backgrounds may offer valuable lenses of reference for them and, through them, to their American students. These teacher educators, as a group, are conscientious in work ethic and resourceful in teaching as they put a variety of instructional strategies to work. In particular, they moved from a teacher-directed, lecture-based approach common in China toward a more student-centered, participatory approach prevalent in the United States. Meanwhile, they worked to draw from the Chinese backgrounds to enrich their teaching practices. This suggests that the U.S. and Chinese educational communities may both benefit from learning from each other. In particular, the U.S. educational community may be better off to take advantage of the unmatched diversity in its faculty force, while preserving the proven ones from its own tradition.

Clearly, while sharing common Chinese linguistic and cultural backgrounds, these participants do not and cannot represent all Chinese teacher educators in the United States. Each of them is a distinctive individual teaching in his or her own field and having different interests or career trajectories. Although it is important not to assume any cultural essentialism (Luke, personal communication, February 9, 2005), the findings illuminate the pedagogical journeys and transformations of nonnative faculty, as well as the potential to utilize their strengths to better educate the next generation of American teachers.

Theoretical and Pedagogical Implications

Help Nonnative Faculty Improve Their Presentation Skills and Cultural Knowledge in English. Previous research has identified the importance of acquiring native-like linguistic and cultural competence by nonnative faculty, and skills for public speaking and presentation (Lang, 2004). As evidenced in the findings, nonnative faculty's accent can complicate their communication with and acceptance by their native-born students. The participants' experiences also demonstrated that having native-like cultural knowledge may be as important as having native-like English. To address such inexplicit "weaknesses" in nonnative faculty, some non-stereotypical, nonevaluative measures may be helpful to them.

For example, universities that have a large number of nonnative professors may offer noncompulsory accent-training workshops, or special-topic courses on student needs analysis or the popular culture affecting their students' thinking and behavior. Additionally, one-on-one partnership with a seasoned colleague on teaching and research can be beneficial. Program-wide curricular discussions on teaching standards and course design may also generate useful feedback to improve teaching. Regardless of the institutional assistance provided, a premise is that, upon being hired, nonnative faculty members deserve to be helped to function more effectively in and outside of their classrooms, and their enhanced teaching and research capacity will pay off over time.

Tap Nonnative Faculty's Native Linguistic, Cultural, and Educational Experiences as Resources. As suggested by previous research (cf. Stevenson & Stigler, 2006; Watkins & Biggs, 1996), and discussed in other chapters, Chinese education stresses teacher-directed and textbook-based learning activities, memorization of foundational knowledge, reflective listening and thinking, and strong discipline and work ethic. The downside is that its test-oriented teaching and learning practices may be too rigid for individual students to realize their creative potential (cf. Ma, 2010; Zhao, 2009). The four participants are influenced by such an educational tradition in China. Meanwhile, they are exposed to the student-centered, participatory educational milieu in the United States, which strives to allow for more personal choices and less discipline and self-discipline for mastery of curricular content. Having lived in both worlds, these educators call to bridge such divergent perspectives for some "middle ground": delivering the required content knowledge, while honoring the students' personal experiences and interests.

For example, most of them place more emphasis on curricular content, while working to respond to their students' personal learning style and participation preference. Other educators can similarly think alternatively and draw complementary elements from other sources (including the Chinese model) to improve the pedagogical practices in both countries. With the unprecedented lived experiences and perspectives from the diverse faculty force in the United States, it is especially meaningful to draw upon the culturally informed educational experiences and perspectives that all nonnative professors bring with them to the U.S. educational scene. More and more of such pedagogical exploration and integration by all diverse educators, when appreciated by the educational community, can be channeled to our collective profession for a more inclusive pedagogical framework. In the end, it is our students who will benefit more from a comprehensive learning experience.

Limitations and Directions for Future Research

As with most research, there are limitations in, as well as unanswered questions resulting from, this small case study. Moreover, these intellectually sophisticated teacher educators may change as they gain more experience in the new teaching realities. Additionally, relying on self-reporting through written survey and oral interview, useful as these research tools are, may not be adequate.

Field observations, student evaluation, and colleague feedback would add valuable information.

However, this study brings to light the lived experiences of a unique cohort of nonnative faculty. The findings may help mainstream educators better understand these nonnative professors' pedagogical integration and transformation as well. It is obvious that the educational community not only has the right to know how nonnative faculty are actually teaching in their respective classrooms, but also has the responsibility to help them overcome any pedagogical hurdles. Equally important, such research may encourage other faculty members to similarly reflect on and sort out their own pedagogical journeys and transformations.

Considering that faculty members who come from non-White backgrounds make up nearly 17% of the faculty force (National Center for Education Statistics, 2009), educators from diverse backgrounds perhaps do not have to cede their prior educational and cultural perspectives in order just to fit in with mainstream norms. Indeed, the multilayered complexities and dynamics embedded in the participants' transitions and transformations may encourage other diverse faculty to honor and experiment with a variety of new pedagogical thinking and practices. Clearly, when all members of the educational community weigh in to contribute to our shared mission, the educational enterprise will grow stronger and better.

SUMMARY OF IMPLICATIONS

For Foreign-Born Professors in the United States

- Recognize your strengths and weaknesses: Nonnative English and lack of insider cultural knowledge can be limiting, and your prior cultural lenses are your asset.
- While in the United States, adjust to the local educational circumstances, but tap your native background as a supplementary resource.
- After returning to your home country, follow the native norms, but adopt complementary elements from the U.S. perspective to inform your home country's educational community.
- Wherever you are, hard work pays off, despite differences in origin.
- Model practical ways in teaching and learning through integrating different perspectives on a "middle ground" basis.

For U.S.-Born Educators

- Interact with your nonnative colleagues. This is the first step to learn who they are, and how you may help them.

- Help them know U.S. students' needs and institutional policies and resources.
- Observe and reflect upon your Chinese colleagues' ways of thinking and learning. This can give you new ideas about different thinking and practices.
- View reach-out efforts as a professional service: When nonnative colleagues are better acclimated, our students gain more, and our collective profession grows stronger.
- Look for "middle ground" possibilities with an open mind and an earnest attitude: This will enable us all to join forces for building a more inclusive educational culture.

NOTE

The actual data collection procedures are as follows. After the consent to participate was obtained, the survey was sent to and received from each participant as an email attachment. It is a qualitative survey, and the open-ended questions may take up to several hours to be responded to thoughtfully. The interview is semi-structured, conducted over the phone one-on-one, tape-recorded, each lasting approximately 1 hour. Additionally, I emailed and called each participant throughout the research process, setting up the survey or interview arrangements, explaining the survey or interview questions, and checking the final findings and interpretations. These less structured forms of communication became part of the data as well. For data analysis, I used the constant comparison method, which involves "a process of comparing instances of each code across segments in order to discover commonalities in the data that reflect underlying meaning of, and relationships among, the coding categories" (Gall, Gall, & Borg, 2010, p. 351). Specifically, I repeatedly read the survey responses, listened to the tape-recorded interviews, cross-checked the notes I took during the interviews, and identified important thematic categories and descriptive codes for each participant to generate overarching themes on the margins of the texts and transcripts. As the analyses proceeded, I continued to expand or modify the codes into major themes around the research questions, ensuring that the three emergent themes were substantiated and triangulated by all data sources.

REFERENCES

Addington, A. H. (2001). Talking about literature in university book club and seminar settings. *Research in the Teaching of English, 36*(20), 212–248.

Applebee, A. N. (1996). *Curriculum as conversation: Transforming traditions of teaching and learning.* Chicago: University of Chicago Press.

Applebee, A. N., Langer, J. A., Nystrand, M., & Gamoran, A. (2003). Discussion-based approaches to developing understanding: Classroom and student performance in middle and high school English. *American Education Research Journal, 40*(3), 685–730.

Creswell, J. W. (2008). *Educational research: Planning, conducting, and evaluating quantitative and qualitative research* (3rd ed.). Upper Saddle River, NJ: Pearson.

Daniels, H. (2001). *Literature circles: Voice and choice in book clubs and reading groups* (2nd ed.). York, ME: Stenhouse Publishers.

Dewey, J. (1902). *The child and the curriculum*. Chicago: University of Chicago Press.

Fishman, S. M., & McCarthy, L. (1998). *John Dewey and the challenge of classroom practice*. New York: Teachers College Press.

Gall, M. D., Gall, J. P., & Borg, W. R. (2010). *Applying educational research* (6th ed.). Boston: Allyn and Bacon.

Han, Y. (768–824 AD). On teachers. In Y. Han, *Collected works of Mr. Chang Li* (n.d.).

Igoa, C. (1995). *The inner world of the immigrant child*. Mahwah, NJ: Lawrence Erlbaum.

Lang, Y. (2004). Cultural shock and conflict: Experiences of first year tenure track native Chinese professors in American universities. *Intercultural Communication Studies, 13*(3), 123–132.

Ma, W. (2008). Participatory dialogue and participatory learning in a discussion-based graduate seminar. *Journal of Literacy Research, 40*(2), 220–249.

Ma, W. (2010). Bumpy journeys: A young Chinese adolescent's transitional schooling across two sociocultural contexts. *Journal of Language, Identity, and Education, 9*(2), 107–123. doi:10.1080/15348451003704792

MaKay, S. L., & Wong, S. C. (1996). Multiple discourses, multiple identities: Investment and agency in second-language learning among Chinese adolescent immigrant students. *Harvard Educational Review, 66*(3), 577–608.

McMahon, S., & Raphael, T. (Eds.). (1997). *The book club connection: Literacy learning and classroom talk*. New York: Teachers College Press.

National Center for Education Statistics. (2009). *Digest of education statistics, 2008*. Retrieved from http://nces.ed.gov/fastfacts/display.asp?id = 61

National Center for Education Statistics. (2010). Highlights from PISA 2009: Performance of U.S. 15-year-old students in reading, mathematics, and science literacy in an international context. Retrieved from http://nces.ed.gov/pubsearch/pubsinfo.asp?pubid= 2011004

Stevenson, H. W., & Stigler, J. W. (2006). *The learning gap: Why our schools are failing and what we can learn from Japanese and Chinese education* (2nd ed.). New York: Simon & Schuster.

Watkins, D. A., & Biggs, J. B. (Eds.). (1996). *The Chinese learner: Cultural, psychological, and contextual influences*. Hong Kong: The University of Hong Kong Press.

Windschitl, M. (2002). Framing constructivism in practice as the negotiation of dilemmas: An analysis of the conceptual, pedagogical, cultural, and political challenges facing teachers. *Review of Educational Research, 72*(2), 131–175.

Zhao, Y. (2009). *Catching up or leading the way: American education in the age of globalization*. Alexandria, VA: ASCD.

PART III

Studying Chinese Educators' Professional Practices to Establish the "Middle Ground"

This section showcases individual Chinese educators' professional practices to integrate the Chinese and U.S. educational perspectives. As such, these chapters suggest common ground between the divergent Chinese and U.S. thinking and practices across the educational spectrum.

Chapter 7 examines how the Chinese as a Heritage Language (CHL) teachers taught writing in CHL classrooms, and what cross-cultural issues emerged during writing instruction. These findings not only show that CHL students, parents, public school and CHL teachers and administrators, policymakers, and researchers need to join efforts to improve CHL literacy instruction and learning, but also that there are implications for the many new Chinese American bilingual schools that are proliferating across the United States, and also for Spanish as a Heritage Language and other foreign language education for all students.

Chapter 8 explores two graduate-level educational research courses at a research university to better understand student perspectives toward the use of indirect and direct instructional approaches employed by a Chinese American professor. Through multiple examples of conflicts in beliefs about learning between Chinese culture and American culture, the chapter shows that the use of indirect and direct instructional approaches depends on specific learning tasks and students' needs. These results point to the importance of making situated pedagogical decisions.

Chapter 9 describes an innovative action research model developed by a Chinese educator with a team of science teachers and teacher educators. This multiyear collaborative action research model, which has already been implemented by more than 100 K–12 science teachers, appears to have wide applications for improving science teachers' effectiveness in both countries. Such research proves the value of striving for a "middle ground" in engaging classroom teachers for professional development.

7

Learning to Write in Chinese in Community-Based Chinese Heritage Language Classrooms

Chang Pu

Like other ethnic groups, many Chinese immigrants in the United States attempt to pass on linguistic knowledge and cultural values to their children who were born in the United States. Additionally, in the milieu of the increasing popularity of the Chinese language as a critical language to acquire and the rapid economic development in China, most Chinese immigrant parents acknowledge the importance of being biliterate in English and Chinese. Thus, if no Chinese English bilingual program is offered in public schools, many Chinese immigrant parents choose to take their children to Chinese heritage language schools if they are available in the local community.

Although approximately 150,000 students are studying in community-based Chinese as a Heritage Language (CHL) schools nationwide in the United States (Asia Society, 2005), heritage literacy development was rarely reported (August & Shanahan, 2006). Previous CHL studies mainly focus on investigating parents' attitudes (e.g., Li, 2005), the role of heritage language schools (e.g., Zhou & Li, 2003), identity development (e.g., Lu, 2001), and language socialization (e.g., He, 2003). These research findings are important to facilitate the development of CHL in the United States; however, fewer studies have looked at CHL instructions and the importance of CHL literacy skills in the eyes of CHL teachers, CHL learners, and their parents.

As a teacher educator in North America, an advocate for heritage language education, and a former student/teacher in China, I became aware that the teaching of writing was approached differently in American and CHL schools. Lave and Wenger (1991) believed knowledge construction is a situated practice and lies in interaction between individuals and the environment; that is, knowledge of teaching is "contextually developed as practitioners respond to the specific context in which they operate" (Tsui, 2011, p. 22). Teacher knowledge can be developed "in the course of engaging in the teaching act and responding to the context of situation" (Tsui, 2003, p. 42). A number of studies (e.g., Tsui & Ng, 2010) used the notion of situated knowledge to understand the relationship between instruction delivery and the teachers' knowledge of the subject. Tsui and Ng (2010), for example, investigated how two English writing teachers in Hong Kong developed effective strategies as a result of their profound understanding of Chinese cultural beliefs and classroom cultures.

Inasmuch as CHL learning and teaching is situated in the American macro-environment, it brings cross-cultural challenges and adjustments to the surface, which blend into the CHL schooling experience. Framed with the conception of teacher knowledge as situated knowledge (Lave & Wenger, 1991), this chapter aims at answering the following questions:

1. How did the CHL teachers teach writing in their CHL classes?
2. How was CHL teachers' knowledge of CHL writing instruction developed?
3. Did any cross-cultural issues emerge during CHL writing instruction?

Knowledge of heritage languages (HL) is an asset for individuals, families, communities, and the nation. HL education plays a significant role in building a multilingual U.S. society. The answers to research questions can help identify the challenges HL teachers are facing and pedagogical gaps in HL education in the United States. With suggested solutions, this chapter aims at helping teacher educators prepare HL teachers to teach HL learners to progress toward high-level proficiency, and develop HL instruction and curriculum materials.

LEARNING TO WRITE IN THE CHINESE CONTEXT

When learning Chinese characters, learners face a rich and complex orthographic structure expressed in a nonlinear form. In addition to forming single characters, strokes are combined to form common radicals, which have certain positional constraints to form compound characters (Wang, Liu, & Perfetti, 2004). Because of the complexity of Chinese characters, writing them correctly becomes an important step toward being literate in Chinese. After words and sentences are learned and polished, the whole essay will be improved consequently and naturally (Liu, 1983). This explains why much time was spent in each lesson to ensure that the pupils were able to write the characters correctly (i.e., the shape of the character and spatial composition) (Ingulsrud & Allen, 2003).

According to Nine-Year Compulsory Education Elementary Curriculum Standards for Language Arts used in Mainland China, knowledge of strokes, correct stroke-writing orders, radicals, and neatness of Chinese character writing is emphasized throughout the 1st-grade to 6th-grade curriculum. Word choice and sentence formation are addressed in 2nd and 3rd grade; in 4th grade, students start learning narrative writing, focusing on concrete descriptions and logical order in writing. Students are introduced to prewriting in 5th grade; in 5th and 6th grade, students are expected to demonstrate skills and applications in composing as well as different writing genres. Nonetheless, writing in the American classroom is understood as "the skill of writing down particular words, in a particular order, to create particular effects" (Fletcher & Portalupi, 2001, p. 1). In the United States, language use and meaning constructions are the key standards in Common Core State Standards (2011) for English Language Arts and Literacy through kindergartners to 5th grade. Even at the kindergartners' level, composing opinion pieces by using a combination of drawing, dictating, and writing is expected.

LITERACY INSTRUCTION IN CHL SCHOOLS

CHL learners usually have acquired basic Chinese communication skills through daily conversations with their family members, but literacy skills in Chinese require formal instruction and practice to expand the functional range of the home-based language (Chevalier, 2004). Wang (2004) looked at types of instructional content to which CHL students were exposed, and found that classroom activities usually include radicals and stroke order analysis, phrase and sentence making, read-aloud, and translation. Similar findings were also reported in Ruan's (2004) study.

HOW WAS THIS STUDY CONDUCTED?

This chapter draws upon the data from a larger study to report on how two CHL teachers taught writing in CHL classrooms, how their practical knowledge of writing instruction was developed, and if any cross-cultural conflicts emerged during CHL writing instructions (see the note at the end of the chapter). In this relatively small Chinese community in an urban area in a Southern state where a

Chinese-English bilingual program in the public schools is unlikely to be established because of the small number of students and limited resources, a community-based CHL school has become a place for Chinese parents to hold on to the hope that their children can learn the Chinese language and culture. Ms. Zhou (pseudonym) came to the United States to obtain a doctorate in biology. When I conducted this study, she had taught at the Chinese school for 1 year. Ms. Li (pseudonym) had taught at the Chinese school for 2 years. Ms. Li earned her master's degree in the United Kingdom and came to the United States to join her husband. The adopted textbook series were published in Mainland China and designed for Chinese children living abroad. Teachers in the CHL school were usually volunteers who did not necessarily have any teaching or language teaching experience. These two teachers were selected to study because of their similar educational and CHL teaching backgrounds; they also reflected the teacher body of the CHL schools in the United States and the high CHL teacher turnover rates due to challenges CHL schools face (e.g., part-time job status). Further, students in these two CHL classes were at the similar age and intermediate Chinese language proficiency level.

WHAT ARE THE FINDINGS?

The presentation of findings below is organized according to the core themes. Although there were additional examples illustrating each theme, length limitations allow me to present just a few.

CHL Instruction

Ms. Li usually started the class with character dictation. She gave students 5 minutes to review characters learned in the previous class and then dictated characters or word phrases to check if students had memorized them. Ms. Li then taught new characters; she explained their meanings and decomposed them into meaningful radicals or parts to help students remember the characters. After spending approximately an hour on new characters and making sentences by using the characters, Ms. Li usually asked students to read the passage aloud. She would correct mispronounced words and check comprehension of every sentence through questions. Ms. Li then called on students to summarize the reading. Target sentence patterns would be introduced. For example, in the lesson of 大自然的语言 [Languages of the Nature], the targeted sentence structure is "... 多么 ... 啊！" [... is/are very ...!]. Ms. Li asked students to make sentences by using the sentence pattern, such as 花园里的花多么美丽啊! [Flowers in the garden are very beautiful!] At last, Ms. Li guided students to complete the follow-up exercises in the textbook, which mainly focused on character writing, vocabulary, sentences, and reading comprehension. If time allowed, Ms. Li would ask students to play a flash card game, which was their favorite activity, according to her students. Ms. Li spread out character or word phrase index cards she had made and then read one card aloud each time. Students who found the corresponding cards would gain stickers to buy snacks at school.

Throughout my observations in Ms. Li's class for one academic year, no instruction on writing composition as opposed to character formation was given in class. However, Ms. Li did assign students two writing assignments during this study. The first writing assignment was to write about Halloween; the second writing assignment was to write about students' weekend. Ms. Li did not demand students to turn in their writings, though; only five students turned them in. Based on the feedback Ms. Li left on student writings, it is evident that Ms. Li focused on the correctness and neatness of Chinese character writing and the coherence of sentences. For example, in Figure 7.1, she circled and corrected every incorrectly written word. To make sentences coherent, Ms. Li added the transitional word "然后" [Then] to the last sentence. Nevertheless, she did not comment on any other writing features, such as organization and idea development.

Figure 7.1. Student Writing Sample in Ms. Li's Class

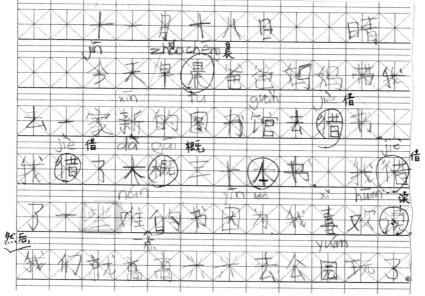

Ms. Zhou had a very similar instructional routine to Ms. Li's: decomposing characters, making sentences, reading aloud, and checking reading comprehension. If time allowed, Ms. Zhou integrated interactive games such as Pictionary to help students review characters. Different from Ms. Li, Ms. Zhou sometimes gave writing-related instructions after reading. For example, she asked students to identify components of narratives: "In this story, when did this story take place? Where? Who? Who are the characters?" However, during my observations, I only recorded four instances of writing-related instruction.

Ms. Zhou assigned writing homework every week. She would provide prompts on the homework notes. For example, when she asked students to write about a person, she wrote on the homework note in Chinese, "Four ways to write about a person: details about how he/she looks, speaks, behaves, and thinks." When grading student writings, Ms. Zhou focused on grammar, character writing, and idea development. During my observations, I recorded three instances that Ms. Zhou used the whole-class time for peer-editing. Typical writing discussions between Ms. Zhou and students can be illustrated through Excerpt 1. During discussions, Ms. Zhou emphasized word choice and the process of revision and editing.

Excerpt: Peer-Editing

Ms. Zhou：我们把作文唸一唸，大家听一听，看有没有要修改的地方. [Let's read our compositions. Let's see if there are things that need to be revised.]

Zi-yue：狮子和狐狸。。。他爬上去正想 从苹果树上抓一只苹果，发现有一个环子，ring。环收紧了，狐狸想下苹果树也下不来，只好等着。 [A lion and a fox . . . he climbed up the tree, thinking to catch an apple, found a ring. The ring was tightened up. The fox couldn't get down from the tree and had to wait.]

Ms. Zhou：你写的是抓是吧？ 应该是一 [You wrote "catch," right? It should be . . .]

May：摘。[Pick]

Ms. Zhou：对。[Right.]

Ms. Zhou：大家觉得还可以吗？ 有问题，就马上举手，我们来帮子越改，完善一下。苹果树，苹果树，这里有点重复。可以去掉一个。大家要听啊，因为editing 也是写作文里很重要的一步。如果要想写得好一些，写完以后- [How do you think? If you have a question, raise your hand right away. Let's help Zi-yue revise it. Apple tree, apple tree, here it is a little repetitive. You can delete one. Listen carefully, because editing is a very important stage in writing. If you want to write a better story, after you finish . . .]

An-bo: First draft.

Ms. Zhou：Yeah. 我们现在正在做这个改的过程。就是要推敲字句 [Yeah. We are in a process of editing. It is about refining words and sentences.]

Chinese rhetorical patterns and the underlying structures, however, were seldom introduced in CHL classes. Both deductive (topic first) and inductive (topic delayed) styles were employed in Chinese writings, although the inductive pattern is more common, with background given first to lead the reader to the main point (Cortazzi & Jin, 1997). Chinese rhetorical style consists of a typical four-part pattern: *qi* (start), which establishes the field or prepares the reader for the topic; *cheng* (sustain), which introduces and develops the topic; *zhuan* (turn), which turns to look at the problem from another angle; and *he* (conclude), which sums up the essay whereby the author's opinion is established (Xing, Wang, & Spencer, 2008). Nevertheless, this four-part pattern was neither introduced to CHL students, nor practiced in their writings. From writing samples collected from these two classes, students mainly adopted the "introduction, body, and conclusion" pattern when organizing ideas. Explicit writing instruction was limited and/or lacking in CHL classes.

Perceptions of Chinese Writing Skills

Both CHL teachers thought that it was important for CHL learners to develop Chinese literacy. Two CHL teachers emphasized that they closely stuck to the textbook series adopted by their school. The pedagogical purposes of that series include equipping students with Mandarin Chinese listening, speaking, reading, and writing skills and introducing Chinese culture to build a strong base for further Chinese language and culture learning. Shockingly, no explicit writing instruction is provided in the textbook series.

Both Ms. Li and Ms. Zhou expressed their concerns about helping students develop writing skills in Chinese. Ms. Zhou commented,

> In some cases, it's hard to expect that they [students] can write in Chinese. Kids are very busy with their other activities to develop their talent so that they can be successful in American society; they do not have much time or many opportunities to practice Chinese writing. Because of the extra work, many students actually do not want to come. I have tried very hard to keep them interested, like using games in class. So, too much work will keep them away from the class.

Ms. Li pointed out that writing was the hardest skill for students to acquire because of the complexity of Chinese characters and the limited time that students devoted to Chinese outside her CHL classroom; hence, she mainly focused on helping students recognize characters and use them to make sentences.

When I asked Ms. Li and Ms. Zhou if they taught literacy strategies in class, they were not sure what literacy strategies were. After I gave them some examples, Ms. Li responded:

To be honest, I haven't thought about it. But, I think for right now I will be very grateful if students can recognize Chinese characters and word phrases, and understand their meanings. So, probably, strategy is not the priority right now. On the one hand, they are still kids whose cognition is not there yet. On the other hand, if you don't know characters and words, it is still useless to know strategies; you still don't know. If they know more characters, they will know how to write gradually.

In order to understand the CHL teachers' perceptions of the relationship between reading and writing instruction, I asked about their views on integrating language skills in instruction. Ms. Zhou believed that it was beneficial to combine reading and writing in instruction. She explained: "Like when we learn and read a narrative text, I ask them to write a narrative." Indeed, some writing homework assigned by Ms. Zhou asked students to imitate the original texts. In contrast, Ms. Li thought that it might be good to integrate reading and writing in instruction, but since writing was hard to achieve, she should focus on reading until students were ready to move to writing. Ms. Li further stated, "They [students] cannot read fluently, so it's too ambitious to expect them to write. Some parents like Eric's mom asked me not to assign writing homework because parents had to keep telling them how to write characters they did not know."

I also gave out 50 questionnaires to parents while they were waiting to pick up their children, and collected 32 completed ones. The purpose of the questionnaire was to understand (1) parents' anticipations of CHL skills to be learned in CHL schools in a rank of their importance, and (2) their children's Chinese language use outside class. The importance of CHL skills was ranked on a 6-point scale, where oral language fluency, the ability to read books, the ability to understand media (e.g., TV), and the acquisition of a repertoire of Chinese words and phrases were the first four priorities selected by parents. The ability of writing Chinese essays and functional writings (e.g., writing a letter), however, was ranked at the bottom as the less anticipated skills to be learned in CHL schools. Additionally, parent questionnaires indicated that reading Chinese books or other text resources (e.g., newspapers) and watching Chinese TV and movies were the two main sources of Chinese language exposure.

Further, I interviewed four parents whose children were in a focus group in the larger study, regarding their anticipations toward their children's Chinese writing skills. They all thought that although Chinese writing skills were important to acquire, it was an impractical anticipation because their children would have fewer opportunities to write in Chinese. One father responded, "It is already difficult to take her to the Chinese school. She is not motivated. If she can learn some Chinese characters and hold a conversation in Chinese, I already feel satisfied. I'll be more concerned if she can't write in English." A mother stated, "We are not expecting he can be as good as us. I expect he, at least, can recognize learned characters and he can learn Chinese stories about morality and tradition."

When asked how they completed their writing assignments, one student responded, "I need to look in my Chinese dictionary to look for characters. My dad doesn't always want to tell me how to write them." Another student said he wrote the essay in English first and then with his mother's help he translated it into Chinese. But I noticed all of them had a good understanding of the process of writing, as one student responded:

> You brainstorm to get ideas. You write down your ideas and pick your
> favorite one. First, you have to have a rough draft. Like you write a
> whole story, but it's not the best, and then you have corrections and
> after corrections on the rough draft till you finish, you write your best
> handwriting, final draft. You copy all the corrections.

Culturally Shaped Chinese Writing Instruction

Culture shaped the way instruction was represented in the classroom (Hinkel, 1999). Culture, in this chapter, refers to a body of shared knowledge "what people must know in order to act as they do, make the things they make, and interpret their experience in the distinctive way they do" (Quinn & Holland, 1987, p. 4). In these two CHL classrooms, instructions mainly focused on rote memorization and language forms, which was consistent with the traditional Chinese teaching method. Both CHL teachers assigned students to copy characters five times on their worksheet and corrected every miswritten Chinese character that appeared on students' workbooks and writings. In addition to correctly writing Chinese characters, CHL teachers often encouraged students to take their time to write every character in a correct stroke order, and to keep every stroke in their appropriate positions to make the character well balanced and fit together. Ms. Li explained that Chinese people believed in the importance of good character writing: "Writing characters is more like a meditation for patience, commitment, and persistence, and it represented the writer's personality." She further commented, "Writing will also develop naturally after the good writing habit is formed and more characters are recognized."

Rushing through the character writing process usually led to the step of students rewriting the characters in CHL classes. "慢一点 [Slow down]" was a very common comment made by the teachers. However, students who were used to American classroom culture, which valued effectiveness and efficiency (Xing, 1995), did not necessarily accept this culturally determined concept of good writing, which was implicitly conveyed by their CHL teachers. Hence, they were very reluctant and annoyed to rewrite the characters, when they thought they had already finished the task. This attitude negatively affected their motivation toward CHL class and the Chinese language.

WHAT CAN WE LEARN FROM THE FINDINGS?

A Situated Perspective to Chinese Writing Instruction in CHL Classes

Observations of literacy instruction in the two CHL classrooms revealed that writing-relevant instruction was lacking while much attention was paid to Chinese character learning. Teacher knowledge of CHL writing instruction was developed as a situated learning experience. CHL teachers' Chinese education background, the textbook-driven curriculum, and traditional perspectives of writing development influenced their instructional foci. The complex structures of Chinese characters and the traditional goal of a good visual impression in writing shaped the way they theorized "learning to write."

Additionally, CHL instruction is situated within the American context where English has much higher and dominant status. CHL students had limited opportunities to use Chinese outside their CHL classrooms, except doing Chinese homework, reading Chinese books, watching Chinese TV shows/movies, and communicating with their parents. According to the questionnaire results and teachers' interviews, it was clear that writing was not the most anticipated skill to be fully acquired through CHL classes. The ability of Chinese writing is not seen as being necessary and important to increase social mobility or to improve intergenerational relationships. Parents' perspectives on the inferior status of Chinese writing skills compared with reading and speaking skills, and the dominance of English language also directly contributed to CHL teachers' decisions on their instruction and the values they placed on different literacy skills.

At the societal level, CHL education has been implemented in a concentric circle within the local Chinese communities. CHL is neither encouraged nor prohibited in private spheres of community lives (Macías & Wiley, 1998) nor recognized by the public. Many mainstream teachers had very limited knowledge about CHL schools, and the linguistic and cultural resources that the CHL schools held (Pu, 2010). Therefore, at the macro level, Chinese language and English language exist in a context of unequal status.

The importance of Chinese language has been recognized in the United States, due to its economic, social, cultural, and political meaning. Former president George Bush launched the National Security Language Initiative (NSLI) in

2006, and requested $114 million in fiscal year 2007 to fund this effort. The NSLI included the plan of building continuous programs for the study of critical need languages (e.g., Chinese) from kindergarten to university (U.S. Department of State, 2006). Sixty-seven of 74 grants awarded under the initiative, as well as 75% of the money, went to Chinese programs (Vu, 2007). However, community-based CHL schools have not taken a share of benefits from the so-called "Chinese language fever" because the funding was given to K–12 and college/university-level Chinese language programs.

CHL Teachers as Cultural and Language Mediators

CHL teachers are not only language instructors, but also mediators of Chinese culture. They are often called upon to explain Chinese cultures, traditions, and values when they appear in textbooks. Their instruction was also shaped by Chinese cultural understandings. The famous Chinese Dang Dynasty poet, Du Fu, wrote in his renowned poem "Fu Zeng Wei Zuo Cheng Zhang Er Shi Er Yun," "A voracious reader makes for an eloquent writer." The verse indicates the emphasis of wide reading as a foundation for writing development, which is consistent with Ms. Li's understanding of teaching writing. Nevertheless, as observations demonstrated, at times, CHL teachers' conception of learning to write led to resistance due to different cultural expectations. They might not realize that such cultural conflicts were carried through their instruction; instead, they related such resistance to students' lack of motivation and interest. Harklau (1999) explained that language teachers needed to raise their awareness of cultural representations, which shaped the interactions of students and teachers in classroom. Hence, CHL teachers might reexamine their instructional modality to identify cultural representations embedded within instruction; by doing this, they can help students who were used to American classroom cultures make a transitional adjustment through explicit discussions of cultural expectations in CHL classrooms, as well as invite them to define Chinese culture for themselves. Indeed, "classrooms can be a space from which we creatively construct, contest, and redefine culture" (Harklau, 1999, p. 130). In order to do this, CHL teachers also need to increase their familiarity with American classroom cultures.

CHL teachers, as mediators of language and culture, should continue their practices of decomposing characters into meaningful parts (e.g., radicals) to help students comprehend and remember how characters are written. They can also extend their efforts to socialize CHL students into Chinese rhetorical patterns for both academic and social texts. Since rhetorical styles not only appear in texts, but also shape the way of speaking and thinking, fostering an awareness of different rhetorical styles enhances biliteracy development and intergenerational relationships. CHL classrooms are ideally situated to take the lead in this venture.

FINAL THOUGHTS

Although this chapter examined two CHL teachers' writing instruction at the individual level, it calls for attention to literacy instruction in heritage language schools in the United States. Also, the numbers of Chinese dual-language programs are rapidly increasing in the United States in recent years; for example, Chinese dual-language programs have increased from 17 to 25 from 2012 to 2013 in Utah (Utah Chinese Dual Language Immersion). The chapter may shed light on curriculum development of Chinese bilingual education. Too often, to improve instruction, efforts mainly focus on the implementation of curricular materials and on increasing teacher knowledge of content. This chapter highlights the multidimensionality of factors that influenced CHL instruction, identifies challenges CHL teachers face when teaching Chinese literacy to HL learners, and helps identify professional development needs and considerations in the areas of curricular and material development when designing HL teacher preparation programs.

Krashen (1998) stated, "without literacy ability in the heritage language, native bilinguals are unable to benefit from the documented economic and academic advantages available to those with dual language proficiency" (cited in Tse, 2001, p. 256). Grounded in local communities, CHL schools play a crucial role in CHL maintenance and Chinese literacy development. Because of the power relations between English and Chinese languages, Tse (2001) suggested, "validation of the heritage language by formal institution, especially mainstream schools contributes significantly to positive attitudes towards knowing and learning the heritage language" (p. 266). Hence, in order to facilitate such pedagogical improvement, it is urgent to raise the public awareness of heritage language schools, and recognize the critical roles they play in emergent bilingual students' lives. We can then empower CHL teachers through professional training with help from educational agents such as local school districts, professional education organizations, and university outreach programs. Training opportunities from the local level would be more accessible to CHL teachers. If collaboration between public schools and CHL schools is established, CHL educators can help public school teachers understand Chinese American students' learning needs and help mediate between Chinese parents and the public schools; meanwhile, K–12 educators can help CHL educators with curriculum and assessment design.

CHL teacher training can focus on helping teachers understand principles of Chinese language and bilingual development as well as teaching heritage language students. Unknown characters are barriers that may bring anxiety and beat down students' confidence in Chinese literacy practices. When teaching writing in Chinese, CHL teachers can teach Chinese words in context and put more emphasis on meaning at the beginning to help students overcome their fear of unknown characters. CHL teachers should also integrate reading and writing into instruction and help students move from the aural to the written registers. They can get to know CHL students' English proficiency skills, and if applicable, encourage students to make full use of their English writing skills, strategies, and knowledge to facilitate Chinese writing.

Indeed, CHL students have limited exposure to the Chinese language. Since literacy takes place in every aspect of daily life, CHL teachers should take the project-/task-based approach to Chinese literacy development, provide more input opportunities, and engage their students in reading and writing real-life texts for real-life reasons. This can also help students understand that Chinese is not just an academic subject; instead, it becomes a real means of communication. In order to reach for a "middle ground," efforts must be made by all agencies: CHL students, their parents, their public school and CHL teachers, public school and CHL school administrators, policymakers, and researchers to strengthen the status of Chinese heritage language and help improve CHL literacy instruction and learning.

SUMMARY OF IMPLICATIONS

For CHL and Chinese Dual-Language Teachers in the United States

- Build upon knowledge of traditional Chinese culture and language.
- Understand Chinese culture embedded in their instruction and compare it with American classroom culture.
- Develop knowledge of language, literacy, and biliteracy development.
- Engage students in reading and writing real-life texts for real-life reasons.
- Help public school teachers understand Chinese American students' learning needs and help mediate between Chinese parents and the public schools.

For CHL and Chinese Dual-Language Teacher Educators in the United States

- Develop appropriate curricular and materials that introduce Chinese language and rhetoric features.
- Provide accessible training and professional development to community-based CHL school teachers.

For American K–12 School Teachers

- Validate students' heritage language.
- Collaborate with CHL schools and help with curriculum and assessment design.
- Adopt CHL schools' cultural, linguistic, and literacy resources into culturally responsive teaching and benefit all students.

For American K–12 School Administrators/Policymakers

- Validate students' heritage language.
- Promote bilingual and heritage language education.

NOTE

To answer research questions, I engaged in observing and audiotaping CHL classes; interviewing CHL teachers, students, and parents; and collecting the graded student writing samples. Also, survey questions were utilized to understand parents' anticipations toward Chinese language skills to be developed through attending the CHL classes.

REFERENCES

Asia Society. (2005). *Expanding Chinese language capacity in the United States*. Retrieved from http://asiasociety.org/files/expandingchinese.pdf

August, D., & Shanahan, T. (2006). *Developing literacy in second-language learners: Report of the national literacy panel on language-minority children and youth* [Center for Applied Linguistics.] Mahwah, NJ: Lawrence Erlbaum Associates.

Chevalier, J. F. (2004). Heritage language literacy: Theory and practice. *Heritage Language Journal*, 2(1), 1–19.

Common Core State Standards. (2011). *The National Governors Association Center for Best Practices and the Council of Chief State School Officers*. Retrieved from http://www.corestandards.org/assets/CCSSI_ELA%20Standards.pdf

Cortazzi, M., & Jin, L. (1997). Communication for learning across cultures. In D. McNamar & R. Harris (Eds.), *Overseas students in higher education: Issues in teaching and learning* (pp. 76–90). New York: Routledge.

Fletcher, R., & Portalupi, J. (2001). *Writing workshop: The essential guide*. Portsmouth, NH: Heinemann.

Harklau, L. (1999). Representing culture in the ESL writing classroom. In E. Hinkel (Ed.), *Culture in second language learning and teaching* (pp. 109–135). New York: Cambridge University.

He, A. W. (2003). Novices and their speech roles in Chinese heritage language classes. In R. Baley and S. Schecter (Eds.), *Language socialization in bilingual and multilingual societies* (pp. 128–146). Clevedon: Multilingual Matters.

Hinkel, E. (Ed.) (1999). *Culture in second language teaching and learning*. New York: Cambridge University Press.

Ingulsrud, J., & Allen, K. (2003). First steps to literacy in Chinese classrooms. *Current Issues in Comparative Education*, 5(2), 103–116.

Krashen, S. (1998). *Condemned without a trial: Bogus arguments against bilingual education.* Portsmouth, NH: Heinemann.

Lave, J., & Wenger, E. (1991). *Situated learning: Legitimate peripheral participation.* Cambridge, England: Cambridge University Press.

Li, M. (2005). The role of parents in Chinese heritage-language schools. *Bilingual Research Journal, 29*(1), 197–206.

Liu, X. (1983). V. Y. Shih (Trans.) *The literary mind and the carving of dragons.* Hong Kong: The Chinese University Press.

Lu, X. (2001). Bicultural identity development and Chinese community formation: An ethnographic study of Chinese schools in Chicago. *The Howard Journal of Communications, 12*, 203–220.

Macías, R. F., & Wiley, T. G. (1998). Introduction. In H. Kloss (Ed.), *The American bilingual tradition* (pp. vii–xix). Washington, DC: Center for Applied Linguistics/Delta System.

Nine-Year Compulsory Education Elementary Curriculum Standards for Chinese Language Arts. (2000). People's Education Press. Retrieved from http://www.pep.com.cn/peix un/xkpx/xiaoyu/kbjd/jxdg/201008/t20100818_663520.htm

Pu, C. (2010). The influence of public and heritage language schools on Chinese American children's biliteracy development. *Bilingual Research Journal, 33*(2), 150–172.

Quinn, N., & Holland, D. (1987). Culture and cognition. In D. Holland & N. Quinn (Eds.), *Cultural models in language and thoughts* (pp. 3–40). New York: Cambridge University Press.

Ruan, J. (2004). Bilingual Chinese/English first graders developing metacognition about writing. *Journal of Literacy, 38*(2), 106–112.

Tse, L. (2001). Heritage language literacy: A study of U.S. biliterates. *Language, Culture, and Curriculum, 14*(3), 256–268.

Tsui, A.B.M. (2003). *Understanding expertise in teaching: Case studies of EFL teachers.* New York: Cambridge University Press.

Tsui, A.B.M. (2011). The dialectic of theory and practice in teacher knowledge development. In J. Hüttner, B. Mehlmauer-Larcher, S. Reichl & B. Schiftner (Eds.), *Theory and practice in EFL teacher education: Bridging the gap* (pp. 16–37). Bristol, UK: Multilingual Matters.

Tsui, A.B.M., & Ng, M. M. (2010). Cultural contexts and situated possibilities in the teaching of second language writing. *Journal of Teacher Education, 61*(4), 364–375.

U.S. Department of State. (2006). *National security language initiative.* Retrieved from http://www.state.gov/r/pa/prs/ps/2006/58733.htm

Utah Chinese Dual Language Immersion. (2012). *Participating schools.* Retrieved from http://utahchineseimmersion.org/about/participating-schools/

Vu, P. (2007). *More U.S. schools pin fortune on Chinese.* Retrieved from http://www.stateline. org/live/details/story?contentId=189934

Wang, M., Liu, Y., & Perfetti, C. A. (2004). The implicit and explicit learning of orthographic structure and function of a new writing system. *Science Studies of Reading, 8*(4), 357–379.

Wang, S-H. C. (2004). *Biliteracy resource eco-system of intergenerational language and culture transmission: An ethnographic study of a Chinese-American community.* Unpublished dissertation, University of Pennsylvania, Philadelphia.

Xing, F. (1995). The Chinese cultural system: Implications for cross-cultural management. *SAM Advanced Management Journal, 60*(1), 14–20.

Xing, M., Wang, J., & Spencer, K. (2008). Raising students' awareness of cross-cultural contrastive rhetoric in English writing via an e-learning course. *Language Learning & Technology, 12*(2), 71–93.

Zhou, M., & Li, X. (2003). Ethnic language schools and the development of supplementary education in the immigrant Chinese community in the United States. *New Directions for Youth Development, 100,* 57–73.

8

Indirect vs. Direct Instructional Approaches to Teaching Research Methodology

Chuang Wang &
Wanying Wang

Research methodology courses are required in all graduate programs in the United States and most students feel apprehensive about these courses. Students' anxiety level rises when they realize that the course is taught by a professor from a Chinese background. When teachers and students from different cultures meet in the same classroom, differences in beliefs, attitudes, and classroom behaviors are expected (Zhao, 2007). Both authors of this chapter had a minimum of 6 years of teaching experience in Chinese universities and a few years of experience in American universities. The first author taught educational research methodology courses, both quantitative and qualitative, to graduate students for 8 years in an American university. The second author was a postdoctoral fellow at the university where the first author was teaching and served as a peer debriefer (Lincoln & Guba, 1985) for this study. Presented in this chapter is the first author's struggle between the choice of pedagogies, indirect and direct instructional approaches in particular, along with student feedback about the effectiveness of these strategies in classes. As more and more U.S. educators are moving toward indirect teaching because this approach is student-centered, motivates the learning, and stresses group-work and problem-solving skills (Prince & Felder, 2006), the authors hope that U.S. educators can revisit the values of direct teaching and not replace direct teaching with indirect teaching in every classroom.

THREE APPROACHES

Direct Instructional Approach

With a Chinese background, the first author is certainly influenced by the traditional Chinese model of teaching, which embraced the Confucian culture. The traditional Chinese model of teaching is one of an empty vessel or pint pot (Maley, 1982). Such a model is essentially knowledge-based in that it is characterized by the transmission of knowledge through an imitative and repetitive process (Paine, 1992; Tang & Absalom, 1998). Teaching methods are largely expository and the teaching process is teacher-dominated (Biggs, 1996). Based on the framework provided by the textbook, a teacher enjoys a certain degree of autonomy in the order of presentation, but he/she needs to follow regulations regarding what students are expected to learn. There is a national standard curriculum that specifies the content knowledge to be covered in each grade level, which reflects the essentialist's point of view (e.g., Bagley, 1907).

As suggested by Brick (2004), Chinese learners are supposed to master the basic knowledge before they can apply what they learned in a creative manner. Therefore, the focus of teaching is not on how teachers and students can create, construct, and apply knowledge in an experimental approach, but on how extant authoritative knowledge can be transmitted and internalized in a most effective and efficient way (Brick, 2004; Jin & Cortazzi, 1995). Hu (2002) summarizes three aspects of the role of a Chinese teacher: (1) a teacher must be a role model of socially preferred behavior for his or her students; (2) a teacher is expected to play the role of mentor or parent; and (3) it is the teacher's responsibility to make sure that all students make progress satisfactorily. Because of the perceived roles mentioned above, Chinese teachers do not want a pedagogical practice where challenging of the authority is allowed. The teacher feels embarrassed if he/she fails to answer students' questions. It is a common belief that a teacher must assume a directive role, having the sole prerogative in deciding what to teach and exerting complete control over the class all the time (Tang & Absalom, 1998). This sense of security to both teacher and student is intended to make class activities fully predictable and to guarantee the smooth delivery of carefully planned contents.

To keep abreast of the transmission model of teaching, students should maintain a high level of receptiveness, wholeheartedly embracing the knowledge they receive from their teacher or books. They are expected to respect and cooperate with their teacher (Cortazzi & Jin, 1996) and not to challenge the transmitted knowledge or present their own ideas until they have mastered sufficient knowledge to make informed judgments (Brick, 2004). As a result, all of these characteristics bear much resemblance to a direct teaching approach. Direct teaching is based on the idea that a highly structured presentation of content allows maximal amount of learning for students. The instructor presents a general concept first and then provides examples or illustrations that test how the idea works. Students are directed to practice, with instructor guidance and feedback, applying and finding examples of the concept at hand until they achieve concept mastery.

Students with different intellectual capacities and learning styles may choose their own way of knowledge accumulation. As a result, teachers are interested in different approaches to effectively assist all students to understand better and learn. Teachers want to bring about better understanding of the material they want to transmit. It is the responsibility of teachers to seek more effective ways of teaching in order to meet the students' needs.

Indirect Instructional Approach

Indirect teaching is built on the claim that knowledge is derived primarily from a learner's experience and interaction with the phenomenon. It occurs when an instructor uses examples and cases to help the students infer a concept or a general principle. From the perspectives of progressive education, learners should have the freedom to choose what to learn and how to learn (Dewey, 1907). Learners look for patterns, raise questions, or make generalizations from their observations. The teacher's role is to facilitate and to provide the context in which students successfully make appropriate generalizations.

Prince and Felder (2006) summarize three characteristics of an indirect instructional approach: (1) Students are responsible for their own learning; (2) students learn by fitting new information into existing cognitive structures and are unlikely to learn if the information has few apparent connections to what they already know and believe; and (3) students solve problems through discussions (active learning) in groups (collaborative learning).

This constructivist framework for the indirect approach is characterized by the widely accepted principle that students construct their own understanding of reality rather than simply absorbing versions presented by their teachers. Proponents of constructivism and cognitive science provide theoretical support for indirect instruction (e.g., Prince & Felder, 2006). Instruction begins with content that has an apparent connection with what students are more likely to know and experience so that they can make connections to their existing knowledge structures. "All new learning involves transfer of information based on previous learning" (Bransford, Brown, & Cocking, 2000, p. 53). Instruction helps students become self-learners.

Effective Approach

The goal of teaching is to help students learn, regardless of whether a direct or indirect instructional approach is taken. Both authors believe a combination of direct and indirect instructional approaches would be most effective if they were used appropriately and fit with student needs. Students approach learning in three ways. Some take a surface approach, relying on rote memorization and mechanical formula substitution, making little or no effort to understand the material being taught. Others may adopt a deep approach, probing and questioning and exploring the limits of applicability of new materials. Still others use a strategic approach. They do whatever is necessary to get the highest grade, taking a surface approach if that suffices and a deep approach when necessary. Instruction should guide students to adopt a deep approach that is important for their professional or personal development. Furthermore, Felder and Brent (2004) maintain that the characteristics of high levels of intellectual development and of a deep approach to learning are essentially the same. A deep approach involves taking responsibility for one's own learning, questioning authorities rather than accepting their statements, and attempting to understand new knowledge in the context of prior knowledge and experience.

The most significant difference with respect to the forms of reasoning is that, in the deductive case, when the required conditions are fulfilled, the truth of the conclusion can be guaranteed. In the inductive case, however, the truth of the premises lends support to the conclusion without giving absolute assurance. Inductive arguments intend to support their conclusions only to some degree; the premises do not necessitate the conclusion. Therefore, inductive reasoning is common in qualitative research, where data are collected and tentative theories are developed through grounded theory (Glaser & Strauss, 1967). After the theory is proposed, repeated testing of the theory steps in with theoretical hypotheses. Deductive reasoning is used to test the hypotheses, where large-scale quantitative data are collected to see if the data support the theory consistently or if the theory needs to be modified. Elaborate structures of irrefutable theorems are built up from a small set of basic axioms and rules.

Literature supports the use of either indirect or direct instructional approach or some combination of the two in light of subjects being taught in class (e.g., Paradowski, 2007; Rivers, 1972, 1975). Paradowski (2007) suggests that two factors affect the selection of teaching methods: the content and the learner. Some research indicates that the indirect instructional method may not suit all learners (e.g., Leech, 1994). "An inductive approach frustrates students who, by dint of their personal learning style or their past learning experience (or both), would prefer simply to be told the rule" (Thornbury, 1999, p. 55). It is suggested that the indirect instructional approach may cater to and be more effective for holistic learners, who learn best by exposure to knowledge in meaningful contexts, but not analytic ones, who form and test hypotheses and extract rules from examples.

The relative effectiveness of these two approaches to teaching was examined in a few studies, but the results were mixed. Herron and Tomosello (1992) found a clear advantage for indirect instruction while Robinson (1996) posits that a direct approach was more effective. Robinson's conclusion was echoed by Erlam's (2003) study, which revealed a significant advantage for the group receiving direct instruction. Rosa and O'Neill (1999), however, found no significant difference in effectiveness. Ellis (2006) points out that it is likely that many factors affect which approach benefits learners more, including the specific structure, the target of the instruction, and the learners' aptitude.

As stated by Prince and Felder (2007), neither teaching nor learning is purely indirect or direct. Like the scientific method, learning always involves activities in both directions. Students use new observations or examples to infer rules and theories (induction), and then test the theories by using them to deduce consequences and applications that can be verified experimentally (deduction). Good teaching helps students learn to do both. Compared with traditional direct teaching, the indirect instructional approach imposes more logistical problems and requires more planning and possibly more resources. An indirect instructional approach is also more likely to invoke student resistance and interpersonal conflicts (Felder & Brent, 2004). Moreover, instructional methods that call for the use of cooperative (team-based) learning produce additional problems, such as the need to assess individual student performance in a team environment and to equip students to deal with the interpersonal and communication problems that inevitably arise in teamwork.

The literature suggests consideration of the content and learner when choosing either direct or indirect approaches, but to our knowledge, none of them extends to graduate-level courses in the context of East and West cultural conflicts between the instructor and students. This study is to examine effectiveness of the use of direct and indirect approaches and student feedback in two educational research method classes taught in an American university.

METHOD

The Instructor

The instructor is a Chinese American professor of educational research with 16 years of teaching experience, 8 years in a Chinese university and 8 years in an American university.[1] He was trained in a predominantly direct instructional method in China for his bachelor and master's degree but in a predominantly indirect instructional method in the United States for his doctorate degree.

Students and Courses

The students are 34 Americans pursuing doctorate degrees in education. Half of the students ($n = 17$) were European American. Fifteen of the students were African American, and two of them were Asian American. Most of the students ($n = 25$) were females and nine of them were males. This distribution of ethnicity and gender is representative of the doctoral students in educational fields at the institution. These students were evenly distributed to two courses: 17 in a qualitative research method course and 17 in a quantitative research method course. The same instructor taught both courses, using an indirect instructional approach in the qualitative research method course and a direct instructional approach in the quantitative research method course.

The adoption of the pedagogy was based on the analysis of the content of the course, student needs, and resources available. The content of the quantitative research method course was mainly statistics with lots of terminologies and formulas to memorize. Students did not have much background (knowledge or experience) working with statistics, especially the computer software used in the course. Each student was equipped with a personal computer with the statistical software installed, which made it convenient for students to analyze data, but the physical structure of the lab made discussion and group-work difficult.

On the contrary, the content of the qualitative research method course was mainly about philosophical paradigms, ethical conducts in research, researcher's subjectivity, interviews, narratives, and observations, on which the students already had some existing knowledge. The classroom was equipped with a computer, a projector for presentations, and easily movable desks and chairs. The delivery of the content knowledge in this course was predominantly indirect, where students worked in groups for projects. Discussions took most of the time. Each student was required to work on an interview project and an observation project, respectively, based upon his/her own research interest. Students were also encouraged to work in groups on the observation project because every student needed a peer for the purpose of peer debriefing. The research paper that originated from these projects was evaluated for student learning in this course.

Measurement of Effectiveness

Student course evaluation forms administered by the institution as well as personal communication between the instructor and students were used as measures of the course effectiveness and to solicit student feedback. There were originally eight items in the course evaluation for which descriptive statistics can be found in Table 8.1. Each item was rated on a 5-point Likert scale where "1" stands for "strongly disagree" and "5" stands for "strongly agree."

RESULTS

Positive Feedback

Overall, there was no statistically significant difference between the two classes with respect to student perspectives about the effectiveness of the course.[2] When we looked into each item, similar results were found with respect to the instructor's

Table 8.1. Means, Standard Deviations, t-Statistics, and Effect Size (Cohen's d) for the Comparison Between Direct and Indirect Approaches

Items	Direct	Indirect	t	d
My instructor was prepared and organized.	5.00 (0.00)	4.88 (0.33)	1.46	0.51
The teaching strategies used in this course helped me understand course content.	4.65 (1.00)	4.06 (1.09)	1.64	0.56
This course challenged me to think about the subject matter.	4.88 (0.33)	4.53 (0.51)	2.38*	0.81
My instructor provided useful feedback about my performance on course assignments.	4.76 (0.44)	4.88 (0.33)	-0.88	-0.31
My instructor used varied evaluation methods that were clear and consistent.	4.64 (0.61)	4.71 (0.47)	-0.32	-0.13
I experienced a positive learning environment in this class.	4.76 (0.56)	4.76 (0.56)	0.00	0.00
Overall, I learned a lot in this course.	4.82 (0.39)	4.59 (0.80)	1.09	0.37
Overall, this instructor was effective.	4.88 (0.33)	4.65 (0.79)	1.14	0.38
Total	4.81 (0.42)	4.63 (0.54)	1.02	0.37

*Numbers in parentheses are standard deviations. $P < .05$.

preparation and organization (Item 1), the teaching strategies (Item 2), the learning environment (Item 6), learning in the course (Item 7), and the effectiveness of the instructor (Item 8). As for the challenge of the course (Item 3), students rated much more positively in the quantitative research method course than they did in the qualitative research method course.[3] This confirms the instructor's beliefs that the content covered in the quantitative research method course is a greater challenge to the students than that covered in the qualitative research method course. Students in both classes experienced a positive learning environment (Item 6), and the means and standard deviations were exactly the same. Although not statistically significantly different, the means for instructor's feedback (Item 4) and evaluation methods (Item 5) were slightly higher in the qualitative research method course where the indirect instructional approach was adopted. This is not surprising because the assessment of student works in the quantitative research method course was simply right or wrong, whereas the assessment of student works in the qualitative research method course consisted of a variety of methods. The instructor provided detailed feedback to each student's work with tracked changes and comments, and students were allowed to revise and resubmit with consideration of the instructor's comments. Students felt that the feedback in the qualitative research method course was more useful than that in the quantitative research method course.[4]

Students also expressed their appreciation of the instructor's use of the pedagogy. One student from the quantitative research method course wrote, "I understood statistics well for the first time! Patience in explaining content—thoroughness explaining—practical assignments—prompt feedback on assignments." Another student added, "At the beginning (first class), I cried on the way home because I felt dumb because I couldn't understand the material. By the end, I realized that I learned a lot and this is one of the best experiences of my program." The use of direct instructional approach in the quantitative research method course was clearly a success, as reflected in a student's words: "Dr. Wang's method of delivery of potentially confusing material was effective in helping me navigate coursework that I was very concerned about." The use of an indirect instructional approach in the qualitative research method course was also appropriate. A student from the qualitative research class commented, "I enjoyed the flexibility of this course. I felt that feedback was helpful. Assignments were also helpful in giving practice to skills/methods learned."

Culture Shock

Culture shock occurs when what someone gets is completely different from what was expected (Carol, 1986). A Chinese teacher usually thinks that it is the teacher's responsibility and obligation to help students learn whereas a student from Western culture might think that the students are responsible for their own learning (Zhao, 2007). Trained in China and with a strong belief that good students come from teachers with high expectations, the instructor presented lots of materials in class and gave weekly homework. One student complained, "I felt this class was very frustrating because I have not had another course that I felt the instructor tried so hard to make a class even more difficult than it had to be." Another student had a similar feeling, "It seemed that he was unable to understand the unpreparedness of many of his students to 'get it'. It seemed that we covered massive amounts of information. I often felt we went too fast." Some students thought that they should not have graded homework every week as doctoral students.

If those complaints of high expectations were not surprising to the instructor, the following feedback from a student really made him truly aware of his cultural differences and his use of English language. One student wrote, "Dr. Wang sometimes offends students who are struggling or who do not understand by suggesting that something 'should not' be hard or that we 'should' understand." Deeply rooted in the belief in the authoritative role of a teacher, the instructor used the word *should* to indicate that the students were supposed to know something or be able to do something because they had been taught in previous lectures. The instructor failed to realize that the use of *should* hurt their feelings and that students could not memorize everything learned in previous lectures. This language would be appropriate in a Chinese classroom, but not in an American classroom, especially in a doctoral-level course.

The use of an indirect instructional approach in the qualitative research course was not without complaints, either. One student apparently did not like the discussion format, saying, "I would prefer to not have discussion. The person-to-person dynamic would be more helpful." The indirect instructional approach looked disorganized to some students: "Sometimes the class felt disorganized. I felt like there were too many different assignments to keep up with." There was certainly disagreement with respect to assignments: "The structure of the course assignments and their due dates were too lenient." One more complaint from the students in the qualitative research method course was about the group-work. Although some students enjoyed the teamwork, some others professed a strong dislike. Some students said that it was difficult for them to meet after class. Some other students complained that someone in their group did not contribute, and still others were not happy that every student received the same grade in a group regardless of the amount of work from each individual.

CONCLUSIONS AND DISCUSSION

This chapter addresses how cultural experiences influenced a professor's pedagogical approach and the student's preference for teaching styles. As globalization leads to increased cross-cultural interactions on campuses around the country, these findings may help professors and students develop a greater awareness around cultural differences and ultimately lead to a more positive learning experience for all students.

Reflecting upon student feedback in numerical data and comments in words, the first author realized the cultural differences of teacher beliefs and student expectations between Chinese and American contexts. The instructor certainly adopted the traditional Chinese empty-vessel model (Maley, 1982) of direct instructional approach in the quantitative research method course. This type of instructional method would certainly fit Chinese students, as suggested by Brick (2004), because Chinese students are used to learning the basic knowledge first and then applying it in practice. Although this approach seemed to be welcomed by most American students in the class due to the difficult level of the content knowledge (i.e., statistics), some American students felt offended by the instructor's use of language and unreasonably high expectations. The instructor's belief that a teacher is a role model and a mentor/parent and is responsible for the students' learning (Hu, 2002; Zhao, 2007) certainly affected his way of teaching and his use of language in the class. This belief is certainly not what American students expected in their own process of learning.

What was surprising to both authors was that not all American students enjoyed group-work. Although cross-culture studies of learning styles suggest that Chinese students are characterized low on individualism and high on collectivism (e.g., Hofstede & Bond, 1984; Kennedy, 2002), researchers must not make the mistake of overgeneralizing cultural tendencies to individuals and groups (Conyne, Wilson, Tang, & Shi, 1999). There is always a variety of learning styles in every cultural group. Group-work is efficient and enjoyable if all group members collaborate well and work together. Group-work collapses if everyone is only concerned with his/her own contribution and time regardless of what cultural background the students come from. The same is true of direct and indirect instructional approaches. A recent study of discovery-based instruction (indirect instructional method) challenged the traditional belief that indirect instructional method is always better than the direct instructional method and added that indirect instructional method should be assisted with guided discovery (Alfieri, Brooks, Aldrich, & Tenenbaum, 2011). Although further research is warranted to explore the effectiveness of different pedagogical approaches, it is certainly important for instructors to consider the content, student, and resources available when choosing which method to use. Whatever approach (direct or indirect) is taken, the instructor should provide an appropriate amount of guidance and support and gradually withdraw that support as students gain more experience and confidence.

SUMMARY OF IMPLICATIONS

For Foreign-Born Professors in the United States

- Come out of your comfort zone and use a pedagogy that meets the needs of the students and is appropriate for the content of the course.

- It is okay to say to your students, "I don't know the answer at this moment, but I will try to get it to you as soon as possible."
- Do not assume that all American students like group-work. Group-work would be efficient and enjoyable only if all group members collaborate well and work together, regardless of students' cultural background.

For U.S.-Born Educators

- Make sure that all students are familiar with the cultural background of the activities in the class. International students may not be familiar with the common games that American students are accustomed to.
- Please monitor the small-group discussions and ask each group to share their thoughts with the whole class after the discussions.
- Please offer your own thoughts as well after listening to students' opinions because students also want to hear from you, especially your guidance, whether or not they think you are an authority on the subject.

For Both U.S.-Born and Foreign-Born Educators

- Direct instructional approach is usually appropriate when students do not have sufficient prior knowledge of the content and efficiency of the transmission of the knowledge is of primary concern.
- Indirect instructional approach is usually appropriate when students have some knowledge of the content and the objective is to challenge their prior knowledge and to expose them to multiple perspectives of that knowledge.

NOTES

1. An exploratory mixed methods research design was used with the QUAL-quan model (Creswell, 2012), in which qualitative data were collected first and were weighted more heavily than quantitative data. The methodological approach is autoethnography (Ellis & Bochner, 2000), where the personal reflection of the first author was used as data together with feedback from students through course evaluations and personal communication between the instructor and the students. The second author served as the peer debriefer to guard against any possible subjectivity of the first author. Qualitative data were analyzed using thematic analysis, and quantitative data were analyzed with independent samples t-tests.

2. $t(32) = 1.02$, $p = 0.32$, although a medium effect size (Cohen's $d = 0.37$) was noted. With a mean of 4.81 for the direct instructional approach and a mean of 4.63 for the indirect instructional approach, the statistics could be interpreted to show that students in both classes viewed the course as effective.

3. $t(32) = 2.38$, $p = .02$, with a large effect size (Cohen's $d = 0.81$).

4. With a medium effect size (Cohen's $d = 0.31$), an increase in sample size could possibly see a statistically significant difference.

REFERENCES

Alfieri, L., Brooks, P. J., Aldrich, N. J., & Tenenbaum, H. R. (2011). Does discovery-based instruction enhance learning? *Journal of Educational Psychology, 103,* 1–18.

Bagley, W. C. (1907). *Classroom management: Its principles and technique.* New York: MacMillan.

Biggs, J. B. (1996). Western misperceptions of the Confucian-heritage learning culture. In D. Watkins & J. B. Biggs (Eds.), *The Chinese learner: Cultural, psychological and contextual influences* (pp. 45–67). Hong Kong, China: CERC and ACER.

Bransford, J. D., Brown, A. L., & Cocking, R. R. (2000). *How people learn: Brain, mind, experience, and school.* Washington, DC: National Academy Press.

Brick, J. (2004). *China: A handbook in intercultural communication.* Sydney, Australia: Macquarie University.

Carol, M. A. (1986). Culture bump and beyond. In J. M. Valdes (Ed.), *Culture bound bridging the cultural gap in language teaching* (pp. 170-178). New York: Cambridge University Press.

Conyne, R. K., Wilson, F. R., Tang, M., & Shi, K. (1999). Cultural similarities and differences in group work: Pilot study of a U.S.–Chinese task group comparison. *Group Dynamics: Theory, Research, and Practice, 3,* 40–50.

Cortazzi, M., & Jin, L. X. (1996). Culture of learning: Language classrooms in China. In H. Coleman (Ed.), *Society and the language classroom* (pp. 169–206). Cambridge, United Kingdom: Cambridge University Press.

Creswell, J. W. (2012). *Educational research: Planning, conducting, and evaluating quantitative and qualitative research.* Upper Saddle River, NJ: Merrill/Prentice Hall.

Dewey, J. (1907). *School and society.* Chicago: University of Chicago Press.

Ellis, C., & Bochner, A. P. (2000). Autoethnography, personal narrative, reflexivity: Researcher as subject. In N. K. Denzin & Y. S. Lincoln (Eds.), *Handbook of qualitative research* (pp. 733–768). Thousand Oaks, CA: Sage.

Ellis, R. (2006). Current issues in the teaching of grammar: A SLA perspective. *TESOL Quarterly, 40,* 83–107.

Erlam, R. (2003). The effects of direct and indirect instruction on the acquisition of direct object pronouns in French as a second language. *The Modern Language Journal, 87,* 242–260.

Felder, R. M., & Brent, R. (2004). The intellectual development of science and engineering students: Teaching to promote growth. *Journal of Engineering Education, 93,* 279–291.

Glaser, B. G., & Strauss, A. L. (1967). *The discovery of grounded theory: Strategies for qualitative research.* New York: Aldine de Gruyter.

Herron, C., & Tomosello, M. (1992). Acquiring grammatical structures by guided induction. *French Review, 65,* 708–718.

Hofstede, G., & Bond, M. (1984). Hofstede's culture dimensions: An independent validation using Rokeach's value survey. *Journal of Cross-Cultural Psychology, 15,* 417–433.

Hu, G. (2002). Potential cultural resistance to pedagogical imports: The case of communicative language teaching in China. *Language, Culture and Curriculum, 15*, 93–105.

Jin, L. X., & Cortazzi, M. (1995). A cultural synergy model for academic language use. In P. Bruthiaux, T. Boswood, & B. Du-Babcock (Eds.), *Explorations in English for Professional Communication* (pp. 41–56). Hong Kong, China: City University of Hong Kong.

Kennedy, P. (2002). Learning cultures and learning styles: Myth-understandings about adult (Hong Kong) Chinese learners. *International Journal of Lifelong Education, 21*, 430–445.

Leech, G. N. (1994). Students' grammar—teachers' grammar—learners' grammar. In M. Bygate, A. Tonkyn, & E. Williams (Eds.), *Grammar and the language teacher* (pp. 17–30). New York: Prentice Hall.

Lincoln, Y. S., & Guba, E. G. (1985). *Naturalistic inquiry.* Newbury Park, CA: Sage.

Maley, A. (1982). Foreign language learning and the search for a new paradigm. *Language Learning and Communication, 1*, 123–135.

Paine, L. (1992). Teaching and modernization in contemporary China. In R. Hayhoe (Ed.), *Education and modernization: The Chinese experience* (pp. 183–209). Oxford, United Kingdom: Pergamon Press.

Paradowski, M. B. (2007). *Exploring the L1/L2 interface: A study of Polish advanced EFL learners* (Unpublished doctoral dissertation). University of Warsaw, Warsaw, Poland.

Prince, M. J., & Felder, R. M. (2006). Indirect teaching and learning methods: Definitions, comparisons and research bases. *Journal of Engineering Education, 95*, 123–138.

Prince, M. J., & Felder, R. M. (2007). The many faces of indirect teaching and learning. *Journal of College Science Teaching, 36*(5), 14–20.

Rivers, W. (1972). *Speaking in many tongues.* Rowley, MA: Newbury House.

Rivers, W. (1975). *A practical guide to the teaching of French.* New York: Oxford University Press.

Robinson, P. (1996). Learning simple and complex rules under implicit, incidental rule-search conditions, and instructed conditions. *Studies in Second Language Acquisition, 18*, 27–67.

Rosa, R., & O'Neill, M. (1999). Explicitness, intake and the issue of awareness. *Studies in Second Language Acquisition, 21*, 511–556.

Tang, D. G., & Absalom, D. (1998). Teaching across cultures: Considerations for Western EFL teachers in China. *Hong Kong Journal of Applied Linguistics 3*, 117–132.

Thornbury, S. (1999). *How to teach grammar.* Harlow, United Kingdom: Pearson.

Zhao, Y. (2007). Cultural conflicts in an intercultural classroom discourse and interpretations from a cultural perspective. *Intercultural Communication Studies, 16*, 129–136.

9

Using Collaborative Action Research for Science Teachers' Professional Development

Meilan Zhang

Other chapters of this book have examined the conflicts and differences between the United States and China from teacher educators' perspectives with the object of finding a "middle ground" that incorporates the strengths of both approaches. This chapter aims to offer an innovative model for teacher professional development that can have important implications for improving teacher effectiveness in both countries. Although understanding of differences between the two countries is undoubtedly important, teacher educators in both countries face common challenges in preparing teachers. Therefore, a model that is well grounded in theories and supported by empirical research is worth the attention of teacher educators in both countries.

The teacher improvement model that I describe in this chapter was developed by a group of experienced science teacher educators and science teachers in the United States and was implemented to inservice science teachers in the United States over 4 years. Evidence collected from these teachers suggested that it was a promising model for improving teachers' content knowledge and pedagogical content knowledge. Therefore, this model has direct implications for teacher educators in the United States and its design principles can be beneficially applied to China's teacher education.

ACTION RESEARCH:
A PROMISING TEACHER DEVELOPMENT APPROACH

In both the United States and China, teachers hold the key for the success of educational reform. There is little argument that it ultimately relies on teachers to achieve the ambitious goals for student learning called for by educational reform efforts (National Research Council, 1996). Research shows that teacher effectiveness is even a stronger predictor of student academic achievements than other important factors such as socioeconomic status and race (Sanders & Horn, 1998). Gordon, Kane, and Staiger (2006) argued that "Public education ultimately succeeds or fails based on the talent and skills of America's 3.1 million teachers in elementary and secondary schools. . . . Without the right people standing in front of the classroom, school reform is a futile exercise" (p. 5). The same argument applies to educational reform in China, whose success depends on its 10 million teachers.

Given the recognition that teachers are at the heart of education, each year, the federal government, states, and school districts invest billions of dollars in various types of professional development for inservice teachers. Yet, the traditional "one-shot" and "one-size-fits-all" workshop-model professional development remains largely ineffective and fails to bring about changes in teachers' classroom practice (Lumpe, 2007). Lieberman and Mace (2008) made the criticism that, "Professional development, though well intentioned, is often perceived by teachers as fragmented, disconnected, and irrelevant to the real problems of classroom practice" (p. 226).

In recent years, action research—teachers as researchers systematically inquiring into their own classroom practice—has gained increasing attention in both the United States and China as a new approach for teacher development (Zeichner, 2003; Zhou & Liu, 2011). As of April 18, 2013, a search on action research in the ERIC database (www.eric.ed.gov) yielded 6,971 results. Similarly, a search on its Chinese translation (*Xingdong Yanjiu*, 行动研究) in a full-text Chinese periodicals database (www.cnki.net) yielded 5,402 results. The new national curriculum reform in China has infused strong momentum to improve teachers through action research (Hu, 2008).

Classroom practice is complex and dynamic, full of uncertainty and ambiguity. There is no one best way to teach a certain topic. A reflective teacher often questions "why something is done." However, teachers do not automatically acquire reflective skills. They need to learn to become reflective practitioners. In fact, teaching is such a physically demanding job that it is not uncommon for teachers to routinely go through a busy teaching day without reflecting on what happens, what works, and what does not (Putnam & Borko, 2000).

One of the ways that teachers learn to become reflective practitioners is to conduct research on their own practice. Through choosing a focus question and systematically collecting and analyzing data to answer the question, teachers have opportunities to observe, understand, critique, and reflect on their teaching. Furthermore, teachers' reflection is enhanced when they share their research with other teachers. By articulating their thinking to peers and responding to challenges of others, teachers confront their inherent personal beliefs, make explicit their decision-making processes, and consider alternatives other than what they are accustomed to (Mitchell, Reilly, & Logue, 2009).

In addition, the education community can benefit from teachers' investigation into their practice to understand what is actually happening in classrooms and how innovative instructional approaches are interpreted and implemented. Teachers as insiders have unique advantages in finding authentic problems to study that are often inaccessible to outside researchers. According to Cochran-Smith and Lytle (1993), "A major contribution of teacher research is that it identifies and investigates a distinctive set of problems of practice that outside researchers cannot address because they do not stand in the same relationship to the practice of teaching" (p. 120).

TEACHERS' ACTION RESEARCH: A ROCKY ROAD

Despite the prominence and attention action research has received in educational communities, however, research is not an easy task for teachers. Christenson and colleagues (2002) found it a "rocky road" to help teachers become teacher researchers. Based on interviews with 74 teachers who participated in a professional development program and conducted research on their practice, Zeichner (2003) concluded that

> Conducting research was often difficult, complex, and sometimes frustrating for teachers, but many teachers valued the intellectual challenges posed by the research experience in comparison to what they saw as the superficial nature of many of their professional development experiences. (p. 309)

Teacher researchers often cited a number of challenges, including lack of time, lack of research skills, and lack of support from colleagues and administrators. Similar challenges have been documented in studies of teachers' action research in China (Hu, 2008; Zhou & Liu, 2011).

First, many teachers are unfamiliar with research and lack specialized knowledge of research. Some teachers confuse action research with library research, equating the former with searching resources for new instructional techniques (Christenson et al., 2002). Moreover, many teachers find research a strange and frightening concept because of their stereotyped view of traditional quantitative research that involves complicated statistics and measurements that are beyond their understanding. Teachers are usually unaware of the interpretative nature of qualitative research that is more frequently found in teachers' action research. Negative and rigid image of research often prevents them from engaging in research (Christenson et al., 2002).

The research process itself is difficult for teachers, too (Zeichner, 2003). Teachers have problems asking specific, researchable questions. Often, their questions are too general and vague. Teachers also have difficulty with the data collection and analysis processes. Many teachers are inexperienced in taking fieldnotes, or developing interview protocols or survey items. Typically, they also lack training in both qualitative and quantitative data analysis.

In addition, lack of time for research is a great concern for teachers (Christenson et al., 2002; Zeichner, 2003). This concern is understandable considering the fact that teachers are not given additional time for research. Many teachers find research a daunting task, adding to their already demanding full-time teaching job. They worry that they will not have enough time to collect and analyze data. Extracurricular demands and family commitments also compete against research for teachers' limited after-school time (Reis-Jorge, 2007).

Another common challenge is lack of support from colleagues and administrators in schools. School culture often discourages teachers from engaging in research. Some principals may not support teachers' action research because research can take time away from teaching. Other principals may find it threatening when teachers advocate for changes in the school system as a result of action research. Colleagues may be unsupportive due to lack of understanding of action research, or due to pressure that they have to do the same thing. Sometimes teachers might face pressure and resistance from parents if they study sensitive issues involving students' family or social background (Reis-Jorge, 2007).

DEVELOPING A COLLABORATIVE ACTION RESEARCH MODEL TO HELP TEACHER RESEARCHERS

In this section, I describe an innovative action research model for teacher professional development, drawing upon my research in a large-scale professional development program for K–12 science teachers, a 5-year project funded by the National Science Foundation with multimillion dollars. This program developed a collaborative action research model based on research on teacher research (Christenson et al., 2002; Zeichner, 2003), professional development, teacher reflection (Schön, 1983), Japanese lesson study (Fernandez, 2002), and problem-based learning (PBL) (Hmelo-Silver, 2004).

The collaborative action research model was developed by more than 20 experienced science teacher educators, science teachers, educational researchers, and PBL experts in the United States. Also, the model evolved based on the research evidence collected from teacher participants each year.

In summary, four principles guided the design of the action research model. First, we allowed teachers to decide the topic they want to study, which we believed is important to motivate teachers to engage in action research and sustain their research effort. Levin and Merritt (2006) observed that allowing teachers to choose their own problems to study is a common feature among successful action research studies. Unlike preservice teachers, most inservice teachers typically do not conduct action research to meet course or degree requirements, but for improving their practice and fostering their own professional growth. Therefore, it is critical for these teachers that their action research is driven by authentic problems that grow out of their practice and are of interest to them. Emphasis on teacher autonomy is one of the defining features that separate this action research model from other action research studies in which teachers were assigned a research topic.

Second, we encouraged teachers to collaborate with other teachers in small groups and meet regularly to share their research. Collaboration with other teachers is essential for effective professional development (Garet, Porter, Desimone, Birman, & Yoon, 2001). Collaboration is also important in action research, as a teacher in the study of Christenson et al. (2002) put it, "A support group is necessary because alone, you would give up" (p. 267). In addition, a potential problem for teachers as insiders to study their own practice is that they may not see what they take for granted (McCotter, 2001). Therefore, outsiders can help to spotlight such blind spots and offer alternative perspectives.

Another important feature in this model is that teachers need to videotape their lessons and use video recordings as one of the data sources to examine their practice. Video is viewed as a powerful tool in teacher learning because of its unique capability to capture the elusive classroom practice for later study (Borko, Jacobs, Eiteljorg, & Pittman, 2008). According to Sherin (2004), "Video allows one to enter the world of the classroom without having to be in the position of teaching in-the-moment" (p. 13). Video recordings allow teacher researchers to replay classroom events and notice aspects of classroom situations that they are too busy to notice during their teaching.

Most existing studies on video-based teacher reflection focused on either individual analysis of video or collaborative viewing and discussion. In few studies did teachers have the opportunity to both individually watch and collaboratively discuss their own video. Jay and Johnson (2002) suggested that both individual reflection and collaborative reflection are important aspects of teacher reflection. In our model, teachers had the opportunity for both individual reflection through watching and editing video on their own and collaborative reflection with other teachers in a group.

In addition, we adopted the PBL approach for teachers to analyze their teaching problems. PBL is an instructional approach widely used in medical schools that emphasizes self-directed study, reasoning skills, and group collaboration in solving real-world, ill-structured medical problems (Schmidt, 1993). These emphases represent the essential features of teachers' action research. Action research is a self-directed process. Teachers are expected to develop clinical reasoning skills to solve problems in practice. Teaching problems are also ill-structured because they often have more than one solution. Therefore, we reasoned that PBL has potential for supporting teachers' action research.

The PBL structure for analyzing teaching problems involves teachers collaboratively identifying relevant *facts* about the problem, developing *hypotheses* to solve the problem, and generating *learning issues* for literature research. The process is guided by one or two facilitators.

It is important to note that this action research model was among the first attempts to employ PBL for teachers' action research. Although video has been used in teacher education for almost 30 years, very few studies have used the PBL discourse structure to guide video-based discussion. Prior research has shown that it is difficult to promote productive analysis and discussion of video (Borko et al., 2008). Teachers often focus on superficial features in their teaching video, for example, "I talked too fast." Also, teachers are often reluctant to make critical comments about their peers' practice. The PBL discourse structure that emphasizes reasoning and identifying learning issues can be a constructive, yet nonthreatening way to promote productive discussion among teacher groups.

This collaborative action research model had been implemented to more than 100 K–12 science teachers over 4 years. The professional development included an intensive 2-week summer workshop and a year-long action research project. In the summer workshop, teachers spent 3 days deepening their science understanding through using PBL to solve science content problems related to the subjects they taught (e.g., why are there moon phases?). They then spent 4 days developing or revising a lesson plan. In the second week, teachers developed their pedagogical knowledge through solving problems in science teaching. They practiced the PBL process to analyze teaching problems using video cases from published resources (e.g., how to handle conflicting experimental data). In addition, they identified a problem from their own practice and developed a research plan for studying the problem. They shared their research problems with other teachers and facilitators and received feedback.

During the school year, teachers conducted research on their self-selected problems, videotaped lessons, and analyzed student work. They met in a small group for 3 hours each month. The group meeting started with one teacher presenting his or her teaching problem to the group and showing video clips of the lessons. To help other teachers understand the context of their video and research problem, teachers prepared handouts that described the lesson topic, their objectives for teaching the lesson, big ideas in the lesson for students to learn, a chronological list of activities in the lesson, their research problem, hypothesis, expected results, relevant student work, and the content of the video clips. In addition, teachers provided focus questions for guiding the discussion of their video. Then the group used the PBL process to analyze the teaching problem by identifying relevant facts, generating hypotheses, and developing learning issues. The learning issues were assigned to each teacher in the group. In the next meeting, the group members presented what they found from the literature research for the learning issues they studied. Finally, teachers shared their experience at the end of the school year in a large group meeting with all of the teachers who participated in the project.

Each year, multiple sources of data were collected from teacher participants, including (1) teachers' action research plans developed in the summer workshop; (2) video recordings of group meetings during the school year; (3) end-of-year written reports, in which teachers described their research processes and summarized their learning; and (4) end-of-year focus group interviews, in which teachers were asked about what they learned from their action research, how their practice was changed, and what had been helpful for their research. In addition, before and after teachers' participation in the professional development, we administered the Science Teaching Efficacy Beliefs Inventory (STEBI) that measures teachers' self-efficacy beliefs about their ability to teach science, and the Horizon survey that measures changes in science teaching practices.

HOW EFFECTIVE IS THE
COLLABORATIVE ACTION RESEARCH MODEL?

We have conducted comprehensive research to understand both the design of the professional development model and its impact on teachers and students. In terms of the design of the model, we studied teachers' needs for professional development, challenges they faced in science teaching, motivation for participating in the professional development, characteristics of problem design, and assessment of teachers' science content knowledge. In terms of the impact, our prior research found that after participation in the professional development, teachers improved their content knowledge and pedagogical content knowledge, enhanced self-efficacy as science teachers, improved classroom practice, and aligned with state curriculum standards. In addition, many teachers reported that they were better able to focus on big ideas in their teaching, and shifted toward student-centered, inquiry-based teaching.

In particular, I have conducted a series of studies on the characteristics and effectiveness of the collaborative action research model, including productive and less productive discourse patterns in teacher learning communities (Zhang, Lundeberg, & Eberhardt, 2011), affordances and constraints of different types of video in support of teacher researchers to reflect on their practice (Zhang, Lundeberg, & Eberhardt, 2010), and in-depth case studies on how teachers' action research promoted teacher development and student learning (Zhang, Parker, Eberhardt, & Passalacqua, 2011). Overall, we found the components of the collaborative action research model, including the choice for studying authentic problems, teacher learning community, analysis of teaching videos, and the PBL structure, created conditions that were conducive for teacher learning in action research. Next, I describe teachers' responses to the collaborative action research model. Pseudonyms are used for teachers.

First, teachers appreciated the choice that they had to study issues that were relevant to their classroom and could be directly applied to improve their practice. Many teachers emphasized the personal usefulness and relevance that their research had to their teaching, as shown in the following responses.

I was not told what to do, but allowed to explore my own issues. I had "ownership" and learned more by doing my own research, then being able to discuss it. It was relevant to my immediate teaching practice. (Emma, kindergarten teacher)

Our discussions and research have personal usefulness and relevance. We have dealt with issues in the "real" classroom, not the "ideal" classroom. (Cathy, kindergarten teacher)

Second, almost all teachers recognized the importance of collaborating with other teachers. Teachers are often isolated in their own classrooms, so they valued the opportunity to share ideas with their colleagues, to hear different perspectives on a teaching issue, and to get feedback from other teachers about their research. When asked how the professional development was or was not useful, many teachers referred to the opportunity to collaborate with colleagues, as shown in the following responses.

The usefulness, I think the main thing would just be [that] you are required for 3 hours to sit down and having people to talk about science with, just because I don't get that very often here. Yes, we have staff meetings but maybe 10 minutes are spent when you are actually talking with other science people in your department. So just having that opportunity to discuss "What are you doing in your classroom? What is working for you?" I think that is huge because we all teach science, I mean people may teach other things but the one thing we all have in common is we all teach science. (Kate, 8th-grade teacher)

Discussing someone else's dilemma has helped me become better in my teaching. It has opened my eyes to what concerns my peers have and how alike we actually are. (Cindy, 6th-grade teacher)

As a requirement of the professional development, teachers videotaped their lessons, analyzed the tapes, and selected clips to present in the group meetings. Many teachers referred to the videotaping as an eye-opening experience. Videos allowed teachers to observe their students and themselves at a distance, which often offered them a fresh view on their teaching. When watching their teaching videos, teachers engage in a different practice from their daily teaching. In the midst of teaching, teachers often face pressure to respond and decide what to do next. With video, teachers can focus on reflection rather than action. Video can be stopped at any moment and replayed multiple times, enabling teachers to attend to particular details in their practice and notice events that are not easily observable during the act of teaching. In addition, watching other teachers' video can help teachers gain different perspectives into classroom practice. These affordances are shown in the following responses by the teachers.

> You have one perception of what is happening when you are going through any experience and a different one when you view it as a witness. (Jim, 7th-grade teacher)

> I think video can allow you to see what is really going on versus what you think is going on. (Jane, high school teacher)

> From video clips of lessons, I saw that they had difficulty observing carefully, describing what they saw, and then making the inferential connections that might lead to an understanding of the relevant scientific concepts. . . . I realized a lot of what they weren't able to do is because I hadn't done my job, which is to teach them process skills. So that became something that I started to really focus on and pay attention to this year a lot. (Wendy, 6th-grade teacher)

In addition, teachers considered the PBL approach useful for guiding their action research. The PBL discourse structure encouraged teachers to engage in pedagogical reasoning by developing hypotheses to account for the problems under consideration. It helped teachers to recognize their knowledge gaps by developing learning issues that need further study.

> I really enjoyed working through the PBL process with my peers. It was a great way to talk about, discuss, and analyze what had worked and what had not worked. Through this analysis the group and I came to several conclusions. (Cindy, 3rd-grade teacher)

In summary, the collaborative action research model provided opportunities for teacher learning in action research.

WHAT DOES IT MEAN FOR TEACHER DEVELOPMENT
IN THE UNITED STATES AND CHINA?

It is important to note that the action research model that I described in this chapter is not a typical model found in teachers' action research in the United States. Instead, it is an innovative model that integrates major trends in some of the best practices of professional development. To my knowledge, this project is among the first in using Problem-Based Learning for teachers' action research on a large scale. Despite the widespread advocacy for teachers' action research, it is still not a common practice among teachers. Berliner (2008) suggested that "In business, it is a well-accepted practice to ask the people closest to the problems to help solve them. We do not do that enough with our approximately 3.5 million teachers and administrators" (p. 255). Moreover, there are relatively few studies that have systematically explored ways to support teachers' action research. Capobianco (2007) noted that "Little is known about efforts to support science teachers as a collective group of teacher researchers, systematically collaborating together to inquire about, test out, and reflect upon pedagogical practices" (p. 2). Therefore, the collaborative action research model that was developed by experienced teacher educators, teachers, and researchers in the United States has important implications for improving teachers in the United States by illustrating conditions for productive action research.

The design principles implemented in this action research model are also important for teachers in China. First, our study found that teachers in the United States greatly valued the autonomy that they had in choosing a research topic that was authentic and meaningful for them. Given the relatively strict top-down power hierarchy in China, teacher autonomy should be emphasized to motivate teachers to participate in action research. In other words, action research should be a teacher-driven, not administrator-driven, endeavor.

Also, the action research model is a year-long process. Systemically collecting and analyzing data is time-consuming and labor-intensive. In general, teachers in China face even greater pressure to perform well on standardized tests than their counterparts in the United States. It is important for teachers and administrators in China to bear in mind that meaningful changes derived from action research often take time to cultivate. The positive effect of action research may not be reflected in standardized test scores immediately.

In addition, due to the pressure to perform well on standardized tests, teachers in China might be more likely to view their peers as competitors rather than collaborators. Because the PBL discourse structure places the emphasis on pedagogical issues under investigation, rather than a teacher's performance, it can be particularly useful to guide discussion in teacher study groups in China.

Similarly, teachers in the United States are facing increasingly greater pressure on standardized tests as a result of the educational reforms in recent years that place accountability on teachers. Therefore, the suggestions made to teachers in China above also apply to teachers in the United States.

Moreover, much of what has been written on teachers' action research that I found in China's educational databases are short, abstract, and overly theoretical descriptions. With a graduate degree from China and over 6 years of research experience on action research in the United States, I often find it difficult to read and make sense of the articles on action research written by educational researchers in China. I believe one of the major reasons that contribute to the difficulty is direct translation of concepts, terminologies, and theoretical frameworks in the educational research from the Western countries, particularly the United States. In fact, the term *Xingdong Yanjiu* (行动研究) itself in Chinese is a direct translation of *action research* in English. Although we do not use the term *action research*, China's educators have long been engaged in studying their own practice in teaching and research groups (*Jiaoyan Zu*, 教研组) and conducting research activities (*Jiaoyan Huodong*, 教研活动), a practice similar to Japanese lesson studies (Fernandez, 2002). Perhaps the term *Jiaoyan Huodong* would be more meaningful to China's educational practitioners and researchers than *Xingdong Yanjiu*. Therefore, I suggest that when introducing foreign terms and theoretical frameworks, researchers in China should be careful in their word choice and ensure that the translation is understandable and meaningful.

In summary, as a promising professional development approach, teachers' action research has received increasing attention in both the United States and China. Yet, action research is challenging and teachers need support to initiate and sustain their research efforts. The collaborative action research model that emphasizes choice for studying authentic problems, teacher learning community, analysis of teaching videos, and the PBL structure has important applications for the teacher education communities in both the United States and China.

SUMMARY OF IMPLICATIONS

For Science Teacher Educators in the United States

- Engaging science teachers in researching their own practice can be both rewarding and challenging. Teachers need support to start and sustain their research endeavors.
- Science teachers are often very occupied by day-to-day teaching, and lack time to reflect on their practice. The Problem-Based Learning framework provides a structured way for teachers to reflect on their practice.
- Science teachers are often isolated in their own classroom. They highly value the opportunity to work with peers to gain new perspectives on their own practice.

- It is hard to observe and reflect on your practice during the heat of teaching. Video recordings of classroom lessons are valuable to help teachers see what they may not be able to see while they are teaching.
- Developing teachers as reflective practitioners through action research is time-consuming and takes great effort. But remember, no pain, no gain.

For Science Teacher Educators in China

- When engaging teachers in action research, it is important to respect teachers' autonomy in choosing research questions of interest to them. Assigning research topics to teachers can discourage teachers from doing action research.
- Just as it takes time to grow crops, it takes time to grow deep and sustained teacher learning. The positive effect of action research may not be reflected in standardized test scores immediately.
- When introducing foreign terms and theoretical frameworks on action research, it is important to ensure that the translation is understandable and meaningful.

NOTE

This material is based upon work supported in part by the National Science Foundation, under special project number ESI–0353406 as part of the Teacher Professional Continuum program. Any opinion, finding, conclusions, or recommendations expressed in this publication are those of the author and do not necessarily reflect the views of any of the supporting institutions. The author is deeply indebted to Jan Eberhardt, Joyce Parker, Mary Lundeberg, Matthew J. Koehler, and the project team for their invaluable contribution to the PBL for Teachers project.

REFERENCES

Berliner, D. C. (2008). Letter to the president. *Journal of Teacher Education, 59*(3), 252–256.

Borko, H., Jacobs, J., Eiteljorg, E., & Pittman, M. E. (2008). Video as a tool for fostering productive discussions in mathematics professional development. *Teaching and Teacher Education, 24*(2), 417–436.

Capobianco, B. M. (2007). Science teachers' attempts at integrating feminist pedagogy through collaborative action research. *Journal of Research in Science Teaching, 44*(1), 1–32.

Christenson, M., Slutsky, R., Bendau, S., Covert, J., Dyer, J., Risko, G., & Johnston, M. (2002). The rocky road of teachers becoming action researchers. *Teaching and Teacher Education, 18*(3), 259–272.

Cochran-Smith, M., & Lytle, S. (1993). *Inside/Outside: Teacher research and knowledge.* New York: Teachers College Press.

Fernandez, C. (2002). Learning from Japanese approaches to professional development: The case of lesson study. *Journal of Teacher Education, 53*(5), 393–405.

Garet, M. S., Porter, A. C., Desimone, L., Birman, B. F., & Yoon, K. S. (2001). What makes professional development effective? Results from a national sample of teachers. *American Educational Research Journal, 38*(4), 915–945.

Gordon, R., Kane, T. J., & Staiger, D. O. (2006). *Identifying effective teachers using performance on the job.* Washington, DC: Brookings Institution.

Hmelo-Silver, C. E. (2004). Problem-based learning: What and how do students learn? *Educational Psychology Review, 16*(3), 235–266.

Hu, W. (2008). Analysis of reasons for difficulties in teachers' action research (in Chinese). *Jiangsu Education Research, 17,* 52–55.

Jay, J. K., & Johnson, K. L. (2002). Capturing complexity: A typology of reflective practice for teacher education. *Teaching and Teacher Education, 18*(1), 73–85.

Levin, B. B., & Merritt, S. P. (2006). Guest editors' Introduction: Action research for teacher empowerment and transformation. *Teacher Education Quarterly, 33*(3), 3–6.

Lieberman, A., & Mace, D.H.P. (2008). Teacher learning: The key to educational reform. *Journal of Teacher Education, 59*(3), 226–234.

Lumpe, A. (2007). Research-based professional development: Teachers engaged in professional learning communities. *Journal of Science Teacher Education, 18*(1), 125–128.

McCotter, S. S. (2001). Collaborative groups as professional development. *Teaching and Teacher Education, 17*(6), 685–704.

Mitchell, S. N., Reilly, R. C., & Logue, M. E. (2009). Benefits of collaborative action research for the beginning teacher. *Teaching and Teacher Education, 25*(2), 344–349.

National Research Council. (1996). *National Science Education standards: Observe, interact, change, learn.* Washington, DC: National Academy Press.

Putnam, R. T., & Borko, H. (2000). What do new views of knowledge and thinking have to say about research on teacher learning? *Educational Researcher, 29*(1), 4–15.

Reis-Jorge, J. (2007). Teachers' conceptions of teacher-research and self-perceptions as enquiring practitioners: A longitudinal case study. *Teaching and Teacher Education, 23*(4), 402–417.

Sanders, W. L., & Horn, S. P. (1998). Research findings from the Tennessee value-added assessment system (TVAAS) database: Implications for educational evaluation and research. *Journal of Personnel Evaluation in Education, 12*(3), 247–256.

Schmidt, H. G. (1993). Foundations of problem-based learning: Some explanatory notes. *Medical Education, 27,* 422–432.

Schön, D. (1983). *The reflective practitioner: How professionals think in action.* New York: Basic Books.

Sherin, M. G. (2004). New perspectives on the role of video in teacher education. In J. Brophy (Ed.), *Advances in research on teaching: Using video in teacher education* (Vol. 10, pp. 1–27). Oxford, UK: Elsevier.

Zeichner, K. M. (2003). Teacher research as professional development for p-12 educators in the USA. *Educational Action Research, 11*(2), 301–326.

Zhang, M., Lundeberg, M., & Eberhardt, J. (2010). Seeing what you normally don't see. *Phi Delta Kappan, 91*(6), 60–65.

Zhang, M., Lundeberg, M., & Eberhardt, J. (2011). Strategic facilitation of problem-based discussion for teacher professional development. *Journal of the Learning Sciences, 20*(3), 342–394.

Zhang, M., Parker, J., Eberhardt, J., & Passalacqua, S. (2011). "What's so terrible about swallowing an apple seed?" Problem-based learning in kindergarten. *Journal of Science Education and Technology, 20*(5), 468–481.

Zhou, J., & Liu, K. Y. (2011). Development of action research in China: Review and reflection. *Asia Pacific Education Review, 12*(2), 271–277.

PART IV

Comparing and Contrasting Science and Mathematics Education in China and the United States to Reach for the "Middle Ground"

This section addresses the issues related to science, technology, engineering, and mathematics (STEM) education, especially on science curriculum, mathematics learning, and instruction. Chapter 10 adopts a personal narrative approach to reflect on differences and similarities in preservice science teacher admissions, curriculums, and student teaching in China, Canada, and the United States. Preservice science teacher education curriculums in China focus on science subject and topic-specific pedagogy, yet the focus in Canada and the United States is more on general pedagogy. Student teaching in China emphasizes teaching few and high-quality lessons, whereas student teaching in Canada and the United States emphasizes teaching more lessons, more subjects, and more grades. Although such differences may be related to different beliefs in terms of pedagogical knowledge vs. pedagogical content knowledge, empirical vs. pedagogical research tradition, and varying degrees of centralization of teacher education, it is useful to study each other's program designs and practices for establishing a more comprehensive science teacher education model.

Chapter 11 analyzes the reasons for the difference between U.S. and Chinese students' mathematics learning. From the learners' side, China's collectivist values, high academic expectations, and extensive investments in children's academics, its centralized school system, rigorous national curriculum, high standards for teacher certification, and group teaching preparation all add up to help its students get higher scores than their U.S. counterparts. From the teachers' side, Chinese teachers typically have greater mathematics content knowledge, collaborate on their teaching more often, develop more coherent mathematics lessons with greater abstraction, and provide students with more opportunities to understand and correct their errors, compared to the U.S. teachers. Interestingly, although Chinese students use mathematics procedures more efficiently and produce more solutions with greater accuracy, U.S. students are more likely to attempt unfamiliar mathematical problems. Based on these differences, both systems may benefit from learning from each other's strengths.

Chapter 12 highlights seven important factors that contribute to Chinese students' mathematics performance: culture, curriculum, textbooks, teachers, teaching, students, and parents. The authors call for a coherent, clearly defined national curriculum, a series of well-developed textbooks, and specialized mathematics teachers trained with content knowledge as needed measures to improve mathematics education in the United States. This suggests how divergent educational perspectives may use each other as a mirror to reflect on and enrich their own practices.

10

Paradigm Contrast

Reflection on Preservice Science Teacher Education in China and North America

Xiufeng Liu

As the world economy is becoming more global, a trend in science education globalization has also become evident (Chiu & Duit, 2011). One characteristic of science education globalization is movement of people and internationalization of experiences (Liu, Liang, & Liu, 2012), which is exemplified by my personal journey. In this chapter, I reflect on my experiences in science education in China and in North America (i.e., Canada and the United States), with an emphasis on differences in approaches to preservice science teacher education between China and North America. As science teacher education continues to be a focus of reform in the United States, China, and many other countries, it is hoped that this chapter would provide some insight based on lived experiences on the strengths and weaknesses of preservice science teacher education in North America and China in order to inform ongoing reform efforts in those countries and beyond.

MY EDUCATIONAL AND PROFESSIONAL EXPERIENCES— FROM CHINA TO AMERICA

More than 30 years ago, I was accepted directly from high school into a provincial teachers college in China, majoring in secondary school chemistry teaching.

After graduation, I became a secondary school chemistry teacher. Two years later, I passed the national graduate student unified entrance exam to study for the degree of Master in Chemical Education. After receiving my master's degree in chemical education, I became a research associate at the China National Institute for Education Research.

In 1989, I was accepted into the science education doctoral program at the University of British Columbia, Canada. Transition from chemistry education to science education was a challenge initially. Not only was I exposed to science content other than chemistry, but also pedagogy from various subjects. It took a while for me to appreciate the commonalities among various science subjects in terms of learning theories, curriculum and instructional approaches, and measurement theories and assessment techniques.

In 1992, while still completing my dissertation, I accepted a lecturer position at a Canadian university, and a year later I was appointed as assistant professor. For the next 10 years, I worked as assistant and associate professor at two Canadian universities. My teaching responsibilities included teaching courses in elementary science methods, secondary science methods, measurement and evaluation, educational research methods, and educational statistics. In addition, I supervised 12 student teachers per year, with student teaching assignments from elementary grades (all subjects) to junior high integrated science to high school individual science subjects (biology, chemistry, and physics). In 2002, I accepted a position at my current university in the United States. Within the graduate school of education, my teaching responsibilities are primarily in elementary science teaching methods, seminars in science curriculums, seminars in science instruction, and measurement and evaluation of science teaching.

In the following sections, I will describe the approaches to preservice science teacher education I experienced in China, Canada, and the United States in terms of preservice teacher selectivity, preservice teacher education curriculums, and student teaching (i.e., school practicum), with a focus on the contrast of the approaches. The last section of this chapter will provide an analysis of the above contrasts from a theoretical perspective and argue for a "middle ground" approach to preservice science teacher education.

CONTRAST ON PRESERVICE SCIENCE TEACHER SELECTIVITY

In the United States, there are two primary sources of preservice science teachers. For small and comprehensive 4-year colleges (both private and public), preservice science teachers come directly from high school. Depending on the college, enrolling into a teacher education program in these colleges can vary from open enrollment, to limited selectivity, to high selectivity. For large research universities in which teacher education is typically a postbaccalaureate study hosted by a school of education, preservice science teachers have successfully completed their bachelor's degree in a science discipline from various universities. Once again, admission criteria can vary greatly from university to university, from almost no selectivity to limited selectivity to high selectivity. Because of the varying degree of selectivity, the academic preparation and potential of preservice science teachers can vary greatly. Some preservice science teachers are academically highly capable and dedicated to the teaching profession, while others are not only academically weak but also motivationally questionable.

Similar to the graduate model of preservice science teacher education in the United States, preservice teacher education in Canada is offered through faculties of education within universities. Although almost all Canadian universities, ranging from doctoral universities to comprehensive master's universities to primarily undergraduate universities, usually have a faculty of education, the overall number of faculties of education in the country is small. Furthermore, preservice teacher education is a 1- to 2-year postbaccalaureate study, leading to a bachelor of education degree. Acceptance into a teacher education program is very competitive. At the two universities in two provinces where I taught for a total of 10 years, admission into the science teacher education program required not only a GPA of at least 3.0 (often greater than 3.5), but also relevant experiences with children, strong recommendations, essays on why the applicant wanted to become a teacher, and a face-to-face interview. The acceptance rate was typically around 30%, and a waiting list was common. One important reason for this highly competitive admission is that each teacher education program typically has a quota given by the provincial department of education. The quota for each program, such as chemistry education, is determined by the predicted demand for teachers in a subject area in the province. Because of the competitive admission, in general the academic and professional quality of preservice teachers in Canada is very high.

The academic quality of preservice science teachers in China is also very high and homogeneous. The Chinese teacher education system is mostly based on the normal university model. That is, only normal universities are involved in teacher education (note: Recently, the Ministry of Education encouraged non-normal universities to get involved in preservice teacher education, but the scale remains very small). Smaller provinces may have only a few normal universities/colleges, while larger provinces may have about a dozen normal universities/colleges, with a total of fewer than 200 in the country. Among these normal universities/colleges, a number of them (e.g., Beijing Normal University, East China Normal University, and Northeast China Normal University) are national key universities. National key universities are first-tier universities directly affiliated with the Ministry of Education; they have priority in receiving central government funding, faculty professional development (e.g., study visit at universities in other countries), and most important, they accept the top high school graduates across the country based on the national unified university entrance examination.

Although the majority of Chinese normal universities are not first-tier universities, compared to the large number of third-tier (i.e., private specialization colleges) and fourth-tier (i.e., 3-year colleges), they still have very high prestige; thus, enrolling into these normal universities remains highly competitive. There are a number of reasons for this high prestige. First, the overall college acceptance rate used to be very low (less than 1% in 1978—the first year the national unified university entrance exam was resumed). The acceptance rate has gradually increased over the years due to government investment in higher education expansion during the 2000s. Currently, the rate is about 50%, although the rate into first- and second-tier universities remains low. Second, a large percentage of youth drop out in the countryside after completing the compulsory 9-year education because they lose hope that they will compete well on the national unified university entrance examination. Third, some normal universities provide free tuition and accommodation, which is highly attractive to talented high school graduates from urban low-economic and rural families. Fourth, normal universities have a priority over other universities in accepting students, i.e., they accept students before other universities. Finally, teaching is a highly respected profession due to the Confucian culture, and in general teachers are well paid.

CONTRAST ON CURRICULUMS OF PRESERVICE SCIENCE TEACHER EDUCATION

Despite the fact that there are various teacher education models in the United States, ranging from 4-year undergraduate to 1- or 2-year postbaccalaureate graduate studies to alternative teacher certification programs, the curriculums of preservice science teacher education are remarkably similar. Besides typical courses in foundations of education (e.g., sociology of education), educational psychology, special education, and student teaching, science education courses typically include only one or two courses on general science teaching methods. Few science education programs offer science subject and topic-specific teaching methods courses.

On examination of current popular secondary school science teaching methods textbooks, we also see overwhelming similarities. The table of contents presented in Figure 10.1 is from a very popular secondary science methods course in North America (Trowbridge, Bybee, & Powell, 2004). In it, we see that, although all the topics deal with science teaching and learning, none is science subject or science topic specific. For example, Newton's laws are core topics in secondary school physics, but no chapter is explicitly devoted to teaching and learning related to Newton's laws. One reason for this general approach to science teaching pedagogy is that preservice science teachers of all science subjects (i.e., biology, chemistry, earth science, and physics) typically take the same science methods course

Figure 10.1. Table of Contents of a Popular American Secondary
Science Methods Course Textbook

I. Introduction
1. Becoming a Science Teacher
2. Beginning Your Instructional Theory
3. Understanding Science and Scientific Inquiry
4. Teaching Science as Inquiry

II. Historical and Contemporary Perspectives
5. Historical Perspectives on Science Education
6. Contemporary Issues in Science Education

III. Goals, Objectives, and Assessments
7. The Goals of Science Teaching
8. The Objectives of Science Teaching
9. Assessment of Student Learning

IV. Understanding the Science Curriculum
10. How Science Curricula Are Developed
11. Integrated Approaches to the Science Curriculum
12. The Science Curriculum and Controversial Issues

V. Planning Effective Science Teaching and Programs
13. Models for Effective Science Teaching
14. Planning for Effective Science Teaching
15. Designing an Effective School Science Program

VI. Strategies for Science Teaching
16. The Laboratory and Demonstrations
17. Questioning and Discussion
18. Educational Technology in the Science Classroom

VII. Understanding Students
19. Individual Differences in Science Classrooms
20. Teaching Science for Differences: Gender and Cultural
21. Classroom Management and Conflict Resolution
22. Student Teaching and Becoming a Science Teacher

together, although it is possible that different learning modules on specific science subjects and topics may be offered by instructors. Another reason is due to the fact that the preservice science teacher education curriculums are already crowded with required courses in a variety of areas (e.g., educational and psychological foundations, special education, diversity and multicultural education, technology, and so on); there is little room for more specialized courses. A third reason is that many university science teacher education programs are small in enrollment, with each cohort having as few as 10 students in all science subject areas, for example. As a result, it is financially unfeasible to offer specialized science pedagogy courses.

In the Canadian preservice science teacher education programs, the content and forms of secondary science methods courses are very similar to those in the United States. In fact, Canadian instructors of secondary science methods courses use the same textbooks as American instructors. Also, the curriculum structure in terms of required courses for preservice teacher education is very similar, with the possibility of an additional one or two courses pertaining to Canadian education context. Reasons for the lack of science subject and topic-specific pedagogy courses in Canada are similar to those in the United States.

However, the curriculum structure of science pedagogy courses in Chinese preservice science teacher education programs is drastically different. Because of the discipline-based normal university model of preservice science teacher education, i.e., all preservice science teachers are enrolled in specific science departments, all science pedagogy courses are discipline-specific. Within each discipline (e.g., biology, chemistry, physics), there are many topic-specific pedagogy courses. Figure 10.2 lists a sample curriculum of science education courses offered in the chemistry department of a normal university in China. As can be seen from the figure, there are two distinct features in Chinese science pedagogy courses. One is that there is a variety of specialized courses addressing curriculums, instruction, teaching materials and textbooks, assessment, experiments, research, problem solving, and so on within a science subject. Another is that within each specialized science pedagogy course, there are content-specific topics.

The table of contents presented in Figure 10.3 is from the textbook *Learning and Instruction of the New Senior High School Science Curriculums: Chemistry* (Wang & Hu, 2006). As can be seen from the figure, all topics are discipline (e.g., chemistry) and content (e.g., chemical reactions) specific. Preservice teachers are expected not only to know the science content of the topics, but also to understand learning theories and pedagogy related to those topics. Students are also expected to become knowledgeable about resources for teaching and learning those topics.

CONTRAST ON STUDENT TEACHING

In U.S. and Canadian preservice science teacher education programs, teacher candidates typically spend one semester in the classroom in addition to prior

Figure 10.2. Pedagogy Courses in a Chinese Chemistry
Preservice Education Program

Course	Textbook
Chemistry pedagogy	Liu (2011)
Teaching chemistry experiments	Wen (2006) Wang & Wang (2007)
Chemistry textbooks and instructional strategies	Wang (2006) Wang & Shao (2003) Wang & Shao (2010) Wang & Hu (2006)
Practice of chemistry teaching skills	Wen & Xu (2007)
Research methods in chemistry education	Tang (2003)
Development of chemistry exercises and problems	Wang & Zhang (2003)

classroom observations in schools. While teacher candidates are in school, it is expected that they will gradually assume the full teaching load of a science teacher, which may mean teaching as many as 4 or 5 class periods out of a 7 or 8 class periods a day, 5 days a week. The expectation of experiencing a full teaching load is further exacerbated by teaching multiple science subjects (e.g., biology and chemistry, or biology and AP biology) and multiple grades (e.g., middle school general science and high school biology). The intention of the student teaching assignments is for teacher candidates to experience as "fully" as possible—to get a "taste" of—what a full-time teaching load is like, so that after they have completed the preservice teacher education program and look for positions, they will know what is expected in a position they are applying for—there are no surprises.

There are obvious benefits from such student teaching assignments. Besides the "no surprises" effect, teacher candidates can also develop an understanding of their strengths and weaknesses in terms of becoming a secondary science teacher. Given that a teacher education program is only the beginning for a science teacher to grow professionally, and much remains to be learned while they are teaching, a realistic self-assessment by a teacher candidate in terms of his or her abilities can facilitate future professional growth. However, there are also potential drawbacks.

Figure 10.3. Table of Contents of a Chinese Chemistry Pedagogy Textbook

SECTION I: TEACHING AND LEARNING MODULE I

1. Teaching and learning elements and inorganic compounds
    1.1. Teaching content of elements and inorganic compounds
    1.2. Teaching design and implementation of elements and inorganic compounds
    1.3. Suggestions for assessment
    1.4. Resources for teaching and learning elements and inorganic compounds

2. Teaching and learning core chemical concepts
    2.1. Teaching content of core chemical concepts
    2.2. Teaching design and implementation of core chemical concepts
    2.3. Suggestions for assessment
    2.4. Resources for teaching and learning core chemical concepts

3. Teaching and learning chemistry inquiry processes and methods
    3.1. Teaching content of chemistry inquiry processes and methods
    3.2. Teaching design and implementation of chemistry inquiry processes and methods
    3.3. Suggestions for assessment
    3.4. Resources for teaching and learning chemistry inquiry processes and methods

4. Teaching and learning of chemistry-technology-society
    4.1. Teaching content of chemistry-technology-society
    4.2. Teaching design and implementation of chemistry-technology-society
    4.3. Suggestions for assessment
    4.4. Resources for teaching and learning chemistry-technology-society

SECTION II: TEACHING AND LEARNING MODULE II

1. Teaching and learning the structure of matter
    1.1. Teaching content of the structure of matter
    1.2. Teaching design and implementation of the structure of matter
    1.3. Suggestions for assessment
    1.4. Resources for teaching and learning the structure of matter

2. Teaching and learning chemical reactions
    2.1. Teaching content of chemical reactions
    2.2. Teaching design and implementation of chemical reactions
    2.3. Suggestions for assessment
    2.4. Resources for teaching and learning chemical reactions

3. Teaching and learning organic compounds
    3.1. Teaching content of organic compounds
    3.2. Teaching design and implementation of organic compounds
    3.3. Suggestions for assessment
    3.4. Resources for teaching and learning organic compounds

Obviously, teacher candidates may feel overwhelmed and even "burned out" at this beginning stage of a teaching career. Given the fact that teacher candidates have to learn so much (from getting to know the school, classroom, curriculum, instruction, students, assessment, and so on) in such a short time, many of them struggle to survive, leaving no time for reflection and learning to implement best strategies. As a result, some teacher candidates may not benefit from this "shock and awe," and during student teaching or shortly after student teaching, their desire to become or confidence in becoming a secondary science teacher has been seriously eroded, leading to early dropout. Ultimately, student learning may be compromised. It is not uncommon for students and parents to complain that they don't want student teachers in the classroom. For this same reason, many teachers, especially experienced science teachers, are reluctant to take on student teachers, because they are concerned that student learning may be compromised and their own teaching continuity may be interrupted.

Student teaching in the Chinese preservice science teacher education programs takes a quite different approach. Although the length of practicum is about the same as that in the United States and Canada, typically one semester, the placement and expectation are quite different. Given that Chinese high schools are usually large boarding schools with thousands of students, a high school can accommodate a large number of teacher candidates each semester. Also, because Chinese preservice teachers are full-time students living on campus, they can freely travel to other areas to practice teaching. Usually, 10–30 teacher candidates are placed to one school, with two teacher candidates to the same class. Teacher candidates must live in their placement schools for the duration of the practicum. It is important to understand that each high school class is also a physical classroom—students take all courses in this same room (i.e., in Chinese high schools it is teachers who go to different classrooms to teach). Because placement of teacher candidates is concentrated in a few high schools, and these schools do not have to be local, there is much flexibility for a university preservice teacher education program to select practicum schools. Typical criteria for selecting a school for student teaching are: (1) attitude of school administration, (2) school reputation and quality of teaching and student learning, (3) number of classes available for placing teacher candidates, and (4) living conditions for teacher candidates.

Once a teacher candidate pair is placed in a class, they are supervised by a cooperating teacher and a university faculty advisor. The university faculty advisor will also be living in the same school as the teacher candidates. The teaching load of a teacher candidate will gradually increase during the semester to a full teaching load. The full teaching load means that the teacher candidate pair assigned to a same class will teach that class once a day every day, which is still less than the full teaching load of a school science teacher for two to three classes a day every day. Therefore, teacher candidates in the Chinese preservice science teacher education programs teach much less than those in the U.S. and Canadian systems.

Teaching less does not mean that teacher candidates have an easier time during practicum. Because the focus of student teaching practicum is to practice best teaching strategies, in order to teach a lesson, the teacher candidate pair assigned to the same class must conduct extensive research, planning, and tryout before actually teaching the lesson. The first lesson to be taught typically requires a week's planning. During this week's planning, besides observing the cooperating teacher's teaching, teacher candidates also talk to some students individually during spare time (e.g., lunch, supper, evening study time, weekend, and so on), review their homework and past exams, and talk to teachers of other subjects (e.g., math teachers, Chinese teachers). They will also search for relevant resources pertaining to the lesson to be taught. Consultation with the university faculty advisor and cooperating teacher is also expected. The teacher candidates then jointly create a lesson plan. They will then teach the lesson to one another as a practice. They may also teach the lesson to their university faculty advisor as a tryout. The person of the teacher candidate pair who teaches the lesson best in practice will then teach the lesson to the real class (it is also possible that the two teacher candidates will coteach a lesson). During the lesson day, the university faculty advisor and the cooperating teacher will observe the teaching. A long meeting to analyze the strengths and weaknesses of the lesson will then follow. Gradually, the teacher candidates will increase their teaching frequency. The same lesson preparation process is involved for teaching all lessons, although gradually it is done with much more efficiency. The above process clearly emphasizes teaching fewer best lessons rather than teaching many lessons.

MAKING SENSE OF THE CONTRASTS

Although there are differences and diversity in approaches to preservice science teacher education within any country, the difference in science preservice teacher education among China, Canada, and the United States as described above is striking. In this remaining section, I try to make sense of the above differences from the perspectives of teacher knowledge, education research orientation, and characteristics of education system.

Pedagogical Knowledge vs. Pedagogical Content Knowledge

Schulman (1986, 1987) conceptualizes teacher knowledge to consist of subject content knowledge, pedagogical content knowledge (PCK) and curriculum knowledge. Grossman (1990) revises the above domains of teacher knowledge to include subject-matter knowledge and beliefs, pedagogical knowledge (PK) and beliefs, knowledge and beliefs about context, and pedagogical content knowledge.

No matter how teacher knowledge is conceptualized, it is now commonly accepted that it is PCK that is most useful in teaching (Gess-Newsome & Lederman, 1999; Loughran, Mulhall, & Berry, 2004). The National Science Education Standards (National Research Council, 1996) state that:

> Effective science teaching is more than knowing science content and some teaching strategies. Skilled teachers of science have special understandings and abilities that integrate their knowledge of science content, curriculum, learning, teaching, and students. Such knowledge allows teachers to tailor learning situations to the needs of individuals and groups. This special knowledge, called "pedagogical content knowledge", distinguishes the science knowledge of teachers from that of scientists. It is one element that defines a professional teacher of science. (p. 62)

Magnusson, Krajcik, and Borko (1999) propose that science teachers' PCK may be defined by an orientation to science teaching that is shaped by teachers' knowledge of science curriculums, knowledge of students' understanding of science, knowledge of instructional strategies, and knowledge of science assessment. This conceptual framework of PCK suggests that science teachers' PCK is both generalized knowledge to science teaching and specialized skills pertaining to specific science domains and topics.

Applying the above conceptualization of teacher knowledge, we can see that, although it is difficult to compare subject-matter knowledge between Chinese preservice science teachers and their North American counterparts, a noticeable difference can be seen in terms of PK and PCK. That is, Canadian and U.S. preservice science teachers likely develop more general PK, while Chinese preservice science teachers likely develop more PCK. This difference is due to differences in the number and types of science methods courses offered and in the nature of practice teaching placement and teaching assignments. It is recognized that development of PCK is an ongoing process, or even a lifelong process (van Driel & Berry, 2012); an early orientation to PCK, as is the case in Chinese preservice science teacher education, can provide science teachers with a jumpstart. For example, Luft et al. (2011) found that preservice science teacher education programs played a role in the beginning science teachers' development of PCK. Specifically, those beginning science teachers with exposure to PCK during preservice teacher education continued modifying their PCK during their beginning years of teaching and eventually developed better PCK than those who did not have exposure to PCK during their preservice teacher education programs. Of course, we cannot claim that teachers in Canada and the United States do not develop PCK during their preservice teacher education programs, because PK is an important component of PCK, and a strong PK could eventually lead to better PCK. But this possibility remains a hypothesis; no empirical evidence is available.

Empirical Tradition vs. Pedagogical Tradition

Another way to make sense of the differences in preservice science teacher education between China and North America is through science education research orientations. Jenkins (2001, 2004) defines two research traditions in science education: the empirical tradition and the pedagogical tradition. The empirical tradition is primarily concerned with development and testing of general science education theories, while the pedagogical tradition is primarily concerned with improvement of science curriculum and instruction in specific disciplines. Because science education research in North America follows primarily the empirical tradition, and Chinese science education research follows primarily the pedagogical tradition, the differences in preservice science teacher education become natural. In fact, research on general science education theories and practices in China remains very preliminary, although the body of discipline-specific knowledge is very solid. On the contrary, there is a strong body of general science education knowledge in North America, but discipline-specific body of knowledge (e.g., chemistry education research) is relatively weak. The differences in preservice science teacher education practices described above reflect this difference in knowledge base.

Centralization vs. Decentralization of Education Systems

The difference in preservice science teacher education can also be explained by characteristics of the three education systems. Education in China and Canada is in general more centralized than that in the United States. Although the teaching profession is considered prestigious in all three countries, only in China and Canada is the high prestige matched with relatively high pay and benefits, while in the United States teachers are overall underpaid, particularly in urban school districts. This difference in teacher pay and benefit between China/Canada and the United States is largely due to different educational funding mechanisms. In both China and Canada, education funding to schools is centralized, i.e., exclusively from governments, while in the United States, funding varies greatly from district to district, ranging from mostly funds from the state government in urban districts to mostly funding from local property tax in suburban districts. The difference in teacher pay and benefits could be one important reason for differences among the three countries in attracting talented high school and college graduates into the science teaching profession.

The centralization of preservice science teacher education in China is also demonstrated in other aspects. Not only is enrollment based on the same national university unified entrance exam, but also curriculums, textbooks, student teaching, and even some course exams (e.g., English) are standardized and uniform. That is, all preservice teacher education programs in the country follow the same curriculums stipulated by the Ministry of Education and use the same course textbooks, which are reviewed and approved by the Ministry of Education. This uniform system helps ensure common high standards for teacher quality. In Canada, standardization of preservice teacher education is mainly done through reviewing and controlling the number of preservice teacher education programs and the admission quota of each preservice teacher education program within a province. In the United States, although each state reviews and approves preservice science teacher education programs, there is no limit to the total number of teacher education programs or the number of preservice teachers to be accepted each year in the state, and only a minimal standard for a university to offer a preservice teacher education program. The difference in degrees of centralization in preservice teacher education programs among the three countries could result in diversity in science teacher education program quantity and quality.

SEEKING THE "MIDDLE GROUND" APPROACH

It is of course difficult to claim which country's preservice science teacher education is better. Recent international comparison studies, such as Trends in Mathematics and Science Study (TIMSS) and Program for International Student Assessment (PISA), could be used as one reference for comparison. Specifically, students in Canada have consistently outperformed students in the United States in science at all tested grades (i.e., 4th, 8th, and 12th). China has not participated in TIMSS studies since 1983, but in 2009 one Chinese city, i.e., Shanghai, participated in the PISA assessment, and students from that city performed the best in science among students of all participating countries. Although as a whole U.S. students have not been among the top-performing countries, a large number of students performed at the highest performance levels in science in both TIMSS and PISA assessments.

It can be stated that there are both strengths and weaknesses in preservice science teacher education in each of the three countries. The United States can learn from China and Canada in increasing the selectivity of science teacher candidates getting into teacher education programs. In order for the above to happen, drastically reducing the total number of teacher education programs in the country through more rigorous accreditation is necessary. While China can learn from the United States and Canada on developing stronger general science pedagogical knowledge for all science teachers so that they will be more effective in teaching integrated science courses, both the United States and Canada can learn from China on developing stronger pedagogical content knowledge so that science teachers will be more effective in teaching high school separate science courses. Both the United States and Canada can learn from China in arrangement of student teaching by emphasizing teaching fewer but higher-quality lessons. Overall, Chinese preservice science teachers need to broaden their science content knowledge and teaching pedagogy so that more interdisciplinary science teaching and learning approaches may be implemented.

Thus, there is a better "middle ground" approach to preservice science teacher education in China and North America. As more and more interactions between China and North America take place as the result of science education globalization, learning from each other will occur, and this book is a good example. The "Cold War" mentality of competition does not need to apply in science teacher education; collaboration in science teacher education will benefit students in all countries. Globalization in science education will be a continuing trend.

SUMMARY OF IMPLICATIONS

For Foreign-Born Science Educators in the United States

- Recognize that your science education background may not be broad enough; try to expand your knowledge base in both science and pedagogy.
- Accept that lack of the U.S. K–12 school teaching experience is a deficiency; take every opportunity to know how U.S. schools and classrooms operate.
- Understand the broader contexts of U.S. K–12 education, such as state and local education laws, teacher contracts, charter and private schools, and so on.
- Recognize that U.S. science education students vary in their science content knowledge and education background; whenever appropriate, provide choices to students for their assignments, projects, exams, classroom learning activities, and so on.

For U.S.-Born Science Educators

- Revisit admission criteria to select only teacher candidates with strong subject-matter knowledge and overall academic potential.
- Offer more science topic- and content-specific pedagogy courses or modules.
- Recognize the value of and assist students in teaching fewer and best lessons during student teaching.
- Create professional learning communities for student teachers during their practicum to learn from each other, school cooperating teachers, and university faculty advisors.
- Be open to best preservice science teacher education theories and practices in other countries.
- Realize the necessity for common high standards in preservice science teacher education while maintaining diversity and uniqueness of individual programs.

NOTE

I sincerely thank Silin Wei of Hangzhou Normal University for providing information on current preservice science teacher education curriculums and instruction.

REFERENCES

Chiu, M-H., & Duit, R. (2011). Globalization: Science education from an international perspective. *Journal of Research in Science Teaching, 48*(6), 553–566.

Gess-Newsome, J., & Lederman, N. (1999). *Examining pedagogical content knowledge: The construct and its implication for science education.* New York: Kluwer Academic Publisher.

Grossman, P. (1990). *The making of a teacher: Teacher knowledge and teacher education.* New York: Teachers College Press.

Jenkins, W. E. (2001). Research in science education in Europe: Retrospect and prospect. In H. Behrend et al. (Eds.), *Research in science education: Past, present, and future* (pp. 17–25). Hingham, MA: Kluwer Academic Publishers.

Jenkins, W. E. (2004). Science education: Research, practice and policy. In E. Scanlon et al. (Eds.), *Reconsidering science learning.* London: Routledge/Falmer.

Liu, X., Liang, L., & Liu, E. (2012). Editorial: Science education research in China: Challenges and promises. *International Journal of Science Education, 34*(13), 1961–1970.

Liu, Z. (2011). *Chemistry pedagogy* (4th ed.). Beijing: Higher Education Press.

Loughran, J., Mulhall, P., & Berry, A. (2004). In search of pedagogical content knowledge in science: Developing ways of articulating and documenting professional practice. *Journal of Research in Science Teaching, 41*(4), 370–391.

Luft, J., Firestone, J. B., Wong, S. S., Ortega, I., Adams, K., & Bang, E. (2011). Beginning secondary science teacher induction: A two-year mixed methods study. *Journal of Research in Science Teaching, 48*(10), 1199–1224.

Magnusson, S., Krajcik, J., & Borko, H. (1999). Secondary teachers' knowledge and beliefs about subject matter and their impact on instruction. In J. Gess-Newson & N. G. Lederman (Eds.), *Examining pedagogical content knowledge* (pp. 95–132). Dordrecht, the Netherlands: Kluwer Academic Publishers.

National Research Council. (1996). *National science education standards.* Washington, DC: National Academies Press.

Schulman, L. S. (1986). Those who understand: Knowledge growth in teaching. *Educational Researcher, 15*(2), 4–14.

Schulman, L. S. (1987). Knowledge and teaching: Foundations of the new reform. *Harvard Education Review, 57*, 1–22.

Tang, L. (2003). *Research methods in chemistry education.* Guilin, China: Guangxi Normal University Press.

Trowbridge, L. W., Bybee, R. W., & Powell, J. C. (2004). *Teaching secondary school science: Strategies for developing scientific literacy.* Upper Saddle River, NJ: Pearson.

van Driel, J., & Berry, A. (2012). Teacher professional development focusing on pedagogical content knowledge. *Educational Researcher, 41*(1), 26–28.

Wang, L. (2006). *Research and case-analysis on chemistry teaching.* Beijing: Higher Education Press.

Wang, L., & Hu, J. (2006). *Instruction and learning of new required curriculum in senior high school chemistry.* Beijing: Beijing University Press.

Wang, L., & Shao, J. (2003). *Design and practice of new chemistry curriculum instruction in junior high school.* Beijing: Higher Education Press.

Wang, L., & Shao, J. (2010). *High school chemistry curriculum analysis and its implementation.* Beijing: Beijing Normal University Press.

Wang, Z., & Wang, C. (2007). *Innovative chemistry experiments in secondary school.* Nanning, China: Guangxi Education Press.

Wang, Z., & Zhang, T. (2003). *Development of chemistry exercises and problem-solving.* Beijing: Higher Education Press.

Wen, Q. (2006). *Research on chemistry experiments teaching.* Beijing: Science Press.

Wen, Q., & Xu, Y. (2007). *Practice of chemistry teaching skills* (2nd ed.). Guilin, China: Guangxi Normal University Press.

11

Family and School Influences on Students' Math Achievement

United States vs. China

Ming Ming Chiu

U.S. students and Chinese students' expectations, attitudes, and achievements in mathematics often differ substantially (Cai, 2000; Chiu, 2010). This chapter synthesizes sociological, psychological, and education studies on societies, families, teachers, and students to show how different factors, especially family and school factors, shape the mathematics achievements of U.S. vs. Chinese students (see Table 11.1). Understanding these relationships can help educators both suitably import methods from other countries to improve student learning and identify constraints that might limit their success in new contexts.

Unlike in the United States, Chinese government exams, collectivist beliefs, and economic rewards have shaped Chinese culture and fostered specific academic expectations for all children. These societal, parental, school, and teacher expectations drive allocation of substantial material and human resources both at home and at school to influence students' academic expectations and academic achievement. Educators accustomed to Chinese school systems and Chinese students can draw upon their Chinese school experiences and teaching strategies but must adapt to U.S. students, who can differ substantially from Chinese students.

Table 11.1. How Chinese vs. U.S. Contexts and Students Differ with Respect to Mathematics Achievement

Dimension	Chinese	U.S.
SOCIETY		
Regular national exams	Yes	No
Cultural values	Collectivist	Individualist
Economic/social rewards linked to education	Tightly	Loosely
Extended family resources	Extensive	Some
Expectations of students' mathematics achievement	High	Varies
National curriculum & teacher certification	Yes	No
TEACHERS		
Teacher's mathematics expertise	High	Varies
Collaborations among teachers	Frequent	Occasional
Direct teaching with strong teacher control	High	Varies
Lesson coherence	Tight	Varies
Degree of abstraction in lessons	High	Low
STUDENTS		
Student performance on routine problems	Higher	Lower
Student performance on nonroutine problems	Low	Low
Student accuracy	Greater	Less
Student efficiency	Greater	Less
Number of solutions	More	Fewer
Attempt problems without known answers	Rare	Often

U.S. VS. CHINESE FAMILY ENVIRONMENTS

U.S. and Chinese societies differ in several fundamental ways. Grounded in government exams, collectivist beliefs, and economic rewards, Chinese people have traditionally supported students' academic achievement. Beginning with the Sui Dynasty, the *Keju* civil service exam system from 606 to 1905 not only selected China's government officials but also gave financial rewards, prestige, power, and fame to the extended family, thereby powering collectivist beliefs, values, and norms (Suen & Yu, 2006). As a result, Chinese people learn that academic achievement tightly aligns with economic success (Reitz & Verman, 2004). In Hong Kong's education-rewarding wage system, for example, a high school teacher earns a manual worker's lifetime wages in 15 years while a professor earns it within 5 years (McLelland, 1991). As a result, Chinese parents, schools, and teachers view academic achievement as the gateway to many professions.

In contrast, the United States' 13 original colonies won their independence relatively recently, retain a frontier individualism, and maintain locally controlled schools within a federal system of 50 states. Valuing freedom and individual choice, most schools are under local control and funded by local taxes (Hoxby, 2001). Until the recent Common Core Curriculum supported by most states (but not all), school districts, or even schools chose their own curricula. Hence, parents can often choose a school for their children by moving into the relevant neighborhood.

U.S. vs. Chinese Families

Chinese parents' beliefs affect their children's mathematics learning through specific academic expectations, educational resources, and homework assistance. Unlike U.S. parents, Chinese parents view effort as more important than ability for learning mathematics (Stigler, Lee, & Stevenson, 1990). Hence, Chinese parents encourage their children to study diligently and expect them to excel regardless of perceptions of their innate ability (Hau & Salili, 1996). Chinese parents further enhance their children's academic motivation by wielding their collectivist beliefs, for example, by reminding them that their success or failure affects their entire family's reputation (Chiu & Ho, 2006). As a result, Chinese parents have higher expectations for their children's mathematics performance, express less satisfaction, and are more likely to recognize their children's mathematics learning problems compared to U.S. parents (Stevenson et al., 1990).

Chinese parents also invest heavily in their children's education (e.g., buying books, tutoring children, and so forth) to motivate them and raise their academic achievement (Lam, Ho, & Wong, 2002). Within a given family budget, buying proportionately more educational resources reinforces family commitment to children's learning, implicitly suggesting further social rewards and incentives for higher achievement (Chiu & Ho, 2006). Extra educational resources also give children more learning opportunities on which they can capitalize to improve their academic achievement (Chiu, 2007). Chinese American parents also spend more time with their children and use more formal teaching methods than European American parents (Huntsinger, Jose, Larson, Balsink, & Shalingram, 2000). Chinese parents are also more likely than their U.S. counterparts to monitor their children's homework or help them academically (Stevenson et al., 1990). Because greater parental homework assistance does not necessarily yield higher student mathematics achievement, however, the benefit might be more motivational than instructional (Chiu & Ho, 2006).

Deeply rooted in Chinese culture, extrinsic motivators such as examinations, mathematics achievement expectations, and social status provide incentives for student learning (J. Li, 2003). Furthermore, Chinese students embrace these incentives, and those with higher extrinsic motivation or higher intrinsic motivations have higher mathematics scores, unlike Western students who perform better only with intrinsic incentives (Chiu & Zeng, 2008). Driven by these intrinsic and extrinsic motivations, Chinese students spend more time doing homework and outperform U.S. students in mathematics (Chiu & Zeng, 2008; Stigler et al., 1990).

U.S. vs. Chinese Children's Mathematics at Home

The mathematics attitudes and behaviors of U.S. vs. Chinese families differ, as do the mathematics performances of their children. U.S. mothers typically value literacy skills more than mathematics skills and emphasize only reading to prepare their children for school. In contrast, Chinese mothers believe that their children should learn both mathematics and literacy skills before attending school to support their academic success (Stevenson & Lee, 1990).

In addition, Chinese parents believe that children establish their mathematics learning trajectories before attending school and that these learning trajectories persist in elementary school; thus, they believe that preschool children who lag behind their peers in mathematics performance tend to fall further behind in elementary school. Hence, Chinese parents put early pressure on their children to learn mathematics.

Chinese parents, grandparents, and other extended family members often help coach children to solve mathematics problems (Chiu & Ho, 2006). Because the Chinese have a collectivist culture, extended family members often live nearby and attend to children's care and education much more than do their U.S. counterparts (Georgas et al., 2001). For example, Chinese adults at home often teach children to recite 1 to 100 and to do addition and subtraction by counting their fingers (Cheng & Chan, 2005). For instance, Chinese adults can ask children to compute "7 + 5 =" with the *counting on* strategy by thinking of 7, opening five fingers and counting up "eight, nine, ten, eleven, *twelve!*"

Furthermore, studies suggest that Chinese children outperform children of other countries in mathematics before formal schooling (e.g., Starkey & Klein, 2008). Chinese preschoolers outperformed U.S. preschoolers on cardinal and ordinal number names (Miller, Major, Shu, & Zhang, 2000), base-10 system, fractions, and using 10-complement (e.g., $9 + 4 = 9 + [1 + 3]$) strategy for early addition (Fuson & Kwon, 1991).

MATHEMATICS INSTRUCTION IN U.S. VS. CHINESE SCHOOLS

Prodded by parents' and society's high expectations of children's mathematics achievement, schools in Chinese societies adopt challenging curricula, require certified teachers, support group teaching preparation, and share the knowledge of expert teachers. Schools in collectivist Chinese societies implement these high expectations through a national mathematics curriculum and standardized textbooks, which are typically more challenging than those in the United States (e.g., Geary, Bow-Thomas, Liu, & Siegler, 1996). To teach these challenging curricula, most teachers in Chinese schools are certified.

Furthermore, teachers often work together and share their knowledge. For example, group teaching preparation is common in urban schools of Mainland China (Ni & Li, 2009). Teachers often work together to understand the teacher manuals, the student textbooks, the curriculum standards, and teaching methods that are believed to be effective. The Ministry of Education in each Chinese society officially approves student textbooks and teacher manuals (schools can only use approved textbooks), endorsing them as effective mathematics teaching (J-H. Li, 2004). In addition, successful teachers ("first-class" teachers) demonstrate their classroom teaching to their colleagues inside and outside their school districts to learn and improve their teaching.

As a result, Chinese teachers often have similar lesson plans for a given teaching unit, with similar learning goals, worked-out examples, homework problems, and presentation structures. In contrast, the lesson plans of U.S. teachers vary substantially, even for teachers in the same school (Cai & Wong, 2006). A highly centralized educational system within a collectivist culture (as in Mainland China, Taiwan, and Hong Kong) aids organizational and administrative efficiency by quickly disseminating socially and culturally favored teaching methods. As Stevenson and Stigler (1992) put it:

> The techniques used by Chinese and Japanese teachers are not new to the teaching profession nor are they foreign or exotic. In fact, they are ones often recommended by American educators. What the Chinese and Japanese examples demonstrated so compellingly is when widely and consistently implemented, such practice can produce extraordinary outcomes. (p. 198)

Taken together, family, school, and teachers' high expectations and investment in educational resources for students' mathematics achievement tend to raise students' standards, increase their motivation, enhance their learning behaviors, and raise their mathematics achievement (Geary et al., 1996). The combination of collective family expectations, challenging mathematics curriculum, and complex lesson activities helps students appreciate the difficult mathematics they must master to perform well on national university entrance exams (Davey, Lian, & Higgins, 2007). Combined with their collective belief that their academic success or failure affects their family, Chinese students are motivated to study diligently while lacking confidence and fearing failure (Lam et al., 2002).

U.S. vs. Chinese Preschools

Unlike many U.S. preschools whose curricula do not prepare students for primary school mathematics (Clements, 2001), many Chinese preschools use an operational mathematics curriculum linked to primary school mathematics (Cheng, 2008). Used since the 1900s, this adult-centered instructional approach introduces mathematics to preschoolers in an accessible manner (Cheng, 2008). Like Montessori schools, the operational learning curriculum concretizes mathematics (e.g., by using a 10 x 10 grid), connects the manipulatives to their respective mathematics concepts (e.g., cardinal and ordinal numbers, place values, arithmetic operations), and organizes them to highlight their systematic structure (e.g., addition, subtraction, and part-whole structures in a base-10 system). As a result, students can create an image of the logico-mathematical system of concepts and operations, thereby preparing them to learn mathematics in elementary schools (Cheng, 2008).

Consider the following preschool mathematics example: Children are shown four faces and asked to identify attributes that may be used to classify the faces into different groups. These four faces feature three attributes: One face has a hat and three do not; two are happy faces and two angry faces; and three are circular faces and one is a square face. Preschool teachers ask their students to observe and analyze the attributes and relationships of the four faces. Then, they guide the students' use of beads to model the relationships as they solve addition and subtraction problems within this universe of 4 (e.g., $1 + 3 = 4, 2 + 2 = 4, 3 + 1 = 4$; $4-1 = 3, 4-2 = 2, 4-3 = 1$). Next, the students develop their understanding of part-whole relations for the numbers 2, 3, and 5–10 by using a 10 x 10 grid to perform classification tasks.

The grid and these part-whole relationships can help preschoolers use composition and decomposition strategies to solve addition and subtraction problems involving larger numbers. For example, consider solving $8 + 7$ with the 10-complement strategy ($8 + 7 = 8 + [2 + 5] = [8 + 2] + 5 = 10 + 5 = 15$). First, teachers guide children to focus on the first addend (8 dots) and decide how many extra dots are needed to make up a row of 10 on the grid (in this case, $2 + 8 = 10$). Second, teachers ask students to split 7 into 2 dots and a remaining portion of 5 dots ($7 = 2 + 5$). Third, teachers guide students to add 8 and 2 to create a row of 10 on the grid ($8 + 2 = 10$). In the fourth step, students add the remaining 5 to the row of 10, yielding 15 ($10 + 5 = 15$). Then, children work independently on addition problems yielding sums greater than 10 (e.g., $5 + 9$). This operational approach helps students acquire the skill components necessary for mathematics competence (Cheng, 2008).

After benefiting from this instruction, Chinese preschoolers outperform Western preschoolers in many areas of mathematics (Miller, Kelly, & Zhou, 2005). Among kindergartners to 3rd-graders solving simple addition problems, Chinese children used verbal counting strategies more often than did U.S. children, who counted on their fingers more often. Decompositions were the primary backup strategy for the Chinese children. In contrast, the U.S. children used finger counting as the backup strategy (Geary et al., 1996). Urban Chinese children who attended regular preschool and kindergarten education usually can count, add, and subtract 0–20 proficiently before entering 1st grade (Zhang, Li, & Tang, 2004). The advantages of these Chinese children can continue through their later years of schooling.

U.S. vs. Chinese Mathematics Instruction

The elementary and high school mathematics curriculum in Mainland China emphasizes *two-basics* (basic mathematics concepts and skills), and Chinese classroom instruction focuses on *refined lectures* and *repeated practice* (Zhang et al., 2004). The two-basics view emphasizes foundational knowledge content and skills over creative thinking (Leung, 2001). Chinese educators argue that repeated practice aids memorization and that greater exposure can help students think about the underlying concepts more deeply (Dhlin & Watkins, 2000; for detailed sociohistorical analyses of the origins of these Chinese beliefs, see Zhang et al., 2004). Hence, Chinese mathematics curricula have four student goals: (1) fast, accurate manipulation and computation of arithmetic, fractions, polynomials, and algebra; (2) accurate recall of memorized mathematics definitions, formulas, rules, and procedures; (3) understanding of logical categorizations and mathematics propositions; and (4) facile matching of solution patterns to types of problems via transfer (Zhang et al., 2004).

To implement these curricula, teachers present well-prepared lessons that include strong teacher control, coherent instruction, and abstract mathematics (*refined lectures*; Zhang et al., 2004). To deliver such refined instruction, teachers in Beijing and Taipei spend over 6 hours each day examining students' work and preparing lessons with colleagues, unlike their U.S. counterparts who rarely work together on student work and lesson preparation (Stevenson & Stigler, 1992).

Teachers often maintain control by direct teaching to the whole class. Direct teaching helps teachers control the lesson flow to maintain class discipline (especially with 40–60 students per class in China), while engaging students in the learning activities (Huang & Leung, 2004). As Confucian culture assigns content expertise to teachers, traditional Chinese students are also more receptive to the teacher's dominant role. Stevenson and Stigler (1992) reported that Chinese teachers led their classes 90% of the time, whereas U.S. teachers did so 47% of the time.

Second, the refined lecture integrates teaching content and classroom discourse through coherent connections that guide students toward each lesson's learning goal (Wang & Murphy, 2004). Chinese teachers' lesson plans also enhance instructional coherence by emphasizing the relationships among mathematics concepts. For example, Chinese teachers from Guiyang in Mainland China helped their students specify the similarities and differences between ratios and fractions to clarify their relationship, whereas U.S. teachers from Illinois did not (Cai & Wong, 2006).

When students make mistakes, Chinese teachers often view them as learning opportunities, use their mathematics mastery to ask leading questions, and help students correct their answers (Stevenson & Stigler, 1992). By so doing, Chinese teachers encourage students to persevere, understand their mistakes, and correct them. In contrast, U.S. mathematics teachers typically have less mathematics knowledge than their Chinese counterparts, often feel uncomfortable with student mistakes, and try to avoid addressing them (Stevenson & Stigler, 1992).

Schleppenbach, Perry, Miller, Sims, and Fang (2007) also compared the coherence of mathematics lessons in 17 Chinese and 14 U.S. elementary classrooms by examining the frequency and content of extended discourses. Extended discourses are relatively sustained exchanges that occur when a student gives a correct answer to a question (by the teacher or by another student) and the teacher asks a follow-up question, instead of simply evaluating the student's answer. Consider this example of extended discourse (Schleppenbach et al., 2007):

Teacher: Is this equation $2xy = 5$ an instance of a linear equation with two unknowns?

Student A: No.

Teacher: Why not?

Student A: The power of each unknown should be one for a linear equation in two unknowns. But for this equation, $2xy$ is one unit and its power is two.

Teacher: The power of this single unit is two; therefore, it does not belong to the type of linear equations in two unknowns. Do you agree or disagree?

Student B: Agree.

Teacher: Could you give an example of linear equation in two unknowns?

Student B: $3x + 2y = 25$

Schleppenbach et al. (2007) found that extended discourse episodes were longer and occurred more often in mathematics lessons in China than in the United States. Furthermore, Chinese teachers plan coherent sequences of lessons that reference and build on one another more often than U.S. teachers do. These well-designed and coherent mathematics lessons reduced ambiguity and confusion, thereby aiding students' understanding of mathematics concepts and skills (Dhlin & Watkins, 2000). As a result, mathematics lessons in China were typically more coherent than those in the United States (Schleppenbach et al., 2007).

Related to instructional coherence, Chinese teachers value and use more abstraction to generalize mathematics relationships compared to U.S. teachers, who value concrete representations more (Correa, Perry, Sims, Miller, & Fang, 2008). Specifically, Chinese and U.S. middle school teachers differ in their use of concrete representation, prediction of student strategies, and assessment of student strategies (Cai & Lester, 2005). Chinese teachers exclusively use concrete representations to mediate students' understanding of the main mathematics concept in the lesson (e.g., diagram of four cups with different amounts of water to help students compute and understand the concept of arithmetic mean). In contrast, U.S. teachers use concrete representations to generate data (e.g., students' heights and arm lengths as data to find their mean height and arm lengths). When students use drawing strategies or estimates that yield correct answers, U.S. teachers scored them higher than Chinese teachers did, as the latter view these strategies as less generalizable.

Thus, the approach of the two-basics curriculum and the refined lecture with repeated practice may contribute to effective Chinese mathematics instruction. The two-basics curriculum can focus student attention on the key mathematics concepts, skills, categorizations, and flexible applications to problems. Meanwhile, the refined lecture with repeated practice instruction can aid teachers' classroom management, increase lesson coherence, and help students generalize mathematics relationships in a series of small steps. Together, these factors might help Chinese students learn more mathematics than their U.S. counterparts.

The importance of classroom instruction is highlighted by findings of similar IQ tests scores by U.S. and Chinese children, similar numeracy skills of Chinese and U.S. adults, but Chinese children's *higher* numeracy test scores (Geary et al., 1996). These observations, along with Chinese students' superior performance on international assessments, point to the capacity of mathematics curriculum and instruction to increase the mathematics achievement of Chinese children (Stigler & Hiebert, 1999).

U.S. VS. CHINESE STUDENTS' MATHEMATICS ACHIEVEMENTS

Taught in a two-basics curriculum and highly directive classroom instruction (Cai & Cifarelli, 2004), Chinese students have stronger computation skills and solve more routine mathematics problems than U.S. students do (e.g., routine question: Springfield and Oakland are 54 km apart. On a map, these two cities are 3 cm apart, and Oakland and Riverdale are 12 cm part. How far apart are Oakland and Riverdale in actuality?). However, Chinese students do not outperform U.S. students on nonroutine problems (Cai, 2000). Consider a nonroutine problem with multiple answers: "Ana earns $100 per day and Bob earns $75 per day. If Ana and Bob want to earn the same amount of money, how many days should each person work?"

Chinese students demonstrate high levels of accuracy and efficiency while solving word problems in mathematics. In particular, they are more likely than U.S. students to use abstract and generalized strategies to solve the problems. Both U.S. and Chinese students were more likely to solve mathematics problems correctly when they used symbolic representations (Cai & Lester, 2005), suggesting that the preference for abstract strategies helps Chinese students to solve the problem. As noted earlier, Chinese teachers urge their students to express mathematics ideas formally and precisely (Lopez-Real, Mok, Leung, & Marton, 2004), while U.S. teachers let their students express mathematics ideas informally (Schleppenbach et al., 2007).

Chinese students also use more conventional strategies than U.S. students do to solve mathematics problems, resulting in accurate solutions (Cai, 2000). When asked if each girl or each boy gets more pizza when seven girls share two pizzas equally and three boys share one pizza equally, the Chinese and U.S. 6th-grade students use eight different strategies to solve the problem. For those who use effective strategies, over 90% of the Chinese students use the conventional strategy of comparing the fractions $1/3$ with $2/7$. However, only about 20% of the U.S. students use this strategy. The majority of the U.S. students use less precise, nonconventional strategies (e.g., three girls share a pizza and the other four girls share a pizza; each of the latter four girls gets less pizza than does each of the three boys).

Chinese students also generate more solutions than do U.S. students. When U.S. 7th- and 8th-graders and Chinese 6th-graders are asked to generate three different solutions to the above pizza problem, about 40% of the Chinese students generate more than one solution, but only about 20% of the U.S. students do so. Again, Chinese students prefer abstract representations such as $7/2 = 3.5$ and $3/1 = 3$; therefore, 3.5 girls share one pizza and 3 boys share for one pizza; so, fewer boys share the same size pizza and each one gets more pizza (Cai & Lester, 2005).

However, Chinese students appear less willing than U.S. students to take risks to solve mathematics problems. Given a problem that they do not know how to solve, Chinese students often leave it a blank, while U.S. students often write down something (Cai & Cifarelli, 2004). Unlike U.S. teachers, Chinese teachers teach students the Confucian doctrine that pretending to know when one does not know is dishonest, and so teachers deduct credit for wrong answers to deter students from guessing.

Despite the small samples involved, these observations raise the question of whether the greater risk aversion is a tradeoff for Chinese students' high performance on basic mathematics concepts and computations (especially with directive teachers and high student-teacher ratios). While directive teaching and coherent instruction in Chinese mathematics classrooms likely reduces ambiguity for students, it might also have deterred students from taking risks or being creative. As globalization has heightened awareness of other countries' school systems' strengths and weaknesses, Mainland China has responded to such concerns by beginning implementation of a new mathematics curriculum that includes mathematical computations, explanations, communications, engagement and disposition toward mathematics.

LEARNING FROM U.S. AND CHINESE EXPERIENCES

Differences between U.S. and Chinese societies, teachers, and students contribute to differences in Chinese vs. U.S. students' mathematics achievements. Unlike in the United States, Chinese societies' government exams have historically rewarded high-scoring individuals and their families economically, socially and politically, driving both collectivist values and high regard for academic achievement. As a result, both immediate and extended Chinese family members have high academic expectations for their children, give them substantial educational resources, teach them mathematics, and encourage them to practice their mathematics skills.

Unlike the U.S. decentralized school system, Chinese school systems are highly centralized; adopt a challenging, national curriculum; require high standards for teacher certification; support group teaching preparation; and share the knowledge of expert teachers. As a result, Chinese national curricula and national teacher certification yield shared practices, namely the two-basics curriculum (basic mathematics concepts and skills) and direct teaching classroom instruction, focusing on refined lectures and repeated practice. Furthermore, Chinese teachers typically have greater mathematics content knowledge, collaborate on their teaching more often, develop more coherent mathematics lessons with greater abstraction, and provide students with more opportunities to understand and correct their errors, compared with U.S. teachers.

Differences between Chinese and U.S. students might also help account for Chinese students' higher average mathematics performance. Encouraged by their immediate and extended family since early childhood, Chinese students often have greater internal and external motivation than U.S. students, both of which are linked to greater mathematics achievement among Chinese students. Compared to U.S. students, Chinese students use mathematics procedures that are more efficient and produce solutions that are more accurate. Chinese students also generate more solutions than U.S. students do. However, U.S. students are more likely than

Chinese students to attempt problems to which they do not know the answer. As globalization touches education, school systems in U.S. and Chinese societies are becoming more aware of each other's differences and may learn from them to improve their children's learning of mathematics.

IMPLICATIONS

As noted in earlier chapters, U.S. and Chinese school systems differ substantially with respect to their societal structures and norms, teacher experiences and practices, and student expectation and achievement. Specifically, Chinese societies have collectivist cultural values; economic and social rewards for academic achievement; national curricula, national teacher certification, and national exams; and extended family support and high academic expectations of students. By collaborating with colleagues with content expertise, educators can design coherent lessons with abstract concepts, direct teaching, and teacher control. Although Chinese students show better performance on routine problems, more accuracy, and greater efficiency, U.S. students show greater openness and initiative, but neither set of students performs well on novel problems.

These differences suggest several possibilities that can aid students' mathematics achievement, including teachers with greater mathematics content expertise, aligning social rewards with academic performance, collaboration with colleagues, and fostering student initiative. Educators generally agree that teachers must have sufficient content expertise in mathematics to help their students learn, especially when addressing nonroutine mathematics problems or student questions. Furthermore, educators can raise student expectations and align social rewards with academic achievement by highlighting exemplars of mathematical thinking and problem solving. Educators can also collaborate with colleagues to create coherent lessons about abstract concepts, thereby helping their students attain these high academic standards. However, U.S. students are less accustomed to direct teaching or strong teacher control, and they take greater initiative on novel problems. Hence, simple adoption of mathematics lesson plans from Chinese educators is unlikely to succeed in U.S. classrooms. Instead, mathematics lessons can capitalize on U.S. student initiative and integrate it with China's higher academic standards. U.S. educators can foster U.S. student initiative to create mathematics strategies by posing novel, difficult problems. Then, teachers can help these students create and use criteria to evaluate and select from these strategies (e.g., effectiveness, precision, efficiency, and so on). Combining student initiative with high standards might aid their performance on novel problems, an area in which neither U.S. nor Chinese students excel—and in which joint research by U.S. and Chinese education researchers might prove fruitful.

SUMMARY OF IMPLICATIONS

For Parents

- Support children's mastery of math.

For Teacher Certification Programs

- Support teachers' mastery of math (e.g., required courses).

For Principals and Department Chairs

- Support teacher collaboration to design, implement, and evaluate lessons (e.g., schedule teacher collaboration time).

For Teachers

- Raise student expectations and align social rewards with academic achievement (e.g., highlight student exemplars of mathematical thinking and problem solving).
- Foster student initiative to create strategies (e.g., pose novel, difficult problems).
- Help students create and use criteria to evaluate and select from these strategies (e.g., effectiveness, precision, efficiency).

NOTE

Most of the studies referenced in this chapter examined Chinese students living in cities in Taiwan, Hong Kong, and Mainland China (e.g., Beijing, Shanghai, and so forth). For a more detailed comparison of mainland China vs. U.S. mathematics textbooks, see Chapter 12.

REFERENCES

Cai, J. (2000). Mathematical thinking involved in U.S. and Chinese students' solving process-constrained and process-open problems. *Mathematical Thinking and Learning, 2,* 309–340.

Cai, J., & Cifarelli, V. (2004). Thinking mathematically by Chinese learners. In L. Fan, N.-Y. Wong, J. Cai, & S. Li (Eds.), *How Chinese learn mathematics:* (pp. 71–106). River Edge, NJ: World Scientific.

Cai, J., & Lester J. (2005). Solution representations and pedagogical representations in Chinese and U.S. classrooms. *Journal of Mathematical Behavior, 24,* 221–237.

Cai, J., & Wong, T. (2006). U.S. and Chinese teachers' conceptions and constructions of representations. *International Journal of Science and Mathematics Education, 4,* 145–186.

Cheng, Z. J. (2008). <學前數學操作式和多元化：幼兒學習評估>. [*Operational Mathematics in Preschool: Children Learning Evaluation*]. Hong Kong: Layout Tuning. (in Chinese)

Cheng, Z. J., & Chan, L. K. S. (2005). Chinese number-naming advantages? *The International Journal of Early Years Education, 13,* 179–192.

Chiu, M. M. (2007). Families, economies, cultures and science achievement in 41 countries: Country, school, and student level analyses. *Journal of Family Psychology, 21,* 510–519.

Chiu, M. M. (2010). Inequality, family, school, and mathematics achievement. *Social Forces, 88,* 4, 1645–1676.

Chiu, M. M., & Ho, S. C. (2006). Family effects on student achievement in Hong Kong. *Asian Pacific Journal of Education, 26,* 21–35.

Chiu, M. M., & Zeng, X. (2008). Family and motivation effects on mathematics achievement. *Learning and Instruction, 18,* 321–336.

Clements, D. H. (2001). Mathematics in the preschool. *Teaching Children Mathematics, 7,* 270–276.

Correa, C. A., Perry, M., Sims, L. M., Miller, K. F., & Fang, G. (2008). Connected and culturally embedded beliefs. *Teaching and Teacher Education, 24,* 140–153.

Davey, G., Lian, C. D., & Higgins, L. (2007). The university entrance examination system in China. *Journal of Further and Higher Education, 31,* 385–396.

Dhlin, B., & Watkins, D. A. (2000). The role of repetition in the processes of memorizing and understanding. *British Journal of Educational Psychology, 70,* 65–84.

Fuson, K. C., & Kwon, Y. (1991). Chinese-based regular and European irregular systems of number words. In K. Durkin & B. Shire (Eds.), *Language in mathematical education* (pp. 211–226). Philadelphia, PN: Open University Press.

Geary, D. C., Bow-Thomas, C. C., Liu, F., & Siegler, R. S. (1996). Development of arithmetical competencies in Chinese and American children: Influences of age, language, and schooling. *Child Development, 67,* 2022–2044.

Georgas, J., Mylonas, K., Bafiti, T., Poortinga, Y. H., Christakopoulou, S., Kagitcibasi, C., et al. (2001). Functional relationships in the nuclear and extended family: A 16-culture study. *International Journal of Psychology, 36,* 289–300.

Hau, K. T., & Salili, F. (1996). Achievement goals and causal attributions of Chinese students. In S. Lau (Ed.), *Growing up the Chinese way* (pp. 121–145). Hong Kong: The Chinese University of Hong Kong Press.

Hoxby, C. M. (2001). All school finance equalizations are not created equal. *The Quarterly Journal of Economics, 116,* 1189–1231.

Huang, R., & Leung, K. S. F. (2004). Cracking the paradox of Chinese learners. In L. Fan, N. Y. Wong, J. Cai, & S. Li's (Eds.), *How Chinese learn mathematics* (pp. 348–381). River Edge, NJ: World Scientific.

Huntsinger, C. S., Jose, P. E., Larson, S. L., Balsink, K. D., & Shalingram, C. (2000). Mathematics, vocabulary, and reading development in Chinese and European American children over the primary school years. *Journal of Educational Psychology, 92*, 745–760.

Lam, C. C., Ho, E.S.C., & Wong, N. Y. (2002). Parents' beliefs and practices in education in Confucian heritage cultures. *Journal of Southeast Asian Education, 3*, 99–114.

Leung, F. K. S. (2001). In search of an East Asian identity in mathematics education. *Educational Studies in Mathematics, 47*, 35–51.

Li, J., (2003). U.S. and Chinese cultural beliefs about learning. *Journal of Educational Psychology, 95*, 258–267.

Li, J-H. (2004). Thorough understanding of the textbook—A significant feature of Chinese teacher manuals. In L. Fan, N.-Y., Wong, J. Cai, & S. Li (Eds.), *How Chinese learn mathematics* (pp. 262–279). River Edge, NJ: World Scientific.

Lopez-Real, R., Mok, A. C., Leung, K. S., & Marton, F. (2004). Identifying a pattern of teaching. In L. Fan, N.-Y. Wong, J. Cai, & S. Li (Eds.), *How Chinese learn mathematics* (pp. 282–412). River Edge, NJ: World Scientific Publishing.

McLelland, G. (1991). Attainment targets and related targets in schools. In N. B. Crawford & E. K. P. Hui (Eds.), *The curriculum and behavior problems in Hong Kong* (pp. 106–128). Hong Kong, China: The University of Hong Kong Press.

Miller, K. F., Kelly, M., & Zhou, X. (2005). Learning mathematics in China and the United States. In J.I.D. Campbell (Ed.), *Handbook of mathematical cognition* (pp. 163–177). New York: Psychology Press.

Miller, K. F., Major, S. M., Shu, H., & Zhang, H. (2000). Ordinal knowledge. *Canadian Journal of Experimental Psychology, 54*, 129–139.

Ni, Y. J., & Li, Q. (2009, March). *Effects of curriculum reform.* Paper presented at the Chinese-European Conference on Curriculum Development, Amsterdam, Netherlands.

Reitz, J. G., & Verma, A. (2004). Immigration, race, and labor. *Industrial Relations, 43*, 835–854.

Schleppenbach, M., Perry, M., Miller, K. F., Sims, L., & Fang, G. (2007). Answer is only the beginning. *Journal of Educational Psychology, 99*, 380–396.

Starkey, P., & Klein, A. (2008). Sociocultural influences on young children's mathematical knowledge. In O. N. Saracho & B. Spodek (Eds.), *Contemporary perspectives on mathematics in early childhood education* (pp. 45–66). Baltimore, MD: Information Age Publishing.

Stevenson, H.W., & Lee, S. (1990). *Contexts of achievement: A study of American, Chinese, and Japanese Children. Monographs of the Society for Research in Child Development* [55(1–2), Serial No. 221]. Hoboken, NJ: Wiley.

Stevenson, H. W., & Stigler, J. W. (1992). *The learning gap.* New York: Simon & Schuster.

Stigler, J. W., & Hiebert, J. (1999). *The teaching gap.* New York: Free Press.

Stigler, J. W., Lee, S. Y., & Stevenson, H. W. (1990). *Mathematical knowledge of Japanese, Chinese, and American elementary school children.* Reston, VA: National Council of Teachers of Mathematics.

Suen, H. K., & Yu, L. (2006). Chronic consequences of high-stakes testing? Lessons from the Chinese civil service exam. *Comparative Education Review, 50,* 46–65.

Wang, T., & Murphy, J. (2004). An examination of coherence in a Chinese mathematics classroom. In L. Fan, N. Y. Wong, J. Cai, & S. Li (Eds.), *How Chinese learn mathematics* (pp. 107–123). River Edge, NJ: World Scientific.

Zhang, D., Li, S., & Tang, R. (2004). The "two basics": Mathematics teaching and learning in Mainland China. In L. Fan, N.-Y. Wong, J. Cai, & S. Li (Eds.), *How Chinese learn mathematics* (pp. 189–207). River Edge, NJ: World Scientific.

12

Demystifying the Math Myth

Analyzing the Contributing Factors for the Achievement Gap Between Chinese and U.S. Students

Guili Zhang &
Miguel A. Padilla

The fact that Chinese students outperform American students consistently in mathematics achievement has been widely recognized over the past 40 years (Ornstein, 2010). In this chapter we identify and analyze seven important factors that contribute to Chinese students' superior math performance: culture, curriculum, textbooks, teachers, teaching, students, and parents. We dissect the influential factors where the differences lie, and describe the differences in math education between China and the United States. The work is based on an extensive literature review and systematic research employing multiple methods, including our distinctive firsthand learning, teaching, teacher-supervising, and research experiences both in China and in the United States; participation in the writing of the *National Unified Textbook* and *Teachers Manual* in China; and in both countries, multiple interviews of elementary students, parents, and math teachers; extensive observation of classroom teaching; and comparisons of math textbooks. In this work, Chinese students refer to students in Mainland China.

Although it stands in unison with the previous chapter regarding cultural, societal, and familial differences between China and the United States, this chapter

East Meets West in Teacher Preparation, edited by Wen Ma. Copyright © 2014 by Teachers College, Columbia University. All rights reserved. Prior to photocopying items for classroom use, please contact the Copyright Clearance Center, Customer Service, 222 Rosewood Dr., Danvers, MA 01923, USA, tel. (978) 750-8400, www.copyright.com

distinguishes itself with its emphasis on an in-depth analysis of China's national math curriculum and math textbooks, the use of specialized math teachers, and teacher support. Additionally and importantly, this chapter provides recommendations for the United States to improve students' math achievement.

FACTORS CONTRIBUTING TO MATHEMATICS GAP BETWEEN CHINESE AND AMERICAN STUDENTS

Culture

Education Is Highly Prized in the Chinese Culture. Children's education is the top priority in Chinese families. In modern China, education is believed to be the basis for social development as well as for individual prosperity. Children are instilled with the common knowledge that those with a higher academic background will have a greater chance for a higher-level life. Education has been one of the government's central focuses in China. In the early 1970s, the Chinese government specified universal primary education as a national goal. In 1985, the government issued a reform plan that called for improving the educational level of the entire population by providing all children at least 9 years of formal schooling.

An Intense Exam and Competition Culture Exists in China. Education competition and examination are prevalent in China and are highly regarded. China's one set of national standards makes national comparisons possible. Chinese students are consistently in competitions with each other, and they depend on the National College Entrance Examination to move up the social ladder. China has an estimated 230 million K–12 students—roughly four times the combined U.S. public and private school population—and only a fraction of them get to enter college, based on higher academic performance. Students must fight for limited spaces in schools and universities. On the contrary, the United States is a wealthy nation, where students have myriad opportunities for educational and economic advancement.

Emphasis on Effort. The Chinese attribute success to effort, and failure to lack of enough effort; while Americans often tend to attribute success or failure to high or low ability, respectively. Attributing success to personal ability could prompt a person to give up when faced with failure. In contrast, attributing success to effort, which is within one's control, often leads a person to sustain hope and persistence, and to increase effort.

Curriculum

A national curriculum contributes greatly to Asian students' superior math performance (e.g., Schmidt, Houang, & Cogan, 2002; Stevenson & Stigler, 1992). There is a national unified mathematics curriculum used throughout all of China to guide textbook content, teacher training, and professional development. Four types of teaching materials—the Teaching and Learning Framework (教学大纲, *jiao xue da gang*), textbooks (课本, *ke ben*), teacher's manuals (教师教学用书, jiaoshi jiaoxue yongshu), and workbooks （练习册, lian xi ce）—constitute China's national curriculum. A national curriculum provides a platform for professional exchanges and the establishment of a knowledge base for effective teaching (Hiebert, Gallimore, & Stigler, 2002).

The education system in the United States has been traditionally decentralized and the U.S. national government does not impose much control over education policy. The U.S. Department of Education is not a central ministry for education that oversees all related national and local services in education (Crow & Silver, 2008). Current American K–12 system has more than 13,000 school district governing bodies that hold almost complete control over the design, administration, and outcome of K–12 schools in the United States. These school boards are commonly led by elected groups of residents. Attaining national educational objectives through a network of independent local school boards is almost impossible.

U.S. mathematics curriculum materials are less focused and more repetitive in terms of content coverage, instructional requirements, and structures (Schmidt, Houang, & Wolfe, 1999), and curriculum policy is less authoritative, specific, and consistent (Wang, 2001). American schools end up circling back through topics over a student's course of study, without teaching basic concepts to mastery (Cavanagh, 2006).

Textbooks

One vs. Many Series. There is one series of elementary math textbooks that has been used dominantly throughout China since 2001: The Compulsory Standardized Experimental Mathematics Series (义务教育课程标准实验数学教材) published by the People's Education Press (the PEP series). Besides the PEP series, there are five other series that are recognized and used, none of which has a comparable influence to the PEP series. In contrast, the decentralization of the U.S. education system has resulted in a much larger variety of textbooks being used in schools across the country. According to Usiskin and Dossey (2004), most school districts in the United States designed their own curriculum/standards within the guidance provided by individual states. The United States has never used a unified set of textbooks. In this study, we selected a representative mathematics textbook series developed by one of the most popular publishers and will refer it as "the U.S. series" for anonymity purposes, to compare with the Chinese PEP series.

Small and Light vs. Big and Heavy. The Chinese PEP series textbooks are consumable paperbacks that measure 5.83 inches in width x 8.27 inches in length, which is roughly half the size of the U.S. textbook. Each book weighs approximately 5 ounces. There are around 100 pages in each textbook. The U.S. series textbook is hardback, and measures approximately 9.2 inches in width by 11.2 inches in length. Each U.S. series textbook contains around 400 pages. They are colorful, and full of color photographs and colored illustrations and figures on almost every page. Each U.S. textbook weighs 2 pounds, 6 ounces to over 3 pounds, nearly as much as all 12 PEP series textbooks put together. Table 12.1 provides a comparison of a Chinese PEP series math elementary textbook and the U.S. series typical elementary textbook. The cost of a Chinese math textbook is only a very small fraction of that of a U.S. math textbook.

Sequential and Intensive vs. Repetitive and Cursory. China's mathematics curriculum is very well sequentially organized, with almost no repetition. The textbooks are short and definitive. Different topics are taught in different grades. The same concept or skill becomes a subconcept or subskill for the advanced concept when it is presented at an advanced grade level. The books pursue a topic thoroughly within a particular grade and do not reteach it.

The U.S. mathematics textbooks reflect a spiraling curriculum, characterized by a great deal of repetition and review, with the result that topics are covered with little intensity (Kim, 1993). Unfortunately, a spiraling curriculum allows just a short time for the learning of each topic and frequently insufficient time for mastery of the topic. Succeeding years grant even less time to cover the material that was supposedly mastered in the previous year (Jiang & Eggleton, 1995). Many teachers feel strongly that they have insufficient time to go over the advanced levels or other topics. "There's just too much stuff in it," they say.

Table 12.1. Measurements of a Typical Elementary Mathematics Textbook in China and the United States

Measurements	Chinese math textbook	U.S. math textbook
Width	5.83 inches	9.20 inches
Length	8.27 inches	11.20 inches
Thickness	0.27 inches	0.75 inches
Weight	5.80 ounces	45.00 ounces

Chinese math textbooks cover more advanced topics and introduce topics at a faster rate than those in the United States. According to the report of the Illinois Council of Teachers of Mathematics (ICTM) China Mathematics Delegation (1988), "the Chinese students are learning a great deal of mathematics, . . . at any grade level, the students we observed seem ahead of our own in terms of both topics studied and mastery thereof. Their curriculum is more intensive" (p. 436). This difference continues to exist in the 21st century.

Teachers

Extensive Content Knowledge. Researchers reported that Chinese math teachers have a deeper understanding about mathematics and its representations (Ma, 1999). They are able to provide clearer explanations, use teaching time more efficiently, develop smoother pedagogical flow, and engage students in inquiry using whole-class instruction (Perry, 2000; Stigler & Hiebert, 1999). Additionally, Ma described a longitudinal coherence in Chinese teachers' thinking about mathematics (1999).

Specialized Math Teachers. Math teachers in China only teach math and typically only have one class preparation and can concentrate on mathematics and become very good at teaching it. Chinese math teachers teach less than 3 hours a day, while American teachers teach 5 hours a day on average. In the United States, elementary school teachers usually teach all the subjects. "We simply don't have the time to sit down to prepare lessons carefully," said a preservice math teacher in the United States. One of the most serious problems reported by over 50% of American teachers was the difficulty of meeting the demands on their time, which is five times higher than the percentage of Chinese teachers who reported such a problem (Stevenson & Stigler, 1992).

Complete Teacher Support. Math teachers in China have the national curriculum as a coherent guideline. They are also provided with all of the needed tools—teacher's manual, textbooks, workbooks, and other materials such as manipulatives. The teacher's manual serves as a rich resource and support to Chinese math teachers. In the manual, a detailed lesson plan is presented for each topic.

American math teachers are only given "a long list of ideas about what should be taught (known as standards) and market-driven textbooks that include something for everyone but very little guidance, tools, or training" (Schmidt, Houang, & Cogan, 2002, p. 10). Without a coherent national curriculum, the teachers in the United States are "simply doing what we asked them" to do: "Teach everything you can. Don't worry about depth. Your goal is to teach 35 things briefly, not 10 things well" (Schmidt et al., 2002, p. 13).

Chinese math teachers frequently have only 2 periods of instruction (out of 6) each day (with one class preparation) with 40 minutes per period, and thus they teach only 10–12 periods per week. They spend the rest of their time preparing lessons, grading homework, helping students, and developing high-order problem-solving exercises. In the United States, teachers have very heavy classroom teaching assignments every day, and typically only have one class period to prepare for classes. They commonly have three to four different class preparations per school day (Becker & Selter, 1996).

Professional Development. Chinese schools do far more to help teachers improve their classroom skills. An elementary school principal in Beijing was surprised to learn that many teachers in the United States teach 20 classes a week. Teachers at his school led only 10 or 12 classes, using the extra time to prepare lessons, meet in groups, and discuss classroom strategies. In China, each school has a small and a large teaching research group. Small teaching research group members are teachers teaching the same subject in the same grade. They often meet to discuss ways of teaching certain topics. Large teaching research group includes all teachers teaching the same subject in the entire school. They usually meet once a week for a half day to study and explore better ways to teach the subject in general.

China has a teaching research office at each level—town, district, city, province, and nation. Open sample lessons are provided regularly about once a month. After the open lessons, new research findings are disseminated by the teaching researchers at the meetings in a written form along with oral explanations. Mathematics journals have articles on teaching specific topics or lessons. High-quality sample lesson plans are provided by the People's Education Press for teachers' reference. One series of textbooks being used nationwide makes all these possible. In the United States, because of diverse textbooks, such research activities become unrealistic and impossible, even if the teachers had the time.

Teaching

Adherence to Curriculum and Textbooks. In China, the teaching of mathematics is guided by a national curriculum and a series of textbooks used virtually throughout the nation. The textbooks strictly adhere to the curriculum, follow the teacher's manual, and study the teaching materials intensively (Ma, 1999). They know the exact content they should be teaching each day. To prepare math lessons, Chinese math teachers scrutinize textbooks and teacher's manuals for their content and analysis of concepts, rationale for presentation, suggested instructional methods, and sample problems (Zhou & Peverly, 2005).

American teachers know that there are misalignments between the textbooks and the state standards. They have to deviate from the textbook's content or sequence in order to meet the state standards. Further, most U.S. teachers hold the view that "good teachers do not follow textbooks, but instead make their own curriculum . . ." (Ball & Cohen, 1996, p. 6). They tend to organize their classrooms much more according to their own desires, resulting in great variability among classrooms.

Instructional Practices. Chinese teachers tend to spend a considerably high percentage of time teaching certain knowledge or skills thoroughly using textbooks. They typically use whole-class instructional format in a formal and controlled manner in which all students are on task and the teacher orchestrates all activities. The U.S. public school system does not provide strong administrative or professional instructional guidance; thus, teachers often determine their own instructional approaches. They could simply "close the door" and teach using any method or content they chose (Desimone, Smith, Baker, & Ueno, 2005).

Chinese teachers use manipulatives as part of the instruction to help students understand the concept or relationship. After using a manipulative, Chinese teachers spend a great deal of time analyzing what the manipulative shows. They always help students understand certain knowledge beginning at a concrete level to pictorial, then to abstract. In contrast, many U.S. teachers use manipulatives as the entire instruction. According to Cai (2004), Chinese math teachers discourage solution strategies that lack generality. In contrast, U.S. teachers heavily emphasize the pragmatic nature of mathematics: As long as it works, students can choose whatever representations and strategies they like.

Despite the general belief that Chinese education is traditional and teacher-centered, the whole-class time is not necessarily teacher-centered lecture. Chinese math teachers often use the whole-class time to engage students in discussions of math problems; therefore, it could be characterized as student-centered (Huang & Leung, 2004). In a Chinese math classroom, the students produce most of the mathematical statements and explanations, whereas teachers in the United States produce more mathematical explanations and statements than the students do (Schleppenback et al., 2007).

Learning Time. Prior to 1995, Chinese students attended school 240 days per year, 6 days a week (Monday through Saturday) for 40 weeks a year. Since 1995, students attend school for 5 days a week, for a total of 200 days a year. There are two long vacations separating the school year: the summer vacation and winter vacation. A school day in China starts early and ends later than in the United States. Students usually arrive at 7:30 for a self-study session in order to get ready for the four class periods in the morning. After the fourth lesson, usually around noon, students get a 1.5- to 2-hour lunch and nap break. Afternoon lessons usually run from 1:30 to 4:30 P.M. Each class period lasts about 40–45 minutes. Mathematics is often taught during the first two periods of the day because early morning is the time when students' brains are believed to be the freshest and sharpest.

American students attend school 180 days per year. Mathematics lessons can be scheduled at any time of the school day. U.S. students often spent about twice as much time on language arts as they do on math. The reason, according to a graduate student in the United States, is "because it's easier for teachers to teach reading. Some of them don't know math well."

Classroom—Serious Learning Place vs. Social Center. The classroom environment is quite different in the two countries. Given the fact that there are about as many elementary and high school students in China as there are people in the United States, one will not be surprised that the size of a Chinese class is usually more than twice as large as a class in the United States. However, one will be very surprised to see that classroom discipline problems are nearly nonexistent in a Chinese classroom. Students' minds follow the teacher very closely.

In contrast, based on our extensive observations of classroom teaching sessions, students in a U.S. classroom seem to have much freedom to do many things other than learning (although sometimes permissions are needed), such as getting up, walking across the room to use a pencil sharpener, washing their hands, going to the school office, the library, or the bathroom. Teaching is interrupted constantly, which makes systematic teaching very difficult. While Chinese teachers spend little time for classroom management, U.S. teachers usually spend a great deal of time to keep class in order.

Homework. Homework is an important form of out-of-school learning. Chinese children are typically assigned homework on weekday evenings, weekends, as well as holiday breaks. American children usually receive homework on weekday evenings, not weekends or holiday breaks, and the amount of homework on weekday evenings is less than that of Chinese children. Chinese children spend much more time each day doing homework than American children.

Students

Great Sense of Responsibility. Being raised in a collectivist society, Chinese children work hard to bring honor to the family. Chinese children also assume the responsibility of taking care of their parents when they become elderly. Thus, Chinese children study hard to acquire a good living with financial stability.

Effort for Success. While U.S. students usually attribute mathematics performance to intelligence, their Chinese counterparts hardly ever attach importance to the intelligence difference; instead, they place greater emphasis on the role of effort (e.g., Stevenson, Lee, Chen, Stigler, et al., 1990). Students in China are deeply influenced by the traditional belief that "effort is everything." To them, perseverance spells success.

High Standards. Chinese students are more critical toward themselves. While 87% of American 5th-graders thought their parents were happy or very happy with their math performance, only 38% of Chinese 5th-graders thought their parents were happy or very happy. Similarly, 83% of American children thought their teacher was happy or very happy with their math performance, compared to 37% of the Chinese children (Stevenson, 1987).

Parents

Dedicated to Children's Education. Chinese parents live their lives centered around enabling their children to obtain the highest academic achievement, and to grow up into successful people (望子成龙). Chinese parents see education as the avenue toward a better future. For peasant families, children's education is the way to improve the family's financial state in the future. Chinese families dedicate a large portion of their time and themselves to their children's schoolwork. Basic math skills are often taught at home even prior to formal schooling. Parents not only tutor their children at home but also help them regularly review math textbooks the students learned before.

Even though American parents also help their children to develop and be successful, they tend to show less commitment to and put less emphasis on their children's academic achievement. It's less typical for American parents to see academic activity as something their children should be involved in after school, and they do not spend a great amount of time monitoring and encouraging their child on academic work.

High Expectations. Like their children, Chinese parents believe that academic achievement is more a product of effort than of natural ability (Tusi, 2007) and the children should do well if they put in enough effort. Consequently, they are much more critical when it comes to their children's academic performance. In contrast, American parents tend to emphasize ability as the most important requisite for success, and therefore are less critical when faced with their children's low academic performance. Stevenson et al. (1990) reported that the average math score with which the American parents would be satisfied was in the 70s, while the average score with which Chinese parents would be satisfied was around the 90s.

CONCLUSIONS

Many factors may have contributed to the existing mathematics achievement gap between American and Chinese elementary students. Some of the leading factors appear to be culture, curriculum, textbooks, teachers, teaching, students, and parents. Among these, we especially stress the importance and the potential game-changing effect of a coherent, precisely defined national curriculum, a series of well-developed textbooks, and specialized math teachers at all grade levels. America needs a more consistent approach to teaching math to replace the potpourri of approaches used in states and school districts. It is apparent that improving American elementary student math performance depends on changes and adjustments at the policy and practice levels.

We also wish to emphasize that American math teachers need more solid math content knowledge. According to a famous Chinese saying, if you want to give the students one cup of water, you should have one bucket of water of your own. Ma's study (1999) calls for teachers to have profound understanding of fundamental mathematics. The American Council on Education (ACE) proclaimed that "a thorough grounding in college-level subject matter and professional competence in professional practice are necessary for good teaching . . . students learn more mathematics when their teachers report having taken more mathematics" (American Council on Education, 1999, p. 6).

We do not suggest that the United States should simply import China's model of curriculum and instructional practices. Teaching practices are culturally dependent and there are many challenges to transplanting effective teaching practices from one country to another. It also should be noted that the American education system has many strengths of its own. To illustrate, the Chinese government is seeking to infuse more American-style flexibility into its math and science curriculum by placing less emphasis on exams and more focus on cultivating students' creative and analytical skills.

The uphill battle on the math gap will be strenuous. The encouraging news is that we have the hardworking and enthusiastic American teachers on board with the reform mission. Teachers at all levels are aware of the mathematics reform discussion (Drake, 2006), and have indicated commitment to moving toward practice that reflects the tenets of reform. American math teachers need to be well trained in mathematics subject areas, be released from the unreasonable demand of teaching multiple subjects, and be equipped with a coherent curriculum, well-written textbooks, high-quality teacher's manuals and supplementary materials to get down to business in the classroom with high expectations for students in mathematic achievement. If we choose to follow such a path, we will have an opportunity to remain competitive globally.

SUMMARY OF IMPLICATIONS

Seven Important Factors Contributing to Chinese Students' Better Mathematics Performance

- In Chinese culture education is highly prized, competition is intense, and effort is emphasized.

- China has a coherent, national unified mathematics curriculum used throughout the country to guide textbook content, teacher training, and professional development.
- China has one series of well-developed math textbooks that are sequential and intensive, used dominantly throughout China.
- The teachers are well-prepared, specialized in extensive content knowledge, clear guidance, complete teacher support, and effective professional development.
- The lessons are usually well-prepared, with more math teaching guided by a national curriculum.
- The students have a great sense of responsibility, effort, and high standards.
- The parents are dedicated to children's education and with high expectations for children.

Recommendations for the U.S. Mathematics Community

- Establish a coherent, clearly defined national curriculum.
- Develop a series of well-developed textbooks.
- Have more specialized and well-trained math teachers, with solid content knowledge at all grade levels.
- Make changes and adjustments at both the policy and practice levels to improve student math performance.

Recommendations for China's Mathematics Community

- Infuse American-style flexibility into the math curriculum by placing less emphasis on exams and more focus on cultivating students' creative and analytical skills.

REFERENCES

American Council on Education. (1999). *To touch the future: Transforming the way teachers are taught. An action agenda for college and university presidents.* Retrieved from http://www.acenet.edu/resources/presnet/report.cfm

Ball, D. L., & Cohen, D. K. (1996). Reform by the book: What is—or might be—the role of curriculum materials in teacher learning and instructional reform? *Educational Researcher, 25*(9), 6–8, 14.

Becker, J. P., & Selter, C. (1996). Elementary school practices. In A. J. Bishop, K. Clements, C. Keitel, J. Kilpatrick, & C. Laborde (Eds.), *International handbook of mathematics education* (pp. 511–564). Dordrecht, The Netherlands: Kluwer.

Cai, J. (2004). Why do U.S. and Chinese students think differently in mathematical problem solving? Exploring the impact of early algebra learning and teachers' beliefs. *Journal of Mathematical Behavior, 23*, 135–167.

Cavanagh, S. (2006). China takes different tack from U.S. in teaching mathematics and science. *Education Week, 25*(41), 6–7.

Crow, M. M., & Silver, M. (2008). American education systems in a global context. *Technology in Society 30*, 279–291.

Desimone, L. M., Smith, T., Baker, D., & Ueno, K. (2005). Assessing barriers to the reform of U.S. mathematics instruction from an international perspective. *Educational Research Journal, 42*(3), 501–535.

Drake, C. (2006). Turning points: Using teachers' mathematics life stories to understand the implementation of mathematics education reform. *Journal of Mathematics Teacher Education, 9*(6), 579–608.

Hiebert, J., Gallimore, R., & Stigler, J. W. (2002). A knowledge base for the teaching profession: What would it look like and how can we get one? *Educational Researcher, 31*(5), 3–15.

Huang, R., & Leung, K.S.F. (2004). Cracking the paradox of Chinese learners: Looking into the mathematics classrooms in Hong Kong and Shanghai. In L. Fan (Ed.), *How Chinese learn mathematics: Perspectives from insiders* (pp. 348–381). Singapore: World Scientific Publishing Co.

ICTM China Mathematics Delegation. (1988). China: Primary and secondary mathematics education in China: Report of the ICTM China Mathematics Delegation (1987). *School Science and Mathematics, 88*(5), 413–438. doi: 10.1111/j.1949-8594.1988.tb11831.x

Jiang, Z., & Eggleton, P. (1995). A brief comparison of the U.S. and Chinese middle school mathematics programs. *School Sciences and Mathematics, 95* (4), 187–194.

Kim, H. (1993). A comparative study between an American and a Republic of Korean textbook series' coverage of measurement and geometry content in first through eighth grades. *School Science and Mathematics, 93* (3), 123–126.

Ma, L. (1999). *Knowing and teaching elementary mathematics: Teachers' understanding of fundamental mathematics in China and the United States*. Mahwah, NJ: Lawrence Erlbaum Associates.

Ornstein, A. (2010). Achievement gaps in education. *Social Science and Public Policy, 47*(5), 424–429.

Perry, M. (2000). Explanations of mathematical concepts in Japanese, Chinese, and U.S. first- and fifth-grade classrooms. *Cognition and Instruction, 18*(2), 181–207.

Schleppenback, M., Perry, M., Miller, K. L., Sims, L., & Ge, F. (2007). The answer is only the beginning: Extended discourse in Chinese and U.S. mathematics classrooms. *Journal of Educational Psychology, 99*(2), 380–396.

Schmidt, W. H., Houang, R. T., &Wolfe, R. G. (1999). Apples to apples. *American School Board Journal, 186*(7), 29–33.

Schmidt, W., Houang, R., & Cogan, L. (2002). A coherent curriculum: The case of mathematics. *American Educator, 28*(2), 10–48.

Stevenson, H. W. (1987). America's math problems. *Educational Leadership, 45*(2), 4–10.

Stevenson, H. W., Lee, S. Y., Chen, C., Lummis, M., Stigler, J., Fan, L., & Ge, F. (1990). Mathematics achievement of children in China and the United States. *Child Development, 61*(4), 1053–1066.

Stevenson, H. W., & Stigler, J. W. (1992). *The learning gap: Why our schools are failing and what we can learn from Japanese and Chinese Education.* New York: Simon & Schuster.

Stigler, J. W., & Hiebert, J. (1999). *The teaching gap: Best ideas from the world's teachers for improving education in the classroom.* New York: The Free Press.

Tusi, M. (2007). Gender and mathematics achievement in China. *Gender Issues, 24*(3), 1–11. Retrieved from http://www.springerlink.com/content/dju5660x2t7733r8/

Usiskin, Z., & Dossey, J. (2004). *Mathematics in the United States 2004.* Reston, VA: National Council of Teachers of Mathematics.

Wang, J. (2001). Contexts of mentoring and opportunities for learning to teach: A comparative study of mentoring practice. *Teaching and Teacher Education, 17*(1), 51–73.

Zhou, Z., & Peverly, S. T. (2005). Teaching addition and subtraction to first graders: A Chinese perspective. *Psychology in the Schools, 42* (3), 259–272.

Conclusion: How Educators from China and the United States May Learn About and from One Another to Arrive at the "Middle Ground"

Wen Ma

This book features a disciplinarily diverse team of educators from Chinese backgrounds who have now been teaching in the United States for many years. As you have read, their chapters include theoretical review, research on their own and other Chinese educators' teaching experiences, research on teacher preparation and professional practices, cross-cultural challenges and innovations, as well as comparative studies on science and mathematics education. Combined, these chapters reveal salient similarities and differences in theoretical underpinnings, pedagogical principles, and practices in Chinese and American classrooms, and some of the larger theoretical orientations between education in China and the United States. Each of these authors has modeled in their professional lives and studies the objective and practice of using and integrating the best of both educational worlds.

Clearly, there is no "best" system. Both the American perspective and the Chinese perspective evolved as a product of their own sociocultural circumstances, and both can be strengthened with complementary elements from the other. The purpose of learning about and from each other is not to lose one's own identity or just to become the other. Rather, each needs to learn from other sources in order to outgrow its own limitations and become better and stronger than it would be otherwise.

VIEWING AMERICAN AND CHINESE EDUCATION
FROM THEIR RESPECTIVE TRADITIONS

As Luke (2011) argued, an educational model is often the product of the complicated sociocultural, political, and economic realities in which it is practiced,
and educational research only has limited value in helping us interpret or repli-
cate any model without thoroughly considering its local contexts and conditions.
Similarly, it is necessary to understand the "local conditions" for America's and
China's education. While the chapter authors have illuminated aspects of these, it
is worthwhile to consolidate some broad comparisons and contrasts between the
two countries' pedagogical perspectives and practices.

Time-Honored Wisdom Following a Confucian Tradition

As noted, Chinese education is rooted in a Confucian-heritage learning culture
(Lee, 2000; Watkins & Biggs, 1996), in which the teacher, possessing a larger body
of knowledge, is expected to skillfully share all he or she knows about the subject
matter with the developing learners through preparing detailed "teaching points"
before class, lecturing exhaustively about the content during class, and answering
student questions and checking their understanding after lecturing. Reciprocally, the
students are required to preview for each class, carefully listen to the substantive
lectures by the more knowledgeable teacher in class, and review the content after
class. Other characteristics of Chinese educational practices include standards-based
practices for learning, instruction, and assessment; mastery of foundational knowledge and skills; and emphasis on strong discipline and self-discipline.

Many other schools of thought, particularly Daoism and Buddhism, have also
influenced Chinese educational philosophy and practices over its long history. In
addition, and less obvious to many, various Western countries have had far-reach-
ing impact on China's entire educational establishment, especially in terms of its
K–12 school structures and content areas, as well as its university system. More
recently, China's population policies, economic reforms, and emerging private
schools further add to the many forces at play. Perhaps one of the most controversial areas is China's reliance on the National Entrance Examinations, the official
selection mechanism for all students to pursue a college education. This examination system turns out to be a double-edged sword: Although it provides an open
and fair platform of "equal score, equal opportunity" for millions of high school
graduates, it has led to intense competition among the students in the examinations. Consequently, tests are infectiously built into core subject areas and each
grade level, resulting in a test-oriented school culture (Ma, 2010).

Within such an educational milieu, classroom teaching and learning activities often center on the standardized curriculum and acquisition of foundational
knowledge and foundational skills rather than on promoting independent and
critical thinking capability of the learner. Not surprisingly, fewer opportunities

are actually created for students to participate in open-ended discussions or active self-discovery projects in order to help them make a personal connection with the curricular content, externalize their developing thinking and understanding, or apply what is learned in real-life situations. This sometimes results in the so-called "high scores, low abilities" phenomenon: Chinese learners are hardworking and perform well on tests, yet some of them do not do so well in applying what was learned to creatively problem-solve (Zhao, 2009), a phenomenon that China's former premier Wen (2006) urged the educational community to address more seriously.

Pedagogical Tenets Fused in Empirical Research and Social Promise

The United States is not only on the opposite side of China geographically, but also educationally in many ways. For example, most U.S. teacher training programs stress learner empowerment and social justice, with education being the gateway for good jobs and participatory democracy. Other core principles include that the purpose of education is to facilitate the learner's holistic development, and all students (including those with disabilities, having low English proficiency, and coming from socioeconomically underprivileged backgrounds) deserve classroom instruction that matches their own learning styles, interests, and needs. To create conducive learning conditions, differentiated instruction, hands-on activities, and group discussions are employed to engage the learners as active meaning-makers, facilitating their thinking and learning to develop in the process of problem solving (Dewey, 1902). The social constructivist perspective on learning (Windschitl, 2002) further advocates viewing the classroom as a social site where the teacher facilitates the students to learn interactively as competent and equal learners, and where knowledge may be explored, negotiated, and constructed through class discussions and hands-on learning activities. As a result, the classroom practices shift from how much the teacher teaches to how well the students think, learn, and apply the knowledge to solve problems.

Class discussion is an example. As dialogic interactions provide needed social contexts for the learners to wrestle with specific curricular content or learning tasks, educators are encouraged to utilize student-led discussion as an important participatory learning tool across grade levels and content areas (Applebee, Langer, Nystrand, & Gamoran, 2003). Not surprisingly, U.S. students are more acculturated to learning through participatory discussions and hands-on projects, and they dislike being lectured to by teachers as authoritative figures (Brookfield & Preskill, 2005).

Similarly, there exist salient differences between Chinese and American philosophical orientation and pedagogical emphasis in other areas, ranging from teacher-student relationships, curriculum and assessment standards, teacher training, licensure and evaluation, educational resources and technology, to homework. These issues and many more are fleshed out in the pages of this book.

Obviously, there are significant differences in the actual instructional practices across socioeconomically, culturally, and demographically diverse school settings in the United States (cf. Anyon, 1981; Kozol, 1992). The high-stakes standardized assessments have pushed many teachers to more test-oriented practices in recent years. Nevertheless, in comparison with China's teacher-directed, lecture-based practices, the rhetorical and instructional emphasis is still informed more by a student-centered participatory pedagogy in the United States. On the other hand, China is a country with a long history and a big population, and there are tremendous regional, socioeconomic, cultural-historical, and demographic variations as well. Therefore, it is prudent not to reduce China's educational thinking and practices to the few generalizations outlined above, just as trying to summarize the American educational perspective into a few principles risks losing its deep complexity and rich texture. Nevertheless, this overview of the scientifically informed, socially responsive orientation in the United States and the time-honored Confucian tradition on the content in China is useful because it provides a general context in which to look at how the two countries' education is shaped by their past histories and contemporary realities.

WHAT IMPLICATIONS CAN BE DRAWN?

As revealed in the chapters, the Chinese educators' collective experiences and perspectives present interesting comparisons and contrasts about teaching Chinese language and Chinese ways of teaching, as well as addressing the math and science achievement gaps between Chinese and U.S. students. More important, these findings not only showcase alternative educational thinking and practices across the spectrum, but also offer alternative conceptual lenses for the educational community to ponder the issue of how China and the United States may both benefit by reaching some "middle ground" between the two divergent perspectives (cf. Stevenson & Stigler, 2006). In addition to the specific "middle ground" suggestions enumerated at the end of each chapter, the following issues that cut across the various chapters are particularly worth noting.

Searching for the "Middle Ground" between Student-Centeredness and Teacher-Directedness

Perspectives within this volume not only shed light on Chinese ways of learning and instruction, but also showcase ways to adapt those practices in an American context. Their ideas can help other educators rethink the degree of student-centeredness and teacher-directedness in the teaching and learning equation. The objective of both systems is that teachers, who are trained specialists of the given curriculum, help the learners acquire the disciplinary knowledge. The learners, as beneficiaries of the learning, respect the teachers, study diligently, and acquire the content.

However, educators from these two traditions handle the teaching and learning tasks quite differently. On the one hand, Chinese classroom practices emphasize standards-based direct instruction, acquisition of foundational curricular knowledge and skills, and hard work through strong discipline and self-discipline. On the other hand, pedagogical practices in the United States emphasize learners' participatory experiences embedded in hands-on activities, inquiry projects, and curricular dialogues. Such differing practices tend to lead to somewhat different learning outcomes: Chinese students often know more foundational knowledge and skills, whereas U.S. students develop stronger independent thinking abilities.

Clearly, both are necessary for a substantive learning experience, and there ought to be some "middle ground": allowing the teacher to lead the acquisition of the content knowledge, while honoring the learner's personal experiences and interests. Therefore, instead of dichotomizing the learned-learner relationship, educators can think dialectically about them and draw complementary elements from the Chinese sources to improve the teaching practices and the learning gains in the United States, or vice versa.

Striving for a More Inclusive Pedagogical Framework

Many of the chapters describe practical ways to reconcile Chinese and U.S. classroom differences, but some of them also examine the notion of "pedagogy shock." Although these educators all worked in their own classes to bridge the differing pedagogical orientations, they share one collective musing: In what ways may complementary elements from the two educational perspectives be integrated for a more inclusive pedagogical framework?

Countless athletes, artists, musicians, students, even ordinary tourists, can all testify about the value of exchanges with their counterparts from other places and cultures. Likewise, educators in China and the United States can, and should, take advantage of such educational exchanges to sharpen their thinking and practices.

Li's (2012) recent book gives a useful explanation for some of the deep-rooted cultural foundations of learning in China and the United States. These divergent perspectives are like the two sides of the same pedagogical continuum. Let's use the difference in mailing address to illustrate two opposing viewpoints: In China, one's address is first framed within a big context and then narrows down: province, city, district, street, house, family (last name), and self (given name); whereas it is the complete opposite in the United States, where "me" (symbolized by the first name) is used as the starting point of observation. This specific difference reflects a simple point: There is often more than one way to conceptualize or tackle things in the world. So are many of the pedagogical practices across the Pacific shores.

Therefore, the increased educational ties between China and the United States not only provide cross-cultural learning opportunities for incoming students, but also afford potentials for educators to utilize the other model as a mirror to critically reflect on their practices and perspectives, and to draw relevant lessons to enrich their own. While doing so, educators necessarily need to continue practicing what has proven to work based on their own traditions and experiences, but they also need to embrace a more pluralistic pedagogical framework. Such cross-pollination, as Brooks (2013) proposed, may "champion other moral/academic codes to boost motivation in places where it is absent" (p. A23).

Tapping Diverse Faculty's Perspectives as Assets

The field of education never just accepts the status quo, and educators will not stop searching for new ways of thinking, teaching, and learning. An unmatchable strength of the American educational community lies in its profound human resources. Pertinent to the purpose of this book, the hybrid experiences and perspectives that Chinese and non-Chinese educators bring to the American scene present rich potentials for the profession. To recognize and tap them as assets is not only to celebrate their contribution to our collective enterprise, but also to enrich all of our students' educational experiences. After all, the society expects the field of education to respond to the challenges brought about by the global age, our profession calls for more simulating new perspectives, and our students deserve it. As such, this book offers fresh ideas to the ongoing theoretical reconfigurations and pedagogical innovations in both countries.

REFERENCES

Anyon, J. (1981). Social class and school knowledge. *Curriculum Inquiry, 11* (1), 3–41.

Applebee, A. N., Langer, J. A., Nystrand, M., & Gamoran, A. (2003). Discussion-based approaches to developing understanding: Classroom and student performance in middle and high school English. *American Education Research Journal, 40*(3), 685–730.

Brookfield, S., & Preskill, S. (2005). *Discussion as a way of teaching: Tools and techniques for a democratic classroom* (2nd ed.). San Francisco: Jossey-Bass Publishers.

Brooks, D. (2013, March 1). How the virtue of learning differs in China. *New York Times*, p. A23.

Dewey, J. (1902). *The child and the curriculum*. Chicago: University of Chicago Press.

Kozol, J. (1992). *Savage inequalities*. New York: Harper Perennial.

Lee, T. H. (2000). *Education in traditional China: A history*. Boston: Brill.

Li, J. (2012). *Cultural foundations of learning: East and West*. Cambridge, UK: Cambridge University Press.

Luke, A. (2011). Generalizing across borders: Policy and the limits of educational science. *Educational Researcher, 40*(8), 367–377.

Ma, W. (2010). Bumpy journeys: A young Chinese adolescent's transitional schooling across sociocultural contexts. *Journal of Language, Identity, and Education, 9*(2), 107–123. Doi: 10.1080/15348451003704792

Stevenson, H. W., & Stigler, J. W. (2006). *The learning gap: Why our schools are failing and what we can learn from Japanese and Chinese education* (2nd ed.). New York: Simon & Schuster.

Watkins, D. A., & Biggs, J. B. (Eds.). (1996). *The Chinese learner: Cultural, psychological, and contextual influences.* Hong Kong: The University of Hong Kong Press.

Wen, J. (2006). *Premier Wen Jiaobao seeks advice from university presidents on how to prepare more excellent talents.* Retrieved from http://news.xinhuanet.com/school/2006-11/28/content_5400168.htm

Windschitl, M. (2002). Framing constructivism in practice as the negotiation of dilemmas: An analysis of the conceptual, pedagogical, cultural, and political challenges facing teachers. *Review of Educational Research, 72*(2), 131–175.

Zhao, Y. (2009). *Catching up or leading the way: American education in the age of globalization.* Alexandria, VA: ASCD.

About the Contributors

Wen Ma is associate professor, Department of Education, Le Moyne College, and president of the Chinese American Educational Research and Development Association. Email: maw@lemoyne.edu. His research interests include participatory discussions across subject areas in K–20 settings, literacy and content literacy strategies, teacher education, English language learners, and the Asian perspective on education.

Ming Ming Chiu is professor of Mathematics Education at the University at Buffalo, State University of New York. He invented two statistical methods: statistical discourse analysis and multilevel diffusion analysis. He studies student differences across countries and models classroom conversations.

Ye He is associate professor in the Department of Teacher Education and Higher Education at the University of North Carolina at Greensboro. Her research focuses on teacher beliefs, teacher development, and the application of strength-based theories in preparing teachers for English learners.

Ran Hu is assistant professor, Department of Curriculum and Instruction, College of Education, East Carolina University. Her primary research interest includes emergent literacy and biliteracy, and teaching reading to students who speak English as a second or foreign language.

Xiufeng Liu is professor of Science Education at University at Buffalo, State University of New York. He was a former high school chemistry teacher and science education researcher in China; he has been involved in preservice and inservice science teacher education in Canada and the United States for more than 20 years. His research focuses on measurement and evaluation in science education, science curriculum policy and opportunity to learn, and public understanding of science.

Miguel A. Padilla is assistant professor of Quantitative Psychology in the Department of Psychology, Old Dominion University. His specific areas of research interest are missing data, mixed effects models, psychometrics, and resampling methods. His applied interests range from educational psychology to program evaluation, but most recently he has concentrated on job satisfaction in academia and alcohol and family dynamics with Michelle Kelley.

Chang Pu is assistant professor of Teacher Education at Berry College, Georgia. Her research interests include language-minority education (heritage language education, ESL, and bilingual education), second language teaching and learning, and classroom-based research in language and literacy development.

Ko-Yin Sung is assistant professor of Chinese in the Department of Languages, Philosophy & Communication Studies in the College of Humanities, Arts and Social Sciences at Utah State University. Her research interests include Chinese language teaching and learning, language learning strategies, language learning attitudes, and computer-assisted language learning.

Chuang Wang is associate professor of Educational Research at University of North Carolina at Charlotte. He received a doctoral degree from Ohio State University and his research interests include comparative education, research methodology, program evaluation, and learning English as a second language.

Wanying Wang is a postdoctoral fellow at the college of education of University of North Carolina at Charlotte. She was awarded a doctoral degree from the University of Hong Kong in 2011. She had 6 years of teaching experience in higher institutions in Beijing, China. Her research focuses on the curriculum innovation of higher education, general education, and comparative education.

Guili Zhang is associate professor of Research Methodology in the Department of Special Education, Foundations, and Research, East Carolina University. Her primary areas of research are in applied quantitative research designs, international comparative studies, categorical data analysis, longitudinal data management and analysis, large-scale data analysis, program assessment and evaluation, meta-analysis, mixed-methods research, and engineering education.

Meilan Zhang is assistant professor of Educational Technology, Department of Teacher Education, College of Education, University of Texas at El Paso. Her research interests include improving K–12 education and teacher education through innovative technologies and approaches. She has conducted research on discourse patterns in teacher learning communities, collaborative teacher research models and case studies, science teachers' needs for professional development, problem-based learning for students and teachers, and effectiveness of technology-supported learning environments.

Binyao Zheng is professor of Educational Psychology and Research, Department of Secondary and Middle Grades Education, Bagwell College of Education, Kennesaw State University. He served as associated director of the Sino-American Education Consortium. His teaching and research interests include learning theories, cross-cultural differences and diversity, character education, and teacher education.

Index

Ability, attributing to success/failure, 28–29
Absalom, D., 16, 98
Abstraction, in math instruction, 150–151
Academic achievement
  Chinese learner paradox and, 66
  Chinese parents' attitude
    toward, 47–48, 167
  differing cultural perspectives on, 28–30
  high-stakes testing and, 10
  in math. *See* Math achievement
Academic freedom, 73
Academic illiteracy/unfamiliarity, as
    challenge faced by Chinese university
    students in Western countries, 12–15
Acculturation, of Western teachers, 18
Achievement. *See* Academic
    achievement; Math achievement
Achievement gap, between American
    and Chinese students, 4
  in math, 147, 149, 151–153, 168
  in math, factors contributing to, 160–168
Action research, 111–112
  challenges of, 112–113
  collaborative model for, 113–118
  implications for, 119–121
Active learners, U.S. students as, 60–61
Adams, K., 137
Adamson, B., 42
Adaptation, cross-cultural
  challenges of, 12–17
  implications and suggestions for, 17–18
Addington, A. H., 66
Administrators
  American and Chinese differences, 17, 19

teacher cultural values and beliefs
    and, implications for, 62
Advance organizer, 34
Advanced Placement (AP) courses, 28
Aldrich, N. J., 106
Alfieri, L., 106
Allen, K., 83
American Council on Education
    (ACE), 168
American individualism, 8–9, 19
American students
  achievement gap and. *See* Achievement
    gap, between American
    and Chinese students
  in China, 4, 7
Ames, R. T., 9
Analects of Confucius, 56–57
Anyon, J., 175
Applebee, A. N., 65, 175
*Asia as Method: Towards
    Deimperialization* (Chen), viii
"Asia-envy," ix
Asia Society, 4, 81
Attribution, cultural differences in, 28–29
August, D., 81
Authoritative style, of student
    behavior management, 36–37
Automation, in math problem
    solving, 33–34

Bafiti, T., 146
Bagley, W. C., 98
Baker, D., 165
Ball, D. L., 165

Wang, Z., 133
Ward, C., 13
Watkins, D. A., 4, 66, 75, 149, 151, 174
Wen, J., 175
Wen, Q., 133
Wenger, E., 82
Wesche, M. B., 44
Western teachers, in China
  acculturation stages of, 18
  challenges faced by, 15–17, 19
  implications for, 39
  misunderstanding of teacher
    role by, 16–17, 19
White, J. A., 10
Wigfield, A., 28
Wiley, T. G., 90
Wilson, F. R., 106
Windschitl, M., 64, 65, 175
Winser, W. N., 10
Wisdom
  in Confucian-heritage learning
    culture, 174–175
  of students, 31
  from teachers, 12
Wolfe, R. G., 161
Wong, M. S., 18
Wong, N. Y., 145, 148
Wong, S. C., 67
Wong, S. S., 137
Wong, T., 147, 150
Wong, W. S. S., 10, 16
Works of Zhu Xi (Zhu Xi), 61
Writing instruction, in Chinese as a
    Heritage Language schools
  American approaches to writing and, 82
  culturally shaped, 89–90
  learning Chinese characters, 82–83
  and reading relationship,
    receptions of, 87–89
  routines used in, 84–87

situated perspective on,
    90–91
study findings, 84–90
study implications, 90–94
study parameters, 83–84
teacher training for, 92–93
teachers of, as cultural and
    language mediators, 91
Wu, Z., ix

Xie, X. Y., 11
Xing, F., 89
Xing, M., 87
Xu, S., 42, 50
Xu, Y., 133

Yang, B., 57, 59
Yang, S. H., 9
Yoon, K. S., 114
Yu, L., 145

Zeichner, K. M., 111, 112, 113
Zeng, X., 146
Zhang, D., 9, 149
Zhang, Guili, 159
Zhang, H., 147
Zhang, Meilan, 110, 116, 117
Zhang, T., 133
Zhao, H., 10
Zhao, Y., 66, 75, 97, 104,
    106, 175
Zheng, Binyao, 27
Zheng, W., 57, 59
Zhou, J., 111, 112
Zhou, L., 15, 16
Zhou, M., 81
Zhou, N. Z., 9, 11
Zhou, X., 149
Zhou, Z., 164
Zhu Xi (Confucian writer), 61
Zion, S., 32